Power Choices

Power Choices

7 Signposts on Your Journey to Wholeness, Love, Joy and Peace

BRENDA WADE, PHD
WITH
TAMARA JEFFRIES

HEARTLINE PRODUCTIONS
SAN FRANCISCO

Power Choices : 7 Signposts on Your Journey to Wholeness, Love, Joy and Peace

Copyright © 2005 by Brenda Wade

All rights reserved. No part of this book may be reproduced, stored in a retrieval system, or transmitted, in any form or by any means, electronic, mechanical, photocopying, recording, or otherwise, without the written permission of the author.

Published by Heartline Productions, Inc., 1533 Eddy Street, San Francisco, California 94115

Design by Erin Barrett
Cover design by Wendy Bass

This book is typeset using Palatino, Optima; titles in Lucida Calligraphy

Printed in the United States of America

1 2 3 4 5 6 7 8 9 10   10 09 08 07 06 05 04 03

DEDICATION

For Kena and Kai, my breathtaking daughters, Brandon and Corbin, my wonderful stepsons, and my beloved husband, Gerald—heroes all.

Contents

Acknowledgments 9

Introduction 11

1. **INVESTIGATION** *Getting Ready for Your Journey* 27

2. **INITIATION** *Answering the Call* 75

3. **INSIGHT** *Crossing the Threshold to the Inner World* 99

4. **INTUITION** *Approaching Our Inmost Being* 143

5. **INTENTION** *Facing the Test* 174

6. **INSPIRATION** *Traveling the Road Home-Renewal and Resurrection* 199

7. **INNOVATION** *Returning with an Elixir for the World* 233

Selected Bibliography 275

Acknowledgments

I AM DEEPLY INDEBTED to Diane Ricksecker, healer, writer, and marketing whiz, who stayed up long nights and worked weekends to complete the editing and research of this project and without whom it simply would not have gotten done. My heartfelt thanks to Tamara Jeffries, who, on the shortest timeline ever, did a beautiful job of rewriting and editing with one hand while dandling her infant daughter, Mali, with the other hand.

I owe a huge thank you to miracle worker Roy M. Carlisle, who boldly shepherded the publishing of this work and kept it on schedule. Many thanks to the golden woman of literary agents, Candice Fuhrman, who kept a steady hand on the tiller and offered insight and encouragement at crucial points. Apryl Renee contributed many hours of typing and great feedback; my thanks.

Thanks are due to my friend and business partner, Tzvia Shelef, who cheered me on and helped out in myriad ways. Dr. Jesse Miller was on hand to contribute pith and wisdom as needed; thank you. Jonathan Young, whose courses at the Center for Myth and Story stoked my love of myth, I am grateful. My dear friend Brenda Richardson, writer extraordinaire, thank you for taking the time to read and advise on the manuscript.

To my clients and friends whose heroic work in transforming themselves formed the backbone of this book, I thank you for generously allowing me to share your stories and for inspiring me and so many others to make power choices leading to love.

My husband, Gerald, kept hearth and home and me together from start to finish. Darling, you made this possible, and I can't thank you sufficiently, but I'll try to think of something.

Introduction

A Change Is Coming

It is only change that is at work here.
— The I Ching

Looking back, I remember when my life long dream was crushed in 1984. For several years, I had been working with troubled youth, and I could see that the traditional approach to education was not meeting their needs. I wanted so badly to open a school that nurtured children not just mentally but emotionally, physically and spiritually, too. I decided not just to dream it but to do it. The curriculum took shape, a perfect property became available, a purchase contract was arranged, and I was busy - raising the funds needed to get my wonderful new school off the ground when out of the blue, my attorney called to say the owners of the property were selling it to someone else. I was devastated. I had invested so much time, energy, creativity and money into this project just to have it yanked away from me. I cried non-stop for two days (feeling like the biggest victim in the world) and then called my spiritual counselor for advice on what to do next. Never one to pull a punch, Jocelyn gave it to me between the eyes, "Don't you get it? This isn't your path. You are supposed to do something else."

I had come to a point in the road marked with a sign that read *Wrong Way* in bright red letters. Despite the fact that I felt so strongly about the school and believed so deeply that it was my calling, clearly it wasn't going to happen. It was time for me to change — change my goals, change my feelings about myself, and change the way that I understood my life. How I wish I had known then what I know now: change is inevitable, and it has a purpose.

Thankfully, we can change. We've all done so many times—often of our own free will. We change our hairstyle, our hair color. We change jobs. We move from one house to another, one city to the next. We change from single status to married. And we're glad to do so. At the same time, we have an aversion to other kinds of change—the changes we don't want. For example, we don't mind changing careers when it's our choice, but we're devastated when we're laid off and have to find another job. We're usually quite happy to change from being single to being coupled, but we're often less eager to change from being coupled to being single. Obviously it's painful even if we're the initiator. And if we're the one being left...well, that's why we have all of those love songs about heartbreak.

Even when our situation is far from being the best, we have difficulty changing because whatever we're dealing with today is, in some way, familiar and comfortable. Research shows that our brains are programmed through repetitive experience to prefer the familiar, whereas change represents a whole wide world of the potentially threatening unknown. So even if we are struggling with an unfulfilling love relationship, a job that crushes our creativity and self-esteem, a hair color we hate, or some other aspect of life that's just not quite right, it's still a way of life we know, and we know how to deal with it.

But if you think of change as the way that nature's seasons shift and evolve, each like a dancer stepping forward to take her turn, you'll see that change in the world can be a wondrous, beautiful thing and a necessary thing. What would life be like without a season to plant, a season to grow, a season to reap or to rest and renew? Think about how bored and sluggish you feel when your life is exactly the same day after day after day. It's through change that we discover and express our creativity. Change allows, maybe even requires, us to develop our inner resources, such as compassion, loyalty and determination. I was talking with a friend who left her job after encountering a number of roadblocks she could not surmount. It was really hard for her to leave her position—it

Introduction

gave her prestige, power, a healthy income, but she is now at the helm of her own company and doing exactly what is most important and meaningful to her. Her life is even better than she could have imagined.

It is only through changing our current circumstances that we can ever hope to step into better ones. For as long as we avoid change, we are, in effect, saying that we will continue to endure the aspects of our lives that bring us pain, that keep us from feeling fulfilled, that keep us from fully being the people we were born to be. Actually, change is good for us on every level. Change is the path to improving our connection with ourselves and with others. Even our brains benefit from change. Researchers have found that if we continue learning into and throughout adulthood, our brain function is both increased and protected. We need change to feel fully alive. Above all, we need the change wrought by spiritual growth to heal the idea that we are separate from one another or from the Divine. But we need to look into the source of our feelings and then find a way to work through those feelings in order to successfully navigate change. To make the most of our situation, we may choose to accept emotional support and mentorship from someone who has been down the path before us.

We each have something in our lives that stands in need of improvement. As a psychologist, I see people every day who come in because they've recognized the need for change and have answered the call to do something about it. In the pages that follow, you'll read the stories of people I've counseled who were completely shut down emotionally and of others I've worked with to fix their broken relationships. Some of my clients wrestle with the challenges of having money and success; others are trying to figure out why success eludes them. Their individual circumstances are quite different, but all my clients have this in common: a need to investigate the cause of their distress, to examine the choices they've made, to see those choices as lessons, and to make choices that serve them better. And my job with them—as it is with you, the reader of this book—is to help them do that.

DO YOU HAVE THE GUTS TO CHANGE?
Free will is one of the greatest blessings and compassionate gifts... given to mankind. — Pearl

I've found that the question "Do you have the guts to change?" offends some people. "Why would someone want me to change?" they ask. "What's wrong with me? And what do you mean, 'Do I have the guts?' Do I look like some kind of wimp?"

Life is about change whether we like it or not, whether we choose it or not, whether we understand it or not; that is what we are here for. We human beings are on a journey, and like all journeys, the journey of life is full of opportunities to grow and learn. In fact, that is the point: life IS change.

Most of us in some way view life as random. We figure something new is just as likely to be bad as it is to be good so we consciously avoid change. Even if all the while, deep down, we know that there are things we'd like to change about our lives and our selves—perhaps many things. And we might wonder to ourselves whether we really could muster the boldness, the bravery, the fearlessness that it would take to make the choice to implement the powerful change our deepest selves call for. When I work with someone who is upset by the question "Do you have the guts to change?" it is often a signal to me, as a psychotherapist, that it's a question they need to explore and answer.

So...do you have the guts to change?

For the moment at least, don't let the question offend you. Instead, let it give you a little jolt. Or a big jolt—whatever jump-start you need to begin to think about what your life would be like if you had the power and confidence and tools to make a change for the better. There's absolutely no need to be offended because here's a little secret: I believe you do have the guts to change. You do have what it takes to make a positive difference in your life, and I have an excellent reason for making this statement. And if you don't believe me, just keep reading. You'll believe me by the time you finish this book.

Introduction

THE WORLD NEEDS YOU

...all may see the continuous process of creation and the part our thoughts and actions play in the world's unfoldment. — Dhyani Ywahoo

Why is change so necessary right now? For the answer, we need to look no further than the state of affairs in our families, in our communities, and around the world. The divorce rate continues to hover at 50 percent although we seem to crave connection and partnership, and we know the emotional and financial devastation that comes with the dissolution of our families. Despite amazing advances in healthcare, our health seems to be deteriorating with cases of cancer, diabetes, hypertension, and depression on the rise. We're an overweight nation; our children increasingly swell the ranks of people who are obese. Among African-Americans, the infant mortality rates are among the highest in the world. Drug abuse has spilled out of urban areas to infect small, rural towns across the county. Around the world, women and girls are still vulnerable to injustices—from being denied the right to vote to being subjected to physical and sexual assault and exploitation. We read about politically motivated wars raging, with innocent children and women becoming the invisible, ignored casualties.

All these things—and the countless other cases of injustice and suffering that people face every day—need to change. People need to be freed from their distress so they can express themselves through the purpose and creativity with which they were born—so they can truly live. But when we look at the major problems in the world and in our communities, they seem so systemic and pervasive—so huge—that they appear to be beyond any one person's ability to change. The reality, however, is that anything that gets corrected in this world is changed by individuals. One person with courage and vision—perhaps leading or working with a group of other like-minded individuals—can bring about change in even the direst situation.

Consider people like Harriet Tubman, Las Madres de la Plaza

de Mayo, Rosa Parks, Mahatma Ghandi, and Nobel Laureates such as Martin Luther King, Aung San Suu Kyi, and Mother Theresa. Each one answered a call. In answering, something deep within them was changed, and they, in turn, changed the world. They did not wait for someone else to change things. Each person took some action that lit a fire among other people and caused major, incredibly important shifts in the course of our history, and you may see this not only among the people in history books, but in your own community. You may know of a man who has decided to mentor troubled teenagers, or a woman who is leading the charge to revitalize her crumbling neighborhood. That artist, standing on a scaffold, painting a mural that will be seen from a busy highway, is doing her part to heal the anger and tension and frustration of the people who drive by. She is changing the world she lives in.

In fact, change can only happen one person at a time. Personal, family, community, and global change begin with the decision of one person who chooses to live her or his life courageously. The root of the word *couer* is "couer," which means heart. Courage is having heart. When we live in a heart-centered way, we choose to speak out, step into action, or take on a cause, and that begins the process of change that can spread from the individual to the community, a nation, and the world. To end homelessness or hunger or poverty, one person—then another one person, then another—simply needs to decide that he or she is going to do something differently.

There's a story I love that speaks to the power of one individual with a bravely different worldview. It is the story of Swami Vivekenanda, who attended the first Conference on World Religions in 1898. The first Indian swami to visit the United States, he had traveled three months by sea from India to New York to reach the conference and to bring Eastern faith to meet Western beliefs. He sat at the conference for three days, watching representatives of each faith offer polite tolerance to the others while subtly but clearly espousing their own view as superior. When at last his turn came to speak, Swami Vivekenanda stepped to the platform, looked out at the audience, and with heartfelt sincerity he simply said, "My sisters and brothers." That's it. Just "my sisters

Introduction

and brothers." A pandemonium broke out; the crowd leapt to their feet and cheered for twenty minutes. Vivekenanda had electrified them with the power of love, wisdom, and truth. How simple and how powerful! By showing true acceptance of all faiths as part of the human family, Vivekenanda struck the common chord.

YOU NEED YOU

Why there's a change in the weather, there's a change in the sea, but from now on there'll be a change in me.
— Ethel Waters, singing "There'll Be a Change Made"

But wait, why aren't we all rushing off to transform the world? What stops us? Before you can begin to think of what you can do for the world at large, you need to free yourself from your own chains. Yes, there is work you can do from your own prison. Nelson Mandela is proof of that; he continued to be an inspiration to the people of South Africa for all of the twenty-seven years he was confined on Robbin Island. But his work didn't begin in prison. It began when he freed himself mentally and decided that the apartheid system in his country was unfair and intolerable. It continued when he was released from prison, and he decided he was not too old, too tired, or too worn down to continue his work. Instead of allowing himself to envision defeat—or even to settle into a mode of complacency—he traveled the world, bringing the situation in South Africa to the attention of people everywhere. Apartheid did not wear him down. He wore apartheid down. Not alone. Indeed, others made the choice to stand with him, but certainly he was at the forefront of the movement.

I was blessed to meet Mandela in Oakland, California, shortly after his release from prison, when he came to deliver a speech at the packed fifty-thousand-seat Oakland Coliseum. He decided to forego an exclusive black tie event that same evening in order to thank the local Long Shoreman's Union present at the coliseum; the dock workers had courageously refused to unload South African ships under apartheid.

As I shook his hand, I felt humbled by the magnificence of his decades of self-sacrifice. This hero, by meeting the extraordinary tests of his life, could do the work he's done because he transcended his own history, his personality, his circumstance—all things that could have stood in the way of his work.

In order to fulfill the purpose we were born to complete—to do our work, to pursue our creative endeavors, to have the relationships and the experiences we're meant to have—we must meet the challenges that would block us. Too often, we carry so much baggage, emotionally and mentally, that we are too weighed down to do much more than inch forward along our path. Sometimes we are too burdened from grappling with the day-to-day challenges of survival to dream at all, never mind pursue the accomplishment of our long-term goals, our deepest desires, or the vocation that is desperately calling to us. In order to carry out your life mission—whether that mission is to nurture your family as a full-time homemaker, to create artwork, to become an entrepreneur, or to pursue a high-powered corporate career—you must clear away the baggage and make the choices that will keep you on your path. Our choices are important because they give us an inner compass to steer by in every aspect in our lives.

In the pages that follow, we are going to take a deep look at the choices you make—consciously or unconsciously—that may be holding you back. We're going to identify and strengthen the places in your life where you seem weakest, and we will fortify those areas where you already have accessed your personal power. Uplifting yourself leads to uplifting others and ultimately to uplifting the world.

WISDOM THROUGH STORY

The hero must enter the special world to solve the problem, answer the question, and return balance. — Stuart Voytilla

Wisdom stories such as classical myths have always held a special attraction for me. As a college student, I was dubbed "the resident mythologist" by an English professor, who came to

Introduction

rely on me to recall any name or event in Greek or Roman mythology or any story from King Arthur's realm. These mythic stories spoke to me strongly, and I knew them all. They fascinated me. I had no way to know that the myths I loved—Pygmalion, Echo and Narcissus, and all things Arthurian— would give me comfort and strength through one of the darkest and most painful chapters of my life. I had arrived at college a terrified seventeen-year-old who had left an abusive childhood home deeply depressed and emotionally wounded. No wonder I felt a morbid kinship with the accursed Sisyphus as he daily heaved the stone uphill only to have it roll back and have to be pushed up again the next morning. I didn't know what I needed from these tales, but some guidance nudged me into these stories, and their teachings shored me up without my consciously realizing it.

My affinity for myths increased when, as a graduate student, I received the enormous blessing of living with the Wilhelm and Samuels family. Richard Wilhelm was best known for his translation of the I Ching, the Chinese "book of changes," an ancient text that is part oracle and part philosophical and mystical teaching. At dinner each evening, I'd sit at the table listening to Helmut, Richard's son, retell wisdom stories from various cultures and traditions. Thus the flames of my love of such stories were fanned.

After I began to practice psychology, the dread of legally mandated continuing education hours—the bane of my existence—became a joy when I discovered classes from the Center for Myth and Storytelling founded by Jonathan Young, a student of Joseph Campbell. What was it that infallibly guided me to the study of the world's religions and wisdom teachings—pursuits which have occupied so much of my adult life? As I look back with the 20/20 vision of hindsight, it seems obvious that something was at work that drew me to mythology, that led me to a family who proved so pivotal in my life, that called me to study the world's wisdom stories. I needed these myths, and I needed to share them.

It's no wonder that myths helped teach me life lessons and meet life challenges. It's what they were designed to do. Teaching stories—whether Norse mythology or African folktales—point the way to growth and transformation. Myth brings us the "wisdom of life," as Joseph Campbell put it, a wisdom that simultaneously reminds us that we are constantly growing and evolving on our life journey and encourages us to call forth the best within us. As a holistic psychologist, I sought to weave these stories into my work wherever it fit for my clients and students.

Because myth and story have been such an important—and effective—part of my life and my work, it has emerged as an important part of this book. In fact, you'll see that the structure as well as the content of what you read in these pages is modeled after the stages of classical myth. Myths are about the hero's journey— whether that hero be Odysseus or Br'er Rabbit or Dorothy in the Land of Oz. Each of us is in the middle of a hero's journey. Yes, you are a hero. And this book is a map you can use to recognize yourself as such, figure out what you are here to do, and move along the path toward accomplishing that mission. Each chapter is a signpost that will help you navigate from one place to the next until you reach your goal: to be the person you were born to be, to access the power you were born to use for the greater good.

This book did not begin as a book that included myths, but I must say they insisted on being revealed here. I can only look back and say they wanted to be part of a work on gaining more love, wisdom and truth. That is why they exist and were passed down from generation to generation. Myths show us again and again that there is a need to go within and to tap the wisdom within our own beings, to access the divine guidance and plain old common sense available there.

TOOLS FOR THE JOURNEY

Although you don't necessarily have to believe in God, you do have to accept that you are not the center of the Universe — Joe Gauld, founder of the Hyde Schools

The tapestry of teaching and teachers in my personal and professional life have built on my Black Southern Baptist roots and

Introduction

my training as a scientist; they have led me to Africa and India, to Native American shamans and mystics. I learned meditation and chanting on retreat in Hawaii, practiced yoga in India while learning the Eastern view of spirituality, attended deeply moving services in synagogues, and prayed in mosques. The more I learned, the more I realized that all faiths teach exactly what the ancient myths teach: that we are here to learn and grow into the most moral, upright, kind and loving people we can possibly be. The schoolroom in which we learn those lessons is the world. All these experiences together have led me to create an amalgam of healing and helping tools—tools encompassing physical, emotional, mental, and spiritual modalities—that I use every day in my practice. I call them my "power tools," and I frequently assign my clients and students homework that requires them to use these tools to facilitate their own self-understanding and growth. You will have the opportunity to do some of these homework exercises. As you read, you will find them woven into each chapter, but you'll also see that they're summarized at the end of each chapter so you can find and repeat them whenever you like.

Some of the of tools we'll be using include Zen breathing exercises to relax the body and relieve stress, emotional release work to heal our wounded hearts, chanting and decrees to harness the power of our intellect, and some of the other spiritual practices I mentioned a moment ago.

THE POWER CHOICES

The end of the hero's journey is not the aggrandizement of one hero.... The ultimate aim of the quest must be neither release nor ecstasy for oneself, but the wisdom and the power to serve others. — Joseph Campbell

How can we each embody the role of shero (a "she" hero) or hero in our own story? "A long time ago, in a galaxy, far, far away," the story of futurist hero Luke Skywalker unfolds through a series of *Star Wars* films. A poor orphaned child, Luke can only find the answers to his own past by traveling a path fraught with

Power Choices

Imperial Storm Troopers, a shadowy nemesis, and the help of an odd, unlikely mentor. Skywalker finds a boon companion in a princess warrior, and in the end he must sacrifice part of himself to be made whole and to fulfill his destiny—which thereby restores balance to the galaxy. The struggles of Skywalker—and other figures of ancient and modern mythology—are struggles that we all face. We must recover the lost part of ourselves and begin to understand it through confronting intergenerational cycles—those habits and messages we've picked up from our parents and ancestors. We have to struggle with our shadow side—the part of us that can fall prey to fear, greed, and power for its own sake. We all need a mentor and a boon companion to travel this journey with, and ultimately we can all make a profound difference by healing and transforming ourselves.

How do we answer the call that we hear in our hearts, asking us to live our lives at the highest level? It begins with listening to our lives and making choices based on what we hear. In these pages, we'll explore seven power choices, decisions that—if you make them consciously, wisely, and with love—will empower you to embark on the quest to fulfill your life purpose through self-transformation. The seven power choices include:

1 INVESTIGATION

Investigation requires taking a deep and courageous look at where you are as an individual, at home and in the world. How does your family, your community, or the world at large call for your talents, abilities, and resources? What is working in your life, and what just isn't? What has happened in your past that may be subtly influencing your current behaviors, actions, and reactions? Being honest with ourselves and seeing things as they are right now is always where we start our amazing journey.

2 INITIATION

Like the warriors in the Native American story of White Buffalo Calf Woman (we'll explore it in more depth later), we need the power of initiation—opening us to new possibilities—

Introduction

and the power inherent in ending one way of being and starting a new beginning. We will all be called at some point to participate in some kind of initiation—some ceremony or experience that will take us from one stage in our lives to the next. It is our choice to accept the initiation or refuse it. We don't have to do what we are asked to do—at least not right away. But if we're wise, we know that the initiation will keep returning in even more clear, if not dramatic, opportunities until we decide to move forward and make the change.

INSIGHT 3

The story of King Arthur's knight Igraine illustrates the concept of the power of insight. Igraine sets off on a journey searching for something he considers very valuable, but before he can reach his goal, he encounters many obstacles and accepts help from people he meets along the way. All these experiences aren't just things that happen—they are lessons designed to teach him more about himself, to help him gain wisdom and an inner confidence that will serve him on his journey. As he celebrates the quest, a search for insight, his journey will be a model for yours as you find your own light in the darkness.

INTUITION 4

By learning how to mine the jewels in our hearts, we gather the wealth of power that resides in our intuition. Intuition involves learning to trust ourselves and our inner guidance rather than rely on the patterns that we inadvertently picked up when we were children. We all have them—those little voices in our heads that tell us not to wear the red dress or that our hair is too curly or that we're not "good enough"—and they can keep us from living our most authentic, rewarding life unless we use new tools to excise them. The stories of the biblical Esther and of Hildegard of Bingen highlight the power of following one's intuition despite the apparent risks.

INTENTION 5

The energy of intention, or focused thought, took Pygmalion from arrogance to love. We often make our intellect, a great ally, into a great enemy by failing to control it. When we let our mind wander without any attempt to rein it in or operate it with some discipline, it runs around like the proverbial drunken monkey—chewing things, breaking things, jumping from place to place making messes and having tantrums. Our minds are absolutely powerful and even more so when we focus our thoughts. In making the power choice to be intentional, we choose to tame our monkey mind and operate with focused attention.

6 INSPIRATION

When we are weary of the journey or feel uncertain that we can continue, we need to be renewed by something that inspires us, uplifts us, raises our vision so we can be reminded of the goal ahead, not the rocks on the road beneath our feet. To find this inspiration, we can use tools that help us see inside our own hearts and find a way to step into our authentic lives with true power. The story of Gautama Buddha's enlightenment shows us the strength and far-reaching impact that can come from following our inspired vision.

7 INNOVATION

Along our journey, we will learn and grow, come into our own power and develop a sense of innovation. We'll see what needs to change, how it can be changed and how we might go about implementing it. In fulfilling our vision, we can take the power we have developed and give it as a blessing to the world. Whether our ideas are as grand as those exemplified by leaders such as Mahatma Ghandi or Mother Theresa or simple yet profound concepts that are meaningful within the lives of our own families and our children, at this stage we carry out our purpose and bring forth love in its many forms. Each of us has a unique gift or contribution. This book will help you to discover or uncover yours.

Throughout this book, we use myth, legend, and real stories to explore the seven power choices and practice ways to use them wisely through the prism of balance. Power without balance is a

Introduction

danger to us and to the people around us. Balance must permeate all areas of our lives. Feminine (receptive, creative) and masculine (active, engineering) qualities must both find their place in our lives. We must balance action with meditation, science with spirituality, East with West, right-brain with left-brain, and work with play. We must also balance inner work and outer work so we are not so strong in one area of our lives that we ignore and weaken another area. You will find many examples in the following pages of people who had to find balance in their lives in order to act on their power choices.

Have you ever looked at yourself at the end of the day and realized you'd hurt yourself and didn't realize it? Or maybe you look in the mirror and say, "I gained ten pounds! How did that happen?" Or maybe you get a notice from the bank saying your checking account is terribly overdrawn. How does something like this happen without you realizing it? You weren't paying attention, and when you don't pay attention, you lose vital information. If you ask me about the leading cause of divorce, I'll tell you it's a lack of attention to one's partner. When you pay attention, you give energy. If you are not giving your energy, how do you expect whatever it is you have (such as a happy marriage) to flourish?

Choices that we make when we're awake; when we're conscious; when we're paying attention are power choices. Can you make power choices? Can you consciously choose to investigate, initiate, seek insight, expand your intuition, set a high intention, be open to inspiration, and be innovative? Of course you can! I have faith in you. We are all ordinary, yet we are imbued with that power which makes it possible to do something extraordinary together. That transformative power, of course, is love. It is through finding the love—for ourselves, for others, for our work, for our history and for our path—that we can move forward into our fullest, most divine sense of power.

To make use of this book, you don't need to believe in any particular religion or have any beliefs in the divine at all. The only prerequisite is your openness to the possibility of your own growth and your own capacity to give and receive love. Simply, if you believe in being a good person and that your growth and fulfillment can benefit others, then this book will work for you.

In this work, together we will swing a rope with a big grappling hook (the hooks they use to scale mountains) around our heads seven times with all the power and momentum we can muster, aiming the hook for the highest mountain peak imaginable. This peak is the world of human beings living balanced, joyful, fulfilling lives at peace with one another. (Hey, if you are going to imagine a high peak, why not choose the highest?) The hook is wisdom, the mountain peak—our high vision, and the rope is our most evolved selves. We each have a part to play in weaving the threads of the rope together.

Power Choices is a road map that gives you signposts along the journey. We are more powerful and better prepared in our lives when we understand where this journey is taking us and why. Then we can get the most out of our lives by consciously - choosing to investigate, accept initiation, seek insight, expand intuition, set the highest intention, be open to inspiration, and benefit the world by using what we've learned along the journey innovatively. We are each ordinary, yet we are capable of heroic endeavors, even in our daily lives. As we learn to travel this journey consciously, we more fully embody the extraordinary transformative power of love.

POWER DECREE
I AM LIGHT AND ENERGY EMANATING TO ETERNITY.

There is one God, and that is love.
One race—humanity
One religion—kindness
One nation—the Earth
— Sathya Sai Baba

Chapter One

Investigation
Getting Ready for the Journey

To not know is bad. To not wish to know is worse.
— Nigerian Proverb

It's 4:00 a.m. Lucy, our heroine, is lying awake, staring at the darkness. Outside her second-floor apartment window, the deep predawn silence hovers—empty but somehow full. "Why am I awake?" she wonders as she pushes her dark curls out of her eyes. "Just once I would like to get a full night's sleep. Is that too much to ask?" she moans. She decides to put the time to good use and extracts her journal from the pile of books next to her bed. Rolling onto her stomach, she adds more teeth marks onto the tip of an already-gnawed pen before she begins to write. At first her words are just random reflections—feelings about herself, thoughts about work, and impressions of family, friends, and a certain special someone. As she writes, she realizes that something is trying to take shape. Her musings seem to be turning into a review of her life. A little surprised by that, she stretches and realizes that she's been writing for more than an hour; it's time for her to get ready for work. As she showers, dresses, and packs her lunch, she thinks to herself, "Well, my life is pretty good, but there's certainly nothing exciting or interesting going on. Perhaps it's time to make some plans—do something different." Then, heading off to work, she locks her apartment door behind her, walks down the steps, and opens the front door to her building....

Lucy is an ordinary person, living an ordinary life, but all that

Power Choices

is about to change. Lucy is about to embark—unexpectedly and reluctantly—on a hero's journey.

Why do I call it a hero's journey? Lucy is just a regular workingwoman, like many of us. She's intelligent, but not a genius; she's attractive, but not a supermodel; and she's a kind person, even though like her namesake Lucy in the *Peanuts* comic strip she has a bit of an attitude. She's definitely not a saint—just like most of us.

So what makes her a hero? What makes anyone a hero? In ancient mythology, a hero was often the offspring of a human and a god—someone born with special strengths and gifts, but also with very human weaknesses and foibles. If we consider the superheroes from our comic books, cartoons, and action films, we see that they are, at their core, human beings like you and me. The difference is that something happened in their lives that enabled them to tap into some special strength that they can use to help save their community from perceived danger or evil. Even when we use the term "hero" to describe a real person as opposed to a mythic or fictional one—the September 11 firefighters come to mind—we are talking about someone who seems to have found something powerful inside that enabled him or her to act with extraordinary courage, strength, or wisdom in the face of great challenges. We admire them for something they've done that stands out as worthy of special respect or appreciation. We look up to them.

Toward the end of 1999, *Time* magazine surveyed readers with the question: "Who was the most admired person of the twentieth century?" The top ten responses included Mahatma Gandhi and Albert Einstein—hardly the big, strong Herculean types we might think of when we contemplate a hero. Most of the people on the list were not particularly glamorous in any way. But the magazine's voters didn't seem to judge according to fame and fortune, celebrity or notoriety. The traits that made these heroes admirable seemed to have more to do with their inner qualities: they embodied courage, compassion, selflessness, integrity, and triumph in the face of impossible odds; these great souls also demonstrated committed service to humankind.

Investigation

When we read about the tremendous work of people like Mother Theresa or Martin Luther King, most of us think, *I could never do what they did.* We don't see that kind of heroism within us. But when we look closely at the lives of those we admire most—the whole picture, not just at the heroic acts—we're reminded that these people are not the offspring of gods and goddesses; they weren't born with silver spoons, special favors, or halos of light around their heads. In fact, many of the great people throughout history rose from modest beginnings and lived very ordinary lives before they received the call to do the things that caused them to be so admired and respected in the world.

Gandhi, the Making of a Hero

We all know of modern hero Mahatma Gandhi's history-making deeds in leading India to independence after three hundred years of British colonialism, but few know the details of the pivotal youthful trauma that played a major role in his personal life. In accordance with the customs of his caste and the era, Gandhi entered an arranged marriage at age thirteen to an illiterate girl. He discovered sex in a big way and reveled in it with his youthful bride. Sometime later, his father fell ill and slipped into a terminal state, requiring the care of his son and the rest of the family. One day, as young Gandhi sat massaging his father's feet, he felt an intense sexual desire and was drawn to return to his bedroom. There he awakened his pregnant wife and made love with her. A knock came at the door, and the servant announced that Gandhi's father was dead.

From the moment of his father's death, Gandhi felt intensely conflicted about his sexuality. Who could blame him? He felt guilty about leaving his father in his hour of passing from this world. He felt even guiltier that it was a sexual urge that drew him away. At the time, he had no way to process the fear and grief that led to his need for primal comfort in the form of intercourse. Nor did he understand that his wife, Kasturbai, pregnant with their child, was the ultimate affirmation of life that he needed at that challenging hour when he needed to prepare to step into his father's shoes. He didn't have access to the gift of modern psychological investigation that might have helped him better understand the implications of his feelings, needs and actions.

After his father's death, things continued to go poorly for Gandhi. He was pathetically, physically small and painfully shy and tongue-tied as a young man. His family sent him to England, where he finished a law degree, but didn't seem to develop much self confidence. He struggled along until his family, fed up with his lackluster professional attempts, sent him to South Africa. The call to adventure came one week later when he was thrown off a train in the middle of the night, despite possessing a first class ticket, because a white passenger could not sit in first class with a "colored" person. Gandhi spent the night shivering alone in the dark, pondering and praying for direction and illumination.

Turning within through reflection and prayer may bring us to a critical truth we must confront. ೞ

So if these humble people can achieve greatness and become heroes in our time, why can't Lucy? Why can't *you*? I believe that we each have a hero living inside us. Yes, *you* are a hero. When I say this to most people, they instantly deny it; we see ourselves as just regular folks—not hero material. But think of it this way. Rather than compare yourself to Superman in all his superhuman glory, remember that he's really just a mild-mannered working stiff named Clark. Spiderman is a bumbling teenager; Cat Woman is a shy, insecure graphic artist; Wonder Woman, although a powerful Amazon Queen, is also a mousy military administrative assistant; the Hulk is a clumsy scientist with a self-control issue. Your hero may not have shown herself to you yet, but she's there inside you.

One great model for how we can relate to the hero within comes, interestingly enough, from *Sesame Street*. One character, Baby Bear, likes to draw a cartoon character he calls "Hero Guy." As the lisping Muppet wields his crayons, he sings his hero's theme song: "He's a hero. He's a guy...." It turns out that Hero Guy is Baby Bear's alter ego—a bear who looks like him and sounds like him—and he helps Baby Bear see his ability to do great things. Hero Guy sends a wonderful message to children—a message that's just as important for us as adults: You can be a hero *and* still be a regular Jo or Joe.

THE HERO'S JOURNEY

Furthermore, we have not even to risk the journey alone; for the heroes of all time have gone before us; the labyrinth is thoroughly known; we have only to follow the thread of the hero-path. And where we had thought to find an abomination, we shall find a god; where we had thought to slay another, we shall lay ourselves; where we had thought to travel outward, we shall come to the center of our own existence; where we had thought to be alone, we shall be with all the world. — Joseph Campbell

Perhaps *because* the lives of people like Gandhi, King, and Mother Theresa started modestly, they offer us ideal examples of the potential we all have for doing great things with our own humble lives. Their lives can serve as a map or a model for our individual journeys. No, you don't need to follow in their footsteps precisely—become a nun or start a movement or make a great scientific discovery. (And you can't do exactly what these heroes did, even if you wanted to. Each person receives her own call and follows her own destiny.) But you can analyze the steps each hero took from birth through the unavoidable challenges they faced to achieve a greatly revered life. And if you look carefully, you'll see that almost every hero's story includes the same basic steps along the journey, even if each hero handled those steps differently.

The hero's journey is the journey we all take in our lives, consciously or unconsciously. Each of us begins life with special gifts and a purpose for which we can use these gifts. The journey is the path we each take toward recognizing our gifts, identifying our purpose, and setting off to do what we came here to do. Along the way, we will learn lessons, gain wisdom, sharpen our focus, seek help, and try new ways of doing our work, but in the end we all want to complete our journey successfully. We want to return home to a hero's welcome—confetti and all. How effective and efficient we are in accomplishing the things we are called to do depends on the choices we make. How long and how difficult our journey will be is determined by the decisions we make today.

At some point we will be called to examine our lives—to consider what needs to change and whether to do something about it, perhaps something that seems difficult. That is the very first step in the journey. For Odysseus, it was to fight the battle of Troy and spend ten years traveling the world. For Madame Curie, it was working long hard hours in a dark, dank lab to ultimately discover a previously unknown element, radium, and the phenomena of radioactivity. For Nelson Mandela, it was to fight his country's repressive apartheid government and spend twenty-seven years in prison for his efforts. For you, it might be to constructively confront your emotionally abusive partner or set boundaries with a codependent parent. They look like very different circumstances, but even if your mission is just to confront your mother, you will face challenges and choices that may seem as difficult as fighting fierce warriors or overturning an entire country's government.

Part of your journey will likely involve testing and recognizing your own strengths, and then using those strengths to overcome the obstacles that face you. Some of us are born knowing that we are destined to greatness—and knowing what great thing we are to do in life—but many more of us have to search for and excavate that heroic quality that lives within us. This book will help you with that search. The goal is not necessarily for you to save the world from evil (unless, of course, that's your mission in life). The goal is for you to truly know and deeply trust the power that lives inside you—the power that enables you to overcome obstacles and do the things that truly bring you fulfillment and joy.

In the pages that follow, we are going to explore seven power choices that will help you to choose triumph over trouble, love over fear, open-heartedness over an emotionally closed-down life. This process will help you choose to tap into your spiritual power so that when your call comes—in whatever form it may take—you will be able to make the highest choice and create the greatest change, doing the work that only you can do.

Investigation

Mufaro's Beautiful Daughters

In the children's book Mufaro's Beautiful Daughters, *author John Steptoe tells a story that exemplifies many of the power choices we all must make. As he tells it, there once lived an African farmer named Mufaro who had two beautiful daughters. One worked in the fields with her father and helped her mother weave and churn. She did her chores cheerfully and made everyone smile with her jokes and singing. The other daughter left the household work to her family; instead, she spent her time arranging her beautiful braids and oiling her lovely brown velvet skin. And if anyone disturbed her beauty rituals, she became very cranky.*

One day, the call went out that the king was seeking a wife for his son. All the eligible young women in the land were invited to come to the capital to be considered as the prince's future wife. Of course, our self-obsessed sister took off for the capital at once. Along the road, she met an old woman who was hungry, a snake who was dying of thirst, and an old man who needed help. In her rush to get to the city, she spurned them all. When she arrived in the capital, she was sent to a tent where the prince was waiting, but when she entered, she found a horrible monster waiting to devour her. She screamed and ran, barely escaping with her life.

Meanwhile, her sister had also set out through the woods toward the capital—more to investigate the proceedings and observe the other girls who were vying for the prince's hand than to pursue him herself. Along the road, she met the same old woman, old man, and snake. In her cheerful, helpful way, she stopped to assist them and to cheer them up. When she finally reached the capital, she was directed to the prince's tent. Inside, she met not a monster, but the handsome young prince himself who praised her for her kindness and proclaimed the good-hearted girl his bride.

If the good-hearted sister had not been curious and started out on a journey to investigate, she would not have met her tests in the form of the beings who needed help. She also had to stop and investigate the circumstances of each needy being to discover what they required and what in her could be of assistance. In passing the tests, she met her fate to marry the handsome prince. Her sister meanwhile, unwilling to investigate these fellow creatures more deeply, set herself apart from life and met a monster in the end—a reflection of her own selfish nature.

In our story, the call for the young women is literal: They are called to the capital to be considered for the prince's hand. The first daughter quickly senses an inner call and seizes an opportunity to leave the small village and a life of manual labor, and she put her greatest gift—her beauty—to work. The second daughter's investigation, though it leads her along the same path, is different. She has been happy with her life, but she wants to see a little more of the world, perhaps have some different experiences. She's not tied to the outcome of her journey; rather, she enjoys the journey itself. Each daughter, in her own way, enters a magical realm of tests and challenges by making the power choice to investigate. Along the way, the second sister made other power choices—developing and practicing insight, intuition, intention, inspiration, and innovation. The way she handled the choices that were presented before her determined the outcome.

We each want to rule the kingdom within us so we can make the difference in the world that we each came here to make. The lesson in this wisdom tale, as well as in the stories of real-life sheroes and heroes, shows us that we may move from ordinary lives to the extraordinary. The way you look at your life and make your choices directly affects your growth and progress. ஐ

CREATING YOUR LIFE WITH YOUR THOUGHTS
Thou canst not travel on the Path before thou hast become that Path itself.
— Helena P. Blavatsky

Have you ever gone to the phone, knowing who was going to be on the line before you answered? Or have you ever awakened in the morning thinking about someone you haven't

Investigation

seen for a long time, and then run into that person? That's thought energy. One of my spiritual teachers, Chow Chow Imamoto, used to say, "The mere thought creates." Just as motion creates kinetic energy, thought creates a form of energy as well. You can (and do!) use your thoughts to create, interpret, and define the situations and circumstances you face each day. Depending on how you think, any given situation can be a wonderful lesson or a grueling trial. Paying attention to our thoughts is a way that we focus thought energy so our thoughts work for us and not against us, giving us more power to meet challenges and transform our lives. The first step in investigation is to look at how we think and to shift that thinking to what is most powerful and life affirming.

For example, suppose someone at your workplace passes by without saying hello. You could assume that the person didn't see you. Maybe she had something on her mind and wasn't focusing on her surroundings; maybe she was in a hurry to get to a meeting. If believe it wasn't anything personal, you let it go.

Conversely you could assume that she snubbed you deliberately. But why would she do that? What have you ever done to her? Think; did you ever say anything mean about her or to her? Could she be upset because you've never invited her out to lunch? Maybe she's avoiding you for some reason. People do that sometimes, for example, when they know someone is getting fired. She *does* sit near your boss' office. Maybe she heard your boss talking about you. Maybe you are about to get laid off or something equally awful and your coworker is avoiding you because she doesn't want to tell you. Oh my goodness, what will you do if you lose your job? You just bought that new car, and now you won't be able to make payments. Then there's the kids' tuition. The bank will foreclose on your house. And your partner will surely leave you then...

See the difference a thought process makes? In this case, your coworker has passed you without speaking and gone about her business. The moment is over. That is, unless you let your mind run wild and create all sort of negative scenarios. Whatever her reason for not speaking to you, there's nothing you can do about it but accept the fact and move on. If you aren't aware of your thoughts, though, you could spend the rest of the day—the rest of the week!—worrying about things you can't do anything about. As we will see when we review the medical research on stress, our thoughts play a major role in heightening or dampening the impact of events on our emotions and bodies.

We like to think that our minds have a life of their own. We even use terms like "My mind ran away with me" or "I'm losing my mind." In fact, we are in control of our thoughts and our reasoning every moment of the day. It takes a bit of practice, but when our mind "runs away," we can run and catch it.

Taking a look at our thoughts and words is one early step you can take on your personal journey.

> ## Power Tool
> ### *Focus on the Positive*
>
> *I first learned this exercise when I took a course on behavior modification for managers. Place a three-by-five-inch index card in the wristband of your watch. Then place a plus mark on the card each time that you think a positive thought. For 21 days, work each day to increase the number of plus marks on your card. In this way, you encourage your mind to focus on the positive.*

The Power of "I Am"

I am courageous in truth seeking. — Unknown

The seven power choices in this book all begin with the letter *I*—and with good reason. Every choice we make begins with the "I"—the self. We identify ourselves as "I." We respond to "How are you?" with "I am fine," "I am not so good," and so on. Spiritual history tells us that when Moses demanded of the burning bush, "Who are you?" the voice responded: "I am that I am." Metaphysical teachers the world over use "I am" to begin powerful

Investigation

affirmations and decrees. In Sanskrit, *Om Tat Sat Om*, the mantra chanted by Tibetan monks, translates to "I am that I am." In spiritual usage, the "I" is not just the *individual*—the small *i*—but the energy that encompasses all of us and every thing.

How big is your *I*? As you do your self-investigation, ask yourself whether you tend to operate in the world with your own individual concerns, perspectives, and needs at its center. Or do you see yourself as part of a bigger picture? This might sound like a trick question because obviously you're not supposed to live a self-centered life, right? Well, actually, it is a trick question because what you're trying to achieve is a balance in which you take good care of yourself first, but you also are aware of the needs of other people in your life, your community, and the world.

How do you know when you're out of balance? It shows up in your thoughts, feelings, and behavior. When they were very young, my children used to love a book I read to them at bedtime called *Little Me and Big Me*. The child who was stuck in "little me" could only respond to challenging situations by having tantrums; the "big me" child could respond with kindness and understanding. It was a great lesson for the children—and it's a good reminder for all of us. Often, even as adults, we respond to life's challenges from the perspective of "little me"—lashing out in anger and defensiveness, expecting the worst, being unkind, taking the low road. We need to practice the same things we try to teach our children: When we face life's challenges, leave the small i at home; put the large I in charge.

As we learn to make more powerful choices, we erase the self-centered "I" and replace it with a universal, inclusive "I am." This all begins with each of us looking closely at our original *I*—our original self. We must face who we are right now so we can accurately determine where we need growth—and make the changes necessary to achieve that growth. The more you get to know your large *I* and exercise that part of yourself, the larger you become in mind and spirit. Our progress toward fully embodying the possibilities of our lives leads us from the small *i*, if you will, to a grand identification with the highest within us.

A Life in Balance

I always try to balance the light with the heavy—a few tears of human spirit in with the sequins and the fringes. — Bette Midler

We not only need to find balance between attending to ourselves and attending to the world around us, we also need to integrate and balance all the aspects of ourselves—including masculine and feminine traits, intellect and emotions, the physical and the spiritual, our inner work and outer work.

Being out of balance in any area of life can be unhealthy, whether it's living too much on one side of a spectrum or the other. The pastor of the Baptist church I attended while I was a student at the University of Washington put it like this: "Most Christians are so heavenly bound that they're no earthly good!" For those folks, the issue is finding a balance between their spiritual lives and their lives on earth. For most people today, the real challenge is dealing with feelings. We aren't a society that embraces or encourages the expression of our feelings so we often don't know how to deal with them at all. It seems that we swing from being "in control" to "letting it all hang out." To be in balance, we have to find a way to curb unhealthy emotional outbursts of anger, sadness, or fear, but we also have to avoid the stifled repression of those feelings. Not being able to work through the emotional fallout from our experiences leads to many of the issues that impede us on our journey.

The Egyptians

In the pantheon of Egyptian gods, one trio of siblings stands out. Isis, the great Egyptian goddess, married her brother Osiris, the grain god. Their jealous sibling, Seth, the god of chaos and of the desert, plotted to take over the throne.

Seth took his opportunity to get rid of his brother at a huge banquet. He'd had a gorgeous coffin made to fit Osiris perfectly. Seth raved about it at the banquet, making Osiris curious to see it. Seth had it brought out and, in a macabre parlor game, told the

Investigation

crowd that he would make it a gift for whomever it fit most exactly. When it was Osiris' turn to try the coffin, Seth's accomplices nailed the coffin shut, held the crowd back, and tossed the coffin into the Nile to be swept away by the currents.

Isis, overwhelmed with grief, cut off her hair and dressed in mourning clothes, but she didn't accept her widowhood. Instead, she set out to look for Osiris. After a long journey, she finally found him in Phoenicia and returned with him to Egypt.

Still determined to do away with his brother, Seth took more drastic action: he cut Osiris into thirteen pieces and spread them across the far reaches of the land. Again, Isis searched devotedly, and finding the parts of her beloved, she gathered them one by one and reassembled them. Anubis, the god of the dead, helped her embalm Osiris and wrap him in linen to await resurrection. But somewhere along the way, Isis managed to have sex with Osiris and conceive a son, Horus. She was also able to eventually breathe life back into her husband. Osiris remained in the Underworld to preside as king. Their story explains why Egyptians believed that their exacting mummification rituals guaranteed the dead eternal life.

The symbolism in the magical story of Isis and Osiris illustrates the lengths to which Isis was willing to go to investigate the entire earthly realm and even the Underworld (the symbol of her own subconscious) to find the pieces, not only to complete Osiris, but to complete herself. Her sexual union with Osiris once he is reconstituted is an act of balance, balancing male and female, life and death, past and future. Horus' conception is the symbolic act of creating a positive future.

We all have within us this deep longing to be complete and in balance, and to create a future of hope and possibility. To reach this goal, it takes our complete willingness to go to any lengths and persist in the face of all odds. The tools found in this book—power tools—can help us in our quest for fulfillment. ✿

Marge

My former client Marge struggled to recover the balance between her intellect and her emotions. Her parents ran a store that took a great deal of their energy and attention. As a child, Marge was often left alone to tend her younger brother. It was her job to be certain that he got home from school safely, was entertained, and stayed out of trouble. She had to prepare dinner for the family and take care of things at home-all this, plus do her own homework and prepare for school the next day. Though she did her best, of course she made mistakes. She simply wasn't old enough to handle the job of parenting and taking care of a household, but her parents didn't seem to recognize that she was only eight-too young to shoulder the kind of responsibility they'd thrust upon her. They constantly criticized her. Completely overwhelmed and unsupported, Marge retreated from her feelings. "What good is it to express my feelings?" she thought. "No one is going to listen to me any way."

As an adult, Marge isolated herself from others and avoided intimacy with anyone for fear that people would make unreasonable demands on her and she'd end up overwhelmed the way she had been as a child. Her work life, as an executive assistant to a high-powered biotech researcher, became her primary focus, and she simply soldiered through just the way she had as a child. The catch? Marge was so depressed that she couldn't eat or sleep. It got so bad that the human resources department at her job intervened and sent her to me for therapy.

Marge moved at her own pace through psychotherapy, which went slowly because she had an especially difficult time trusting me enough to open up. Her first real breakthrough was recognizing how hard it was for her to allow herself to become vulnerable. This caused her to realize how alone she had been as a child. Once she admitted that to herself, she was able to see how the pattern she created to

Investigation

defend against that loneliness had affected every aspect of her adult life and was then able to change it.

LINKING BIOLOGY AND BIOGRAPHY

I see my body as an instrument, rather than an ornament.
— Alanis Morissette

In a scene from the biographical movie *Ray*, a young Ray Charles saw his brother drown in a washtub. Only five years old at the time, Ray froze in terror during the incident, neither comprehending what was happening nor knowing what to do. Wild with grief, his mother intimated that his brother's death was his fault. Nine months later, he contracted the illness that left him blind. This profound childhood trauma surfaced years later when he underwent treatment for drug addiction. He could get clean and sober only when he could verbalize the trauma and finally release his own grief.

"Your biography is your biology," says Niravi Payne, a therapist who specializes in a mind-body approach to fertility issues. She means that the things that happen to you in your life have a definite impact on your body function and your health. It took the work of Dr. Ronald Glaser, director of Ohio State University's Institute for Behavioral Medicine Research, and his wife, Dr. Janice Kiecolt-Glaser, pioneers to in the field of psychoneuroimmunology (mind-body medicine) to discover the exact connection. During times of stress, the adrenal hormones released into the bloodstream send the body the signal to fight or flee, telling it to shut down all nonessential functions, including the immune system, reproductive functions, and neurotransmitter production. After all, you don't need those functions if you are in peril. Any stressor—taking final exams, caring for a chronically ill person, arguing with your spouse—affects the endocrine, immune, and nervous systems in particular. So Ray Charles' illness makes sense in the context of mind-body medicine: The trauma of seeing his brother drown, compounded by the guilt and blame his mother heaped onto his grief, compromised his immune system in a severe and permanent way.

In my practice, it is actually quite common for clients who have worked through their negative emotional patterns to find that their headaches, backaches, upset stomachs, and other physical symptoms disappear. My client Stan could hardly believe how much better he felt—emotionally and physically—after we'd been working together for a while. "I just had no idea that these old childhood feelings and patterns of thinking were causing the physical problems," he told me.

As you investigate your life—looking carefully at what's working and what's not—think about the physical ailments you experience. Do you have headaches? Could that mean there's too much on your mind? Or does your back hurt the way it might if you were burdened by a heavy load all the time? If you have problems with your reproductive organs, perhaps you should look at your sexual history or your current practices. Are you comfortable with how you express yourself sexually? Look at where you experience pain, tension, disease, or other chronic problems. If you know your leg hurts because of an old football injury, you can let that go. But if your ailments are vague and unexplained, they might have a source in your mind.

One of the pioneers in the area of mind-body work on a more emotional level was Louise Hay, who some thirty years ago began to notice that people with certain thought and emotional patterns manifested particular physical symptoms. For example, she found that repressed anger surfaced as a sore throat and that fear triggered stomachaches. She recommended that people feeling ill should systematically change their thoughts in order to bring about deep healing. Ahead of her time and ridiculed in many scientific circles, evidence now bears out the connection Hay highlighted between thoughts and feelings and bodily disturbance. Whether the very specific correlations she made will also prove true remains to be seen, but she was certainly on the right track.

None of the mind-body connections are new if we examine Eastern medicine, however. Dating back three thousand years or

Investigation

more, the ancient system of Chinese medicine includes acupuncture, herbs, chi kung, tai chi, and the Tao of Revitalization, the latter perfected by the Yellow Emperor, considered the father of Taoist medicine. The Eastern approach has always taken into account the need for emotional control and balance and the impact that imbalance has on the physical body. The emphasis is placed on preventing illness, which makes sense because under the old Chinese payment tradition, the doctor got paid for keeping you well rather than trying to heal you when you're already ill. Sounds good doesn't it?

In my holistic practice in San Francisco, I work closely with my colleague Helen Ye, an experienced acupuncturist, who says that before she begins to treat a patient, she guides them through a checklist that includes questions about the emotional stresses in their lives. She can then diagnose and treat the physical problem. Thoughts, emotions, and the body are integrally linked and investigation of one area yields information about another.

A recent sign of acupuncture's efficacy is that most health insurance will now cover it. I long ago, while undergoing a stressful internship, became a believer in acupuncture after only three treatments cured a painful knee inflammation that had bothered me for months. I was able to stop my cortisone shots and avoid the surgery my orthopedist had predicted.

PASSING EMOTIONAL HISTORY FROM GENERATION TO GENERATION

Each generation will reap what the former generation has sown.
— Chinese proverb

The impact of trauma extends beyond those events experienced in one's lifetime to the following generations. Things that happened in your great-grandmother's life may continue to influence your own. And it seems quite clear that, *even if we don't know* about the trauma or losses of prior generations, they stretch out their arms and clasp us in their chilling, infectious embrace. It

Power Choices

may be hard to believe, but this intergenerational transmission is the subject of much literature in the field of psychology and mental health; I have witnessed it many times in my twenty-five years of psychotherapy practice.

For example, Marvin and Faith came in to see me for marital issues centering on the breakdown of their sexual relationship. As we talked about their history, they told me about an unplanned pregnancy that occurred while they were dating in college. They hid the pregnancy from family and friends by traveling the semester the baby was due. When the child was born, they placed him up for adoption. After graduation they married and had three children, including a daughter, also named Faith, who had entered college by the time the couple came to me. When I heard the story, I advised them to share the secret of the adopted child with their daughter. I explained to them that patterns have a way of repeating themselves, and secrets have a way of coming out. Hearing this, Faith snapped, "That's the most ridiculous thing I've ever heard. She doesn't need to know."

There are certain times when being wrong is more comfortable than being right. One of them occurred when Faith and Marvin's rosy-cheeked, eighteen-year-old daughter came in to see me. She was pregnant and was planning to put the child up for adoption during an extended trip to the South, ostensibly to visit her dad's family. Sound familiar?

Faith and Marvin's story was not an isolated incident. Research has demonstrated this kind of intergenerational patterning over and over. Particularly obvious are patterns related to major traumas such as the Holocaust. Martin S. Bergmann and Milton E. Jucovy, in their now historic book *Generations of the Holocaust*, demonstrate the effect that experiences parents suffered in the war have on their children.

Susan was born within a year after allies liberated her parents from a concentration camp. The family immigrated to the U.S., where her sister and brother were later born. Susan's primary complaint when she came to see me was an inability to make decisions and an extremely high level of anxiety. She reported that in childhood, her parents had been extremely volatile and very controlling; they second-guessed everything that she said or did and criticized her at every turn. It's easy to see why people who had all control over their lives taken away might become controlling and critical. It was also clear to me from Susan's account of her family that her parents had not availed themselves of psychotherapy in order to heal the extreme trauma of their imprisonment and the losses they had suffered. This became work for the next generation.

I deal with intergenerational trauma and its impact on people a great deal in my book *What Mama Couldn't Tell Us About Love*, coauthored with Brenda Lane Richardson. African-Americans, as well as many other groups who have faced oppression, have long internalized the belief "I'm not worthy" because of the systematic nature of racism, oppression, and degradation. Out of that belief in our own unworthiness comes an imbalance regarding risk taking: we fear taking *appropriate* risks, but we tend to take *inappropriate* risks, such as having unprotected sex, experimenting with drugs, choosing romantic partners who are "unhealthy," even being habitually late. The media and larger cultural messages play their part here too. Witness the press' differing characterization of behavior after Hurricane Katrina's devastation, depending on whether the person performing the behavior was African-American or Caucasian-American. People taking food from a store were called resourceful in meeting their basic needs—unless they were African-American, in which case they were termed "looters". We tend to interpret media messages according to our own personal, often subconscious beliefs. It's like fitting a square peg into a square hole. It clicks into place.

Unfortunately, the primary way of coping with loss and pain in prior generations can best be described as strategic silence. We just keep our mistakes and painful experiences to ourselves in the hope that if our children or grandchildren don't hear about our mistakes, they won't repeat them. Rather than keeping quiet about our past, however, we need to talk about what happened to us and to those who came before and not only tell what happened, but talk about how we *feel* about what happened. And if our parents and grandparents are keeping mum about something, we need to work to get them to open up. I can't begin to count the number of people who have related to me, "I don't know why my mother is so angry and my father is so shut down. I know nothing about their childhoods. They won't talk about it." That is a huge, flashing, red, neon sign that says "Dig right here!" With a little gentle, nonjudgmental probing, we can learn about those who came before us, and thus learn about ourselves. That will enable us to break through these patterns to greater wisdom, self-love and true power.

I recommend that you set up a tape recorder and interview the oldest living member of your family. Tell them you are putting together a family history (later you will be), and ask them to provide as much history as they can. Especially important are any losses in the family or dramatic changes in circumstances.

POWER TOOL
GENOGRAM

One of the most valuable power tools you can have at your disposal is a family genogram. Genograms, created by psychologist Murray Bowne in 1978 and then adapted by fertility therapist Niravi Payne, are diagrams of a person's family history. This tool is invaluable in helping you better understand what and how past experiences and beliefs have affected your life and what you can do to change their effect on you. In fact, most people find that just creating a genogram is therapeutic in and of itself.

A genogram covers three generations of relatives: yours, your parents', and your grandparents'. (If someone other than your parents raised you, you may include both your biological parent and the person who raised you.) Don't worry about knowing details such as their birth dates; instead, record their life choices, behaviors, and other clues to their emotional history. When you look at the completed document, you'll be able to see the patterns that repeat themselves and gain clues to your own behavior.

COLLECTING INFORMATION

To build your own genogram, begin with a clean notebook. Make a heading by each relative's name. The heading should describe this person's dominant life experience, for example "orphaned at age eight" or "alcohol abuser." Record the pertinent emotional experiences that shaped the attitudes of your grandparents, your parents, and yourself. The grandparent who was orphaned found a way to cope with this experience for good or for ill; what was it? Did this relative cope by keeping people at a distance, or did he do the opposite and cling too tightly? Or in the case of a relative who was an alcohol abuser, was she a "mean drunk" or a person who seemed to always be "sleeping it off"? What were the consequences for other family members; what repercussions did it set off for the rest of the family?

If the person in question is still alive, ask him directly whether he is willing to talk about his experiences. I've included suggestions for some questions to ask. Or you can stimulate your memory—and that of your subject—by looking through old family albums.

As you are remembering past events, you may feel sentimental. That's natural. But also be realistic about your life. No one's family is perfect. For example, many intact families got along well and didn't experience any major family dramas, but the grownups were often scrambling so hard to make their lives work that they couldn't provide the emotional nurturing the children needed. If that sounds like your family, you would note that you experienced a scarcity of nurturing or support.

It's also important to ask yourself what part of your family story you're leaving out because it's too painful to consider. Many people find that their own situation was fine, but they were affected by trauma that someone else in the family experienced. For example, if you had a great, loving relationship with your mother, but she and your father couldn't get along, that's an experience worth noting.

What questions can you ask yourself and others to look more deeply into your family's past history? Let's explore some of the types of questions you can ask about your relatives. The following is just a sampling; questions can overlap among relatives, so duplicate questions are not repeated under subsequent relatives. And, of course, there are many more possible questions that you can ask on your own.

YOUR GRANDMOTHER

- What events contributed to her beliefs about scarcity, risk taking, family, relationships, and so on? These events may have been, for example: financial ruin, poverty, physical abuse, abandonment, infidelity, the idea that children should be seen but not heard.
- Did she marry? More than once? How old was she?
- Were there other men in her life besides her husband?
- Did her mate's work cause him to be away a great deal? If so, how did she respond to this?
- Were there any major losses or catastrophes in her family?
- What was her relationship like with her parents?
- Was there addiction in the family (for example, food, alcohol, spending, or drugs)?
- What events impacted her beliefs about loving or being in love?
- How did she feel about her spouse? What was their

Investigation

relationship like?
- Who was "in charge" in her household?
- How are you or your mother like her?

Your Mother
- What were your grandparents' financial and marital circumstances when your mother came along?
- Did she have any major addictive behaviors? What were they?
- What is your earliest memory of her?
- What was her relationship with her father? With her mother?
- What was her relationship with her mate (your father, stepfather)?
- How were her love relationships similar to those of her mother?
- How was her father like her mate?
- If she had siblings, what were their relationships like?
- How have your relationships mirrored hers?

Your Grandfather
- What role models did your grandfather have for how men treat women?
- What was he taught about women? How did he treat women? How did he treat his wife? His mother? Your mother?
- What were his attitudes about working, earning a living, and money?
- How did he relate to his children?

Your Father
- What role models did your father have for how men treat women? What was he taught about women? How did he treat women? How did he treat his wife (your mother)? His mother?

- If your father was absent, how does that fit into the general pattern in your family?
- What were his attitudes about working, earning a living, and money?
- How did he relate to his children?
- What is your earliest memory of him?
- How have your experiences, including relationships, finances, and family, mirrored his?

Your Life

- What do you remember your parents saying to you about men? About women? About relationships?
- What was the nature of your parents' relationship? How were they getting along when your mother was pregnant with you?
- Do you have a favorite expression? Did any family member have the same expression?
- What messages did you hear about scarcity or abundance?
- What was your relationship with your father like?
- What is your earliest memory of your father, either stories you heard or things you experienced?
- What was your relationship with your mother like?
- What is your earliest memory of your mother, either stories you heard or things you experienced?
- If you have siblings, how were those relationships growing up?
- What would you be reluctant to tell a stranger about your father? Your mother? Your siblings?
- What is your attitude about men? Women? Children? Relationships? Money? Work? Play? Spirituality?

Culling Information Bytes

Once you have compiled your information under

Investigation

each relative's name in your notebook, start at the first section, working your way through to the end. With a red marker, circle up to four experiences for each family member (mother, father, both grandmothers, both grandfathers) that most shaped them and most influenced your attitudes and beliefs about life. Now paraphrase each of these 24 experiences into information bytes. (You may list a different number of experiences if you had a less traditional family.) Let's say your grandfather worked hard but drank heavily, wasted the family's money, and cheated on his wife. His description may be "hard-working, extravagant alcoholic/womanizer." When you have at least twelve information bytes, you're ready to compose your genogram.

CONSTRUCTING YOUR GENOGRAM

One of the most attractive aspects of a genogram is its sheer simplicity. You will need to know only six symbols to put together the emotional map of your life. These symbols appear in the legend portion of the following sample about Kim, a woman we will soon discuss.

These symbols are placed in their proper order representing the members of your family. Start with yourself and then draw the lines that link you to your parents, grandparents, using the notations that indicate their gender and marital status and whether they are living or deceased. As you can see from the sample pictured that each generation is placed on its own line. So you and your siblings would occupy one line, your parents another with their siblings and so on. So this ends up looking like a family tree-but with symbols and notations as well as names.

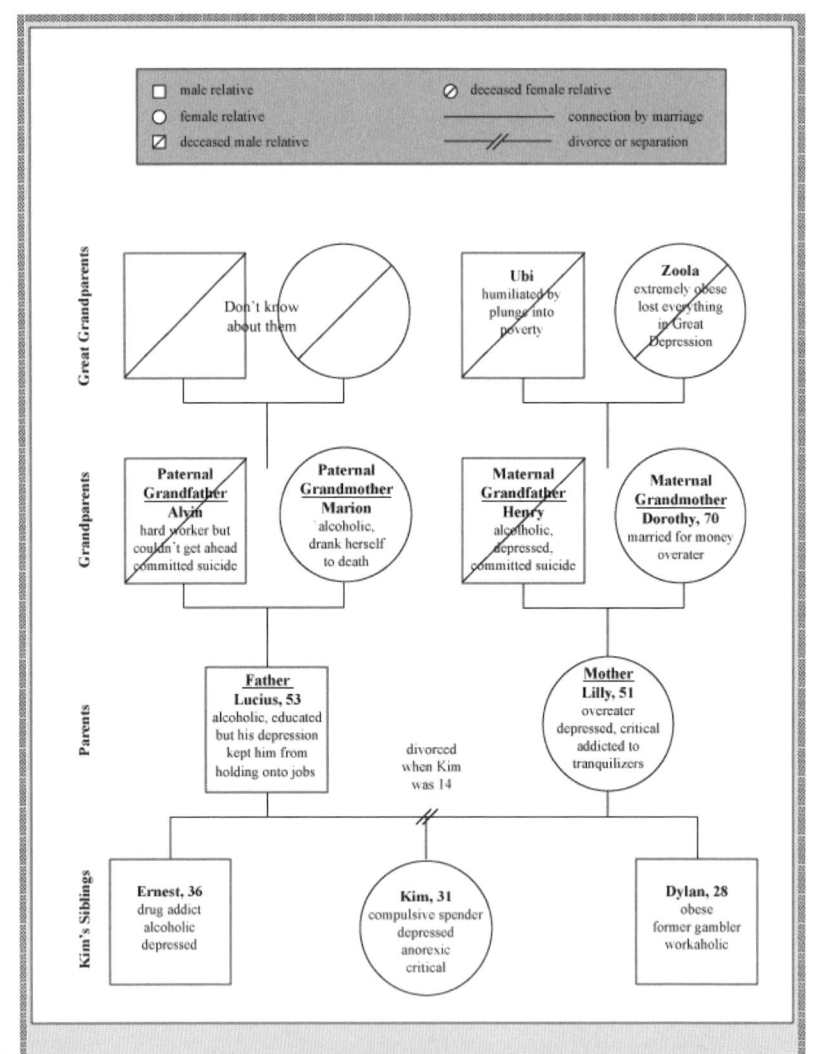

Power Choices

Genogram

Legend:
- ☐ male relative
- ○ female relative
- ☒ deceased male relative
- ⊘ deceased female relative
- ———— connection by marriage
- ——//—— divorce or separation

Great Grandparents:
- Don't know about them
- **Ubi** — humiliated by plunge into poverty
- **Zoola** — extremely obese, lost everything in Great Depression

Grandparents:
- **Paternal Grandfather Alvin** — hard worker but couldn't get ahead, committed suicide
- **Paternal Grandmother Marion** — alcoholic, drank herself to death
- **Maternal Grandfather Henry** — alcoholic, depressed, committed suicide
- **Maternal Grandmother Dorothy, 70** — married for money, overeater

Parents:
- **Father Lucius, 53** — alcoholic, educated but his depression kept him from holding onto jobs
- **Mother Lilly, 51** — overeater, depressed, critical, addicted to tranquilizers
- divorced when Kim was 14

Kim's Siblings:
- **Ernest, 36** — drug addict, alcoholic, depressed
- **Kim, 31** — compulsive spender, depressed, anorexic, critical
- **Dylan, 28** — obese, former gambler, workaholic

4 | REVIEW YOUR GENOGRAM

Now, look for the patterns that emerge in your genogram. What experience has repeated through the generations? After sketching your genogram with your information bytes, you will be surprised at the power inherent in the words on the page. Your genogram will offer you a new perspective concerning your life. Keep it handy and take good care of this valuable family record. What to do with

Investigation

> this information and how to break the patterns that don't work for you will be presented throughout the remainder of this book.

KIM

Kim, a thirty-one-year-old office manager, began seeing me because she was worried about her compulsive overspending and her quickly unraveling relationship with her live-in boyfriend, Leroy. He was also thirty-one, a construction worker and a recovering marijuana addict. Kim admitted that she was overly critical of Leroy, especially now that he had "gotten his act together." She was also depressed and had to force herself to eat. The lack of appetite was significant. For Kim, not eating was life-threatening; she had been struggling with anorexia since high school. The theme running through Kim's life was one of deprivation—not loving herself enough to eat, not having enough money, not feeling enough passion to sustain a relationship that she wanted.

Kim felt certain that her problems were related to her conflicted relationship with her mother, who was severely overweight, depressed and exhibited hyperirritability (she was always angry and very mean to Kim). But I encouraged Kim to go even deeper, because, when one family member appears to be causing another's behavior, the problem was usually the cumulative effect of intergenerational patterns. Kim was able to trace her family back to her maternal great-grandparents. At five-foot-ten and 250 pounds, Kim's great-grandmother towered over her much-smaller husband. Together, this seemingly mismatched couple built one of Atlanta's first prosperous black businesses. Then came the Great Depression; they lost everything and died penniless.

Having seen her parents lose all they had worked for, their daughter—Kim's maternal grandmother—married a local undertaker, assuring herself of some financial stability. But Kim's grandfather suffered from depression and eventually committed suicide. His grieving wife soothed herself with food, becoming as obese as her own mother had been. The family traits of overeating and depression were passed on to Kim's mother, who was one hundred pounds overweight.

The paternal side of Kim's family tree had its own pattern: a suicidal grandfather; a grandmother who drank herself to death after her husband died; and a father, the only child of this troubled union, who was both depressed and alcoholic. Though highly educated, Kim's father was unable to hold a job.

The intergenerational belief on both sides of Kim's family tree was this: life is unbearable until you find a way to insulate yourself from the pain. The insulation on her father's side was alcohol, on her mother's side, food. Both responses showed themselves in Kim's generation. Kim and one of her siblings had eating disorders (Dylan was a compulsive overeater). Kim also spent compulsively, her younger brother was a compulsive gambler, and her older brother abused drugs and alcohol. Though these seem like unrelated addictions, the fact that each of her siblings demonstrates any addictive behavior is significant. Recent genetic studies demonstrate a link between all addictive illnesses.

Looking back over her parents' disastrous marriage, Kim said, "Mom was extremely cold toward Daddy, and she put him down all the time about not being able to bring in enough money. Early on, she turned on me because she was extremely jealous of my relationship with Daddy. When he got drunk, he taunted her about being fat. He didn't get along with my brothers either, especially Dylan because Daddy hated to see his son become overweight. I was the only one he paid attention to. He said I was the only normal one in the family."

Emotionally abandoned by her mother, Kim secretly concluded that the real reason her mother rejected her was because she was inadequate. Kim believed she wasn't smart enough or pretty enough nor could she do enough to warrant her mother's love and care. Desperate to keep her father's love, if she couldn't have her mother's, she concluded that the only way to secure his affection was to be "skinny enough." But that was deep in her subconscious. On the surface, she thought she was rebelling against her mother's overeating, when her undereating was actually the flip side of the same coin. In addition, Kim's lack of nurturing caused her to struggle with another ailment that had been passed down through her family and that usually goes hand-in-hand with addictions: depression. Although Kim refused to drink, she tried to self-medicate her despair by spending.

With addictions running amuck in her family, she was drawn to Leroy, who smoked marijuana several times a day. People raised in families in which there are chemical addictions (drugs or alcohol) or behavioral addictions (gambling, overeating) are unconsciously attracted to mates with similar issues; we are drawn to the familiar. And it's no coincidence that when Kim's boyfriend stopped using drugs, she lost interest in him and began to find fault with him. Kim believed men were supposed to be unreliable and addicted—because that's what her beloved father demonstrated. But clean and sober, Leroy could no longer be an emotional stand-in for her unreliable, addicted father. At the same time, her belief that she wouldn't have to feel pain if she could be skinny enough began to surface, and she lost her appetite.

Kim continued to work in therapy to break through her family patterns. One of the affirmations she used repeatedly was, "I am enough, and I deserve to have enough love, money, and food. Life is full of abundance."

Kim had the courage to use therapy and a program of self-transformation that reached back across the generations to conduct an extensive investigation and discover the hidden roots of the issues in her life. The results? Kim is now a healthy weight; she's no longer undereating or overspending. She is happily married and has become a role model for her siblings. Seeing her demonstrate a new, better way of living, her siblings have started asking her for counsel about making changes in their lives.

THE FOUR LEVELS OF CONSCIOUSNESS

Our bodies mirror our thoughts, emotions, and experiences.
— Dr. Christiane Northrup

As human beings, we have four levels of human consciousness: physical, mental, emotional, and spiritual. Our body, emotions, mind, and spirit are completely interdependent; what affects us in one area will also have an impact on other areas. Thus, when we're feeling strong emotions—say, madly in love or just plain mad—we may lose our appetite. Or when we're upset, we may find ourselves feeling physically ill or unable to concentrate.

An upset in one area may be a clue as to what is going on in the other areas of our lives. The body's ills point to the emotions and the emotions point to our thoughts, while the thoughts may point to our spiritual life or lack thereof.

The ancient hermetic axiom "As above, so below"—the greater controls the lesser—is a universal law that describes the interaction of behavior between the four levels. There's a hierarchy here. The body is on the lowest level; spirit is on the highest. Our thoughts trigger certain feelings, as in our earlier example of the person who ruminates on why her coworker walks by without speaking. The result of that rumination could be feeling angry or sad, feelings which can certainly upset the body and result in fatigue or headache and so on. The spirit, as you will see later, has a profound

Investigation

impact on our thoughts, but a body in pain can also pull the spirit down or drain our energy. All of the parts work together; one can help heal or hurt the other. Let's investigate the state of affairs on each level of consciousness.

BODY 1

Our body is the reliable vehicle that's here to take us to where we want to go. Just as we need to make sure that our car's engine is lubricated with the proper amount of oil and the gas tank is filled sufficiently to get us to our next destination, so it is with our bodies. It's essential to take care of our bodies—with a healthy diet, sufficient sleep, and vigorous exercise—if we're going to pursue our destination in this life.

But taking care of our bodies also means paying attention to the other levels of consciousness, especially our emotions. Stress, negative thought patterns, and spiritual depletion can put demands on our bodies that don't leave us with enough energy and stamina to effectively handle change—even those changes that we want to make. Conversely, since all the levels are connected, by making simple, positive physical changes—staying physically healthy—we can often find the challenges in other areas become less burdensome.

EMOTIONS 2

The spelling of the word *emotion* tells us that such feelings are *energy* in *motion*. By their very nature, emotions cannot stay still; they change, ebbing and flowing, every moment. You may find yourself crying over a tear-jerking movie one moment then laughing at a silly commercial the next. Our range of emotional expression is linked to both the patterns we've created during our lives, as well as to the patterns our ancestors have exhibited before us.

In his book *Raising an Emotionally Intelligent Child*, Dr. John Gottman discusses scientific discoveries that have been made in recent years around the role of emotions. "Researchers have found that even more than IQ, your emotional awareness and abilities to handle feelings will determine your success and happiness in all walks of life, including family relationships," he says. Since emotions are so fluid, we have an amazing capacity to direct and shape the energy associated with emotion in ways that either support or inhibit us, and which impact those near us. How we manage, express, and act upon our emotions establishes whether we feel empowered to move forward or not.

3 MIND

Western society reveres the mind. We like to feel smart and to be associated with smart people. Having someone call you bright, intelligent, or a genius is a high compliment. Yet the mind can play tricks on us. It is notoriously unreliable. (Just ask any detective questioning witnesses about events at a crime scene.)

On the other hand, research consistently shows the evident connection between what we envision in our minds and what occurs in our lives. As far back as the second century AD, Marcus Aurelius believed, "If you are distressed by anything external, the pain is not due to the thing itself but to your own estimate of it; and you have the power to revoke it at any moment." Today some researchers think that we can influence our own success, health, and happiness by the way we think. There's a plethora of medical literature showing the mind's impact on the body. Research has shown that a positive attitude and nonfatalistic thinking has improved the health of people with potentially terminal diseases such as cancer or HIV— increasing longevity, reducing the severity of physical symptoms, or even inspiring complete healing. Other studies have shown that the simple act of keeping a weekly gratitude journal can reduce a sick person's physical symptoms. Having our mind work for us in this way, as opposed to against us, is one of the keys for smooth transitions or transformations.

4 SPIRIT

The spirit is often neglected when one discusses issues of health, transformation, or fulfilling one's life purpose. Yet the spirit clearly impacts whether or not we feel supported in the world, whether or not we feel that there is something greater than ourselves that can assist us through any challenge, and whether or not we feel that we have a purpose for being alive. How can this not impact our thoughts, our emotions, and our bodies? The fact is, it does. Research now shows that regular prayer and a spiritual practice can enhance health and well-being. Dr. Jeff Levin, in his fascinating book *God, Faith and Health*, reviews the research that connects the dots between health and a variety of spiritual beliefs and practices.

Research has also found a wide array of spirituality's long-lasting benefits, including decreased rates of illness, less recidivism, and fewer emotional disorders such as depression. One such experiment compared those who never attended church with those who attended services at least weekly: Church attendees reduced their risk of illness leading to death by almost 50 percent. Other studies showed that positive impacts could last as long as eleven years. Dr. Levin writes, "For sure, there is no medication that can work so effectively for so long."

Whether we define spirit as something that is divine or not, it is spirit that provides meaning beyond the small i that we discussed earlier. This sense of a greater connection in the circle of life is paramount in the effectiveness of any life transformation.

Each of these levels of consciousness is powerful and important in its own way, and in order to be as powerful as we can be in our own lives, we need to keep all four levels strong and in balance. We also need to make the connections between them. It may seem obvious, but many people tend to forget that the whole being is greater than the sum of its parts. Thus, strengthening the weakest link within you will cascade positive change throughout your life. When these four levels are individually strong and collectively integrated, they make up a powerful, wonderful whole.

As you begin the hero's journey, it's important for you to assess where you are in terms of these four levels of consciousness. Do you have a life of the mind, but very little spiritual connection? Do your emotions rule you? Are you physically strong enough to handle the everyday things that you have to do? Your answers to such questions will help you determine what tests you might face on your life journey and what skills you have in your repertoire to address those challenges. Your goal is to have access to all four levels of consciousness as you face any challenge. With all your resources available to you, you'll be better able to approach a challenge appropriately and be more likely to see success.

POWER TOOL
THE POWER QUOTIENT CHECKLIST

MIND YOUR PQ

The Power Quotient Checklist is designed to measure our awareness and growth-physically, mentally, emotionally, and spiritually. This is dramatically different from an intelligence quotient, or IQ, which measures cognitive processes only. Essentially the PQ measures how well we pay attention to our inner being. Real power, according to Dr. David Hawkins, author of Power vs. Force, *reflects states of consciousness that lead to greater peace, love, and joy.*

How do you discover your PQ? Prepare by doing a relaxation exercise. (See the Meditation box in this chapter.) Then give the first response that comes to you as you look at each of the questions below. Don't think too much about a question or overanalyze it. This isn't a test in the typical sense; it's an opportunity to see where you have been paying the most attention. Scoring instructions follow.

THE POWER QUOTIENT CHECKLIST

For each question below, rate yourself on a scale of 1 to 5.
5 = I highly agree
4 = I agree
3 = I'm not sure; I neither agree nor disagree
2 = I disagree
1 = I strongly disagree

Investigation

PHYSICAL
____ 1. I feel in shape, well, and at an ideal weight.
____ 2. I feel energized throughout my day.
____ 3. I am at my peak physical condition.
____ 4. I exercise regularly.
____ 5. I practice good nutrition and take supplements.

EMOTIONAL
____ 6. I generally feel happy.
____ 7. I never feel hopeless, helpless, worthless or depressed.
____ 8. I find it easy to express my emotions.
____ 9. I check in regularly with my feelings and the feelings of those around me.
____ 10. I never react with anger or frustration rather than expressing how I feel to others.

MENTAL
____ 11. My thoughts about myself, my life, and the people I live and work with are persistently positive.
____ 12. I look at the challenges in my life as an opportunity to learn something new.
____ 13. I never blame others or feel guilty.
____ 14. I set aside time to still my mind so I can see more clearly what I need to do or understand.
____ 15. I never focus on the bad things that can happen to me.

SPIRITUAL
____ 16. I never feel disconnected or isolated.
____ 17. I feel connected to my source, and I have a sense of myself as one with life and with others.
____ 18. When solving a life problem, I rely on my inner guidance or spiritual sources for help.
____ 19. I have a regular spiritual practice and/or am

part of a spiritual community or group.

____ 20. I feel that I am continually growing spiritually and helping others do the same.

HOW TO SCORE THIS SELF-ASSESSMENT

CALCULATE YOUR SCORE

Add your results for each area and enter them below.

Physical Total: _____
Emotional Total: _____
Mental Total: _____
Spiritual Total: _____

ANALYZE THE RESULTS

Look at the final scores for each of the four levels of consciousness. If you achieved a score of 20 or greater, you are evolved in that area. If you scored 15-20, you are adequate. If you scored 10-15, you are losing power in that part of your life. If you scored 10 or below, you are running a power deficit.

Look at where your scores indicate your power is adequate or evolved. Were you always confident in those areas of your life? If not, what life lessons brought you to this point? Think about the inner work you've done to get here. Celebrate your growth and evolution.

The areas with the lower scores indicate where you have the strongest need to make positive power choices. What makes you feel differently about yourself in those areas? Is there any obvious experience that accounts for your lack of power here?

List the two areas in which you scored lowest; these are the areas you want to focus on.

The areas I need to focus on are:
_____ *and* _____

Investigation

> ### HOW TO APPLY YOUR PQ
> *Your PQ score gives you data that you can apply as we continue through the remaining chapters of* Power Choices. *On your journey you will want to give special attention to the areas with the lowest scores. These are the areas where you have the greatest potential for growth.*

WHY IS IT SO DIFFICULT TO CHANGE?

Myth is the original self-help psychology. — Liz Greene and Juliet Sharman-Burke, *The Mythic Journey*

One of the features in any mythic story is the hero's struggle to transform him- or herself. And it's usually quite a struggle because change just *ain't* that easy. But just why is it so difficult? Modern science posits five reasons as to why change is so difficult.

1.. *We won't ask for the help we need.* We need help to change, but we tend to view asking for help as a sign of weakness, especially in American culture where we prize our individualism, independence, and efficiency. Our cultural reverence for masculine traits makes it very difficult to utilize the more feminine trait of seeking help and support.

2. *If we ask for assistance, our helpers aren't effective.* Many helpers—experts, advisors, spiritual leaders, mental health providers—haven't done their own work. It's hard to lead people to where you have never been. You can read a map to someone, but unless you know the landmarks and the terrain, you can't give them effective directions. Even people who are trained to help and who make their livelihood from it, often don't use their own tools and advice. For example, when I gave the keynote address to the California Convention of Therapists in 1995, I asked my 1,500 assembled colleagues to raise their hands if they were in therapy. Only a sprinkling of hands went up. I told them, "If your hand isn't up, you have no right to practice. If you aren't actively engaged in your own transformation, you don't have the energy available to help someone else effectively. Haven't you noticed that the people who come to see you have the same issues that you have?" They all responded with a hearty, affirmative laugh.

3. *We think there's no "cure" for our problems, so why bother to try to change them?* We misunderstand the nature of emotional distress and how treatable it is. Most people simply don't have enough information to recognize and correctly interpret the symptoms of depression and other emotional disturbances, nor do they have the information about how accessible and treatable emotional distress is. Dr. David Satcher, during his tenure as the United States Surgeon General, made understanding depression the core of his platform because he felt that Americans needed to grasp the tremendous health hazards of depression.

4. *We're too ashamed to admit we need to change.* Feelings of shame besiege us when we have a problem because we see problems as failures, flaws, or mistakes that we should have avoided rather than as opportunities to learn and grow. Shame is a debilitating emotion. Unlike guilt, which says, "I have done something wrong," shame says, "I am wrong."

5. *We don't feel worthy of the energy investment it would take to change.* It follows that if we feel ashamed of ourselves, we also feel unworthy. I find that many people can't begin to change until they incorporate the idea that they are worth taking care of and that their lives are important enough to be lived fully and successfully.

Perhaps because of these five powerful factors, people hold the common belief that a human's ability to change herself is limited. You've probably heard the fatalistic comments, "Well, you know, folks don't ever really change." "You can't teach an old dog new tricks." "That's just how she is; she'll never change." "You knew I was this way when you married me; it's too late to change me now." To some extent, these are true. Alan Deutschman reported in a 2005 magazine article that only ten percent of heart surgery patients made the lifestyle changes their doctors recommended—changes that would help them avoid further heart problems and prolong their lives. The article, published in *Fast Company*, concludes that even a life-threatening crisis won't bring about sustained change. Nor do scare tactics work; we just go into denial and keep doing what we've been doing. Knowing intellectually all the many reasons we might need to make a change doesn't seem to motivate us to do anything about it.

It's not that we're not capable of change. We now know, based on current research, that we have a much greater opportunity to grow and evolve than we had imagined—whether that growth is on the physical, emotional, mental, or spiritual level. By the time we're adults, many of our behaviors and thought patterns are well established, but our brains aren't completely hardwired. Our brains, even as adults, as still very plastic—meaning we can actually change our thinking and our behavior.

So, how do we bring about change? How do we begin and sustain the growth that can not only save our lives, but fill them with joy and purpose? It starts with that joy and purpose thing. We're not likely to be motivated by "shoulds" or even "musts," but if we're convinced that changing will help us feel better, function better, be happier and more fulfilled, we're more likely to give it a shot. So the first step is to figure out: how could your life be better? Then think about how making a given change will help you live a happier, more peaceful life. For example, if you tell yourself you need to exercise more, you need to support that idea by imagining how, once you get fit, you'll be to be able to go biking with your children or dance all night with your lover.

Making a change also requires us to shift our worldview in some way. The habits and patterns we've established are accompanied by certain conscious or unconscious thoughts. (For example, many overeaters consciously think, "This bowl of ice cream won't do any harm. What does it matter; I've never been able to lose weight anyway." Unconsciously, they are often avoiding something or seeking the protection that their "fat" gives them.) We must change how we view the world, especially our place in it. That may mean surrounding ourselves with success stories—inspirational people who have accomplished the thing we set out to do. Or we may need to put ourselves in counseling in order to unwind some of the thinking that has been holding us hostage.

If we're going to change, we need to go at it fiercely. The change should be sweeping and severe. For most, the cold turkey approach seems to work best. Don't try to wean yourself off cigarettes or just have one less drink tonight. Quit smoking. Today. Forever. Empty the liquor cabinet. Check yourself into rehabilitation. Do something major because you're likely to see results more quickly, and that will motivate you to keep going. The area where this is less likely to work is weight loss. Drastic diets can lead to the well-documented yo-yo effect that many dieters face; if food is the issue, Overeaters Anonymous with its holistic approach may be the best solution.

Once we decide to change, we need support. Research shows that people who find some way to get encouragement for their efforts are more likely to sustain them. That may mean you should get a jogging partner or join a therapy group. You might adopt the slogan that Twelve-Step programs espouse: "Together we can do what we could never do alone."

Even if you do none of these things—even if you avoid change with every fiber of your being—change is inevitable. It's going to happen to you whether you resist it or embrace it. You may as well do the latter. That's what this book is all about. I want to help you heighten your consciousness, identify and get rid of your inherited or self-imposed obstacles, and put your efforts into directing the powerful flow of change in a way that helps you meet your personal goals.

APPLYING INNER TOOLS
So many people know me. I wish I did. I wish someone would tell me about me.
— Joseph L. Mankiewicz, *All about Eve*

To make the most of the power tools in this book, we work from the inside out. It does no good to pretty things up physically

Investigation

before we work on what's going on inside us. That's why so many people who have gastric bypass surgery or cosmetic surgery find that afterward they still aren't happy. Because they fixed the saddlebags and the crow's feet, but they didn't address their deeper issues—the depression that causes them to overeat, the self-esteem issue that causes them to feel badly about their looks. It's important to look at our inner lives first because whatever we create on the inside is the infrastructure and the support for the life we create on the outside—the life that shows to the world. In fact, current research is showing that inner work—whether it is prayer, meditation, or chanting—has massive physical-and mental-health benefits.

More than thirty years ago, Dr. Herbert Benson, president of the Mind/Body Institute and associate professor of medicine at Harvard Medical School, conducted revolutionary research that demonstrated that the regular practice of relaxation techniques acted as an antidote to stress and actually improved overall health. He coined the phrase "the relaxation response" after he noted the physiologic changes that appeared in the body of his research subjects when they repeated a word, phrase, sound, or prayer repeatedly. His research and that of other scientists has shown quite clearly that the relaxation response decreases muscle tension, heart rate, and blood pressure.

I've found that many of the clients in my practice, with as little as five minutes a day of inner work (such as meditation or prayer) easily and quickly shift to more positive feelings and interactions. The practices' effectiveness is increased if they do their inner-work techniques at the same time each day. Your body establishes rhythms, called diurnal cycles, such that it knows when it's time to eat or to sleep. Likewise, it learns when it should be open for the inner work you do. Thus, your practice will go more smoothly and be more effective if it is done consistently at the same time each day. Doing it in the same place—especially in a place set aside for just that purpose, with some kind of altar or place to focus your energy-helps these built-in rhythms serve you and will strengthen your practice of personal growth tools.

Power Tool
Meditation

Meditation is a simple but powerful process that has been the cornerstone of my holistic therapy practice for more than twenty years. My clients who apply this tool with me in the office for even a couple of minutes feel more relaxed and peaceful. There are many, many meditation forms and techniques. Some people chant; others are silent. Some rake the sand in Zen gardens; others walk labyrinths. But the simplest form requires taking time from all of our doing to just be—finding time to sit in quiet contemplation. Here's how I suggest that my clients begin a meditation practice.

1 Get comfortable. Sit in a quiet place where you will be uninterrupted for at least ten minutes. Settle yourself into a position where your body can just relax and fall into stillness. Have a notebook and pen next to you.

2 Breathe. Take three deep, full breaths-filling your lungs to capacity and them emptying them completely. With each breath, think, "I am relaxing and letting go." (Remember, it's mind over matter.) Continue to breathe and repeat the phrase in your mind until your mind begins to relax your body.

3 Visualize light. Picture a beautiful, brilliant light sitting at the top of your head-a light glowing like a sun. Let the rays from this sun penetrate your body, starting at the top of your head and flowing down through every part of your being, right down through your toes. When you visualize yourself full of light, repeat to yourself three times, "I am light."

This technique prepares you to relax and open your mind and body, so you can take in fresh, positive energy that will enable you to answer the questions and face the challenges that come to you in life. I recommend that you do this relaxation exercise at the beginning and the end of each day in order to reap the full benefits of taking a moment to let go. Meditation, in conjunction with the other exercises you'll find throughout this book, can be wonderfully beneficial to you as you travel on your life journey.

Investigation

Mazu: The Girl Goddess

An inspiring example of someone who experienced tremendous growth is Mazu, the Chinese goddess of the sea. Mazu, originally named Lin Mo Niang, was born in AD 960 on a small island in the straits of Taiwan. Her very birth was auspicious: it is said that the birthing room filled with a brilliant light and the fragrance of flower blossoms the moment she came into the world. As she grew, it became apparent that she was extraordinarily gifted with remarkable intelligence, a photographic memory, and supernatural powers.

She was only four years old when she stood before a statue of the goddess Quan Yin and received her gift of second sight—the ability to know events that would happen in a distant time or place. At age thirteen, she became the student of an elderly Buddhist priest who taught her the secret mysteries of Taoism. Two years later, Lin Mo and her friends, all wearing beautiful new dresses, went to a pool to see their reflections in their new clothes. A sea creature sprang from the water holding out a bronze disk. The other girls ran away terrified, but Lin Mo calmly accepted the bronze. From that moment, her powers grew daily—as did the respect of her neighboring villagers.

They relied on her vast knowledge of Chinese medicine and on her miraculous healings. Because she could predict changes in the weather, sailors and fishermen listened for any warnings from her before they went out to sea.

Lin Mo was twenty-eight when she told her family that it was time for her to leave them—indeed, to leave the world. Her neighbors watched as she walked up a mountain near her home. When she reached the top, a dense fog surrounded Lin Mo and celestial music filled the air. Lin Mo was carried into the heavens in a golden glow of light, leaving the trailing curve of a rainbow where she had last been seen.

In honor of her compassion, devotion, and spiritual enlightenment, Buddhist leaders named Lin Mo a deity; even the Chinese government declared her a goddess. Her life teaches those who honor her about the need to be mindful of the balance of opposites *in our lives—whether it be the masculine and feminine, kindness and ferocity, nature and civilization, or the unity of mind, body, emotions, and spirit. Even as a young girl, this remarkable being was willing to investigate, through her studies with her Taoist teacher and her willingness to step forward and accept a gift from the unfamiliar sea creature. Her story gives us an example of the role of investigation in acquiring knowledge and power of the best kind: that which serves others.* ৯

Embracing the Power of the Feminine

What is most beautiful in virile men is something feminine; what is most beautiful in feminine women is something masculine. — Susan Sontag

Most of the heroes we've met in this chapter are actually *sheroes*—women who have faced difficult initiations and gained strength from their own willingness to embrace something new, something feared, something that would change them in ways they couldn't predict. They remind us that women are often called to find within themselves traits that are considered masculine, and men are required to call on feminine traits so we can create greater balance and more harmony in our lives.

All of us—men and women—need balance between the masculine, action-oriented, aggressive aspect of our nature and the feminine, creative, inward-looking part of ourselves. If we don't have both, we are working with only half the tools available to us. No one way of being is going to work for us in every situation. To approach a delicate situation with aggression or a difficult situation too timidly just won't get you the results you need. It's like trying to use a Phillips screwdriver on a straight-head screw. It doesn't work.

Imagine our world if we allowed balance to reign. What would be different if we sought balance rather than power over others? Suppose we focused on the power we have over *ourselves* and the basest parts of our being—angry hurtful behavior, feelings that run wild like an untrained dog let loose in the backyard digging up the

Investigation

flowers and turning over the garbage cans, destroying the beauty around it. We modern heroes like the ancient heroines, must incorporate a quest for balance in all that we do; we must stop, seek inner guidance (which will be our focus in the next chapter), ask for support, access and share feelings, and nurture ourselves as well as those around us in a compassionate positive way. Again and again, the research shows that these elements lead to growth and sustained change. These qualities are essentially feminine, though they are present in men as well as in women. In fact, this really has nothing to do with gender. The question is: to what extent do we seek to develop these strengths so we can maximize the potential inherent in choosing initiation?

In antiquity, the fabled Amazon queens reigned in Africa, Asia Minor, and the Middle East. These priestesses ministered to the needs of their people medically, artistically, and spiritually, and they went to war when needed as well. Now that's quite a balancing act! Many legends and wisdom stories have their roots in the lives of historical events and the people who acted them out. For example, Sigmund Freud (of all people, for he was a biologist not a mythologist) identified the tale of Medusa as the story of an African warrior priestess. The snakes that supposedly served as her hair were actually the traditional coiled braids for which African women are famous to this day.

The world's religious teachings also honor the feminine. One beautiful example of the feminine in spirituality is found in Jewish mysticism. Malkhut (Kingdom) is also known as Shekinah (Presence). In earlier Jewish literature, Shekinah appears frequently as God's immanence, but is not overtly feminine. In Kabbalism, Shekinah becomes a full-fledged woman—the daughter of Binah, God's feminine half. Shekinah is "the secret of the possible, receiving the emanation from above and engendering the varieties of life below," according to D. C. Matt in *The Essential Kabbalah: The Heart of Jewish Mysticism*. The feminine aspect in this description of Shekinah embodies creative possibility.

The goddess—whether as the Hinduism's Lakshmi or Durga, Buddhism's Quan Yin or Tara, the Egyptian Isis or Yoruba Yemaya or Native American White Buffalo Calf Woman or the Greek goddess Gaia, mother earth herself—always nurtures and embodies a fierce compassion for her people. I love the passage from the *Gnostic Gospels* in which the writer speaks with a feminine voice, declaring:

> *For I am the first and the last,*
> *I am the honored one and the scorned one.*
> *I am the whore and the holy one.*
> *I am the wife and the virgin....*
> *I am the barren one,*
> *And many are her sons....*

There is healing power—physical, mental, emotional, and spiritual—in seeking to recover the lost feminine.

LET THE INVESTIGATION BEGIN

I know of no more encouraging fact than the unquestioned ability of a man to elevate his life by conscious endeavor. — Henry David Thoreau

We've covered a lot of ground in this chapter, examining many different areas of our lives. Our lives—our bodies, our emotions, our beliefs—are pretty complex, aren't they? A life is a lot to cover. But the more completely we examine our own lives, the better prepared we are to face the journey we're about to embark upon. Before you start anything, it helps to know what you're dealing with.

Questions, techniques, and power tools are sprinkled throughout this chapter and the ones that follow. You can read the chapter and then do the work, or you can set the book aside and do the exercises when you come to them. It depends on your reading and learning style. But do work to answer all the questions and put the techniques into practice. And continue to use the words from this chapter as inspiration as you move forward.

Investigation

QUESTIONS

1. What physical (body) change would bring the greatest benefit and joy to your life?

2. What emotional change would bring the greatest benefit and joy to your life?

3. What mental change would bring the greatest benefit and joy to your life?

4. What spiritual change would bring the greatest benefit and joy to your life?

POWER TOOLS

1. FOCUS ON THE POSITIVE

Look for what is right. What is right about you, your relationship(s) work and everyone and everything in your life. Take the time each day to strengthen your positive focus. Come up with a minimum of five positives every day in any category, but especially in an area that poses a challenge right now.

2. GENOGRAM

Construct your personal genogram. The patterns that emerge will amaze you. Then, if you have a mate, that person may want to make one as well. It can be helpful to see how your family patterns dovetail. (Trust me they will.)

3. POWER QUOTIENT CHECKLIST

Now that you have collected the information from the Power Quotient Checklist, decide on one thing that you want to change for the better about yourself or your life, and write it down. By the time you reach the end of this book, you are going to see some new possibilities.

4. SPEND SOME TIME CONDUCTING A BODY SCAN

Where in your body does your "emodar" fire? (Emodar is my word for the signal that shows up in your body indicating that you are having strong feelings.) Is it a tightening in your stomach or shoulders? An ache in your chest or throat? A creeping headache or backache? Like Achilles with his mortal heel, we all have one area of our bodies that is more vulnerable than others. This area is your friend. It will cue you in so get to know it well. One of my clients learned to recognize the burning in his stomach as fear and then to talk about what triggered the feeling and to seek support rather than shutting down, —a behavioral pattern that had brought his marriage to the brink of divorce.

Power Decree
I Am a Truth Seeker.

> *We spend most of our time and energy in a kind of horizontal thinking. We move along the surface of things...[but] there are times when we stop. We sit sill. We lose ourselves in a pile of leaves or its memory. We listen and breezes from a whole other world begin to whisper.* — James Carroll

Chapter Two

Initiation
Answering the Call

It was this awesome force within Lighteningbolt that drove him into the mountains to join his teacher Goose Flying.
— Hyemeyohsts Storm

Lucy steps out *onto the sidewalk, only having time to notice that the sky looks overcast, when boom! she suddenly crashes into an old man whose wheeled walker has gotten away from him. As they both tumble to the ground, a bag that had been attached to the walker breaks loose and rolls away. "My bag," he yells, "Get it! Get it!" But Lucy can only roll over and try to sit up. She puts her hand to her brow, groggily mumbling, "I must have hit my head. It hurts like the dickens." The old man can't get up at all, but he is dragging himself along on his belly, clawing frantically for the bag that is slowly rolling toward the open work hole just ahead. Out of nowhere, two kids on skateboards swoop by them, lunging for the bag. Just as they reach it, the tip of one of the boards hits the bag and knocks it into the hole. "Stop!" screams the old man. Lucy can only sit and stare. "You've got to get the bag!" the old man yells at her desperately. "Please, please help me!" Lucy finds her way to her feet, and goes over to peer into the hole. It's deep and dark; she can't see the bottom. "I'm sorry, mister. It's too deep. I can't go down there." One of the skateboarders has circled around, and as she looks up, he is heading straight for her....*

It starts as an ordinary day in the life of an ordinary woman. Lucy is headed for work when she is suddenly entangled in something unexpected, awkward, difficult, and possibly

Power Choices

dangerous. She is encountering the force of change; the power of initiation is at work. Often as we embark on our own mythic journey, we meet the unexpected and must respond whether we want to or not. Sometimes we choose change; sometimes change chooses us.

We begin in the ordinary world where we investigate who and exactly where we are. Now once we've looked at where we are, we are called to initiation, the step that actually starts us on our journey. Initiation can mean one of two things. The first definition has to do with new beginnings—starting something new. In the second situation, an initiation can be a ritual or ceremony—often a rite of passage such as a bar mitzvah, a quinceanna, or a graduation that marks a person's transition from one stage of life to another. In some cultures, the initiations include some kind of test that culminates in you having learned something new or proven your strength, wisdom, or ability to handle important matters. Regardless, the ceremony ushers you into a new state of being.

There are three ways we typically receive the call to initiate:

1 Though your life looks good on the surface and there's nothing significantly wrong, you feel the urge to break out or grow in some way. For example, things are fine at your job, but you feel bored and in need of greater challenge. You begin to have a niggling feeling that behind your facade lie issues and concerns that need your attention—if not now, then soon.

2 You know that something specific in your life needs your attention, and you want to address it, but you don't know what to do about it. Perhaps you have a serviceable, but far from familial relationship with your in-laws. Up to this point, you've just let it go and pretended it was fine.

3 You're slammed with a major life crisis, and you have to respond to it immediately. What the two warriors' experience in the myth that follows is an example of that. (Sometimes if we don't address number one—that first little niggling feeling—it evolves and escalates into number three, a crisis you can't avoid.)

Initiation is the call to actually do something about these things.

It is the first indication we have that we need to take a step—the critical first step that will lead us to a place of growth, ultimately leading to greater peace and fulfillment. When we're going through an initiation, we are making a choice to move forward.

White Buffalo Calf Woman

The Native American wisdom story of White Buffalo Calf Woman speaks to the initiation of individuals and of a people. Two warriors hunting buffalo came upon a white buffalo calf. As the men neared her, the calf changed into a beautiful, young woman. One of the warriors instantly began to lust after her. Sensing his feelings and offended by them, White Buffalo Calf Woman asked him to approach. As he rushed forward, a black cloud fell on him. When it cleared, all that was left of him was his bones. The other warrior, observing all this, fell to his knees in prayer. Having gotten his attention, White Buffalo Calf Woman instructed him to return to his people and inform them that she would appear to them in four days carrying a sacred bundle.

Four days later, she appeared to the tribe as a white buffalo calf descending on a cloud. Stepping down, she rolled on the ground and changed from white to black, then to yellow, then red. But when she arose, she was once again White Buffalo Calf Woman. She stayed with the people for four days, teaching them sacred songs, dances, and ceremonies as well as the ancient traditional ways. She instructed them to be responsible caretakers of the land and to act from the knowledge that the children are the future of the people.

When she left, she pulled a white buffalo calf pipe from her bundle and placed it into their care. She promised to return for it one day, bringing harmony and spiritual balance to the world. The people should look for the birth of a white buffalo calf to signal that she would soon return.

In this story, White Buffalo Calf Woman's appearance is

exciting and significant, but we should also pay attention to what happened to the two warriors. Like our Lucy, they set out on an ordinary day on an ordinary mission, but they met the extraordinary. The first warrior is so caught up in his normal thoughts and in his physical responses that he fails to recognize a magical event is taking place. He wants that woman; he is not paying attention to the fact that, only a second before, she changed from a calf into a woman right before his eyes. (A sure sign that something unusual is about to happen, don't you think?) He is doomed by his own base and unconscious response.

The second warrior, more aware, meets this event with proper reverence and he not only avoids his own demise, he also becomes an instrument of fate, ushering in a renewal for his people. He recognizes that the color white is a portent of divinity and newness. And he knows that the transformation from animal to human form presages something magical about this White Buffalo Calf Woman. He listens to her message and faithfully carries her words back to his people, so they, too, can be aware and prepare.

Along with the color white and the transformation from animal to human form, the number four is important here. It symbolizes the four directions on the medicine wheel: east, south, west, and north. The number four also speaks to the four levels of consciousness when she stays for four days and then she turns the four hues of human beings and of the four seasons. The number four symbolizes balance. Indeed, White Buffalo Calf Woman brings with her the magic and power to sustain the people on the journey of life. Essentially, the songs, dances, and peace pipe she leaves with them are totems and signposts by which they can steer their lives. Initiation can be a sudden experience or it can be a ritual, but in this case, the encounter with White Buffalo Calf Woman and her powerful spiritual symbols entail an initiation in both uses of the word.

Initiation

A Change Is Coming

Change is the constant, the signal for rebirth, the egg of the phoenix.
— Christina Baldwin

Have you ever been in a situation where there were signs that something was about to happen—but you didn't recognize them until after the fact? I think we all have, at some point, had that *"Oh, I should have known..."* moment. For most of us, it's quite a bit more subtle than a buffalo descending from the sky. Perhaps you see your company's sales sag a few months before your CEO announces a series of layoffs. Or you find that your partner is spending more and more time at work before she comes to you and utters the fateful phrase: "We need to talk...." Maybe your sweet child is starting to become more defiant and withdrawn as a teen, and you're waiting for the other trendy designer sneaker to drop.

If you're in tune with your environment, you can sometimes get an inkling of what's to come. Some mothers say that they notice their toddlers eat like little pigs for a few days just before new teeth come in. There are folks who can predict snow by the way the moon looks, or forecast rain based on how their bones feel. One woman I know says that when she loses her keys or locks them in the car, she knows she should take note of what's going on around her—something is about to happen, and she needs to prepare for a shift somewhere in her life. Even if you can't do anything about the change that's coming, just being ready for it is half the battle.

But subtle signs are easy to overlook when you're busy, exhausted, and distracted by the many other things you have to cope with. That's why balance is so important; if we're spending too much time on the things that exhaust, distract, and distress us, we can't pay attention to the smaller signs, the quieter messages that tell us change is about to come. And when we can't pay proper attention, we aren't prepared to effectively meet that changes and challenges that are about to enter our lives. The more you're able to stay in balance, the better you're able to pick up the subtle signs that tell you you're about to be called to action.

Research on the impact of subliminal stimuli definitely shows that we pick up cues that we are not aware of that will influence our responses to people and events. For centuries meditation teachers have encouraged meditation as a way to quiet the mind in order to more deeply access the information available in the subconscious and intuitive parts of the mind. Even if we encounter initiation suddenly, we are better prepared by knowing how to identify an initiatory experience and to approach it with useful tools.

FACING YOUR LIFE; FACING YOUR FEAR
Courage is fear that has said its prayers.
— Dorothy Bernard

Initiation is an important signpost to pay attention to because it leads you to a critical crossroads moment. You are being called on to make a move of some kind. The question is: which way will you turn? Will you move at all? You can look at your life, see the need for change and do nothing. That's how many, many people respond to things. Rather than take some kind of action, they pull the proverbial cover over their heads and refuse to deal with their high blood pressure, their increasingly abusive spouse, or the job stress that's driving them to drink.

One reason people avoid the initiation phase is that it is, frankly, frightening. In fact, that is one of the ways you know you are going through an initiation: You find yourself faced with something that seems difficult. Maybe it's something that wouldn't be too hard for someone else (think Mother Theresa), but it feels too hard to *you*.

When I was called to write this book, my first response was one of fear. I had to face my old, familiar fear of "taking up more space in the world." Along the way, I had learned that I didn't really deserve to do my work on a really large scale. So the moment I began to think about doing something bigger—reaching more people with the messages, the lessons and the teachings I had to share, and having a greater presence in the world—I also started to think about all the reasons I shouldn't do it. "Somebody might not

Initiation

like what I have to say," I told myself. "They might be offended by me taking up all that space. This will backfire on me. If I get too big, I'll be bound for a fall." People will sneer, 'Who does she think she is?'" Or here's one that I've found a lot of people have: "I'll be shot." That one, I believe, comes from the live on-the-air broadcast assassinations of the Kennedys and King.

Mind you, I've written books before. I've been on national television. I've been interviewed for articles for major magazines. This was really nothing new. But I was scared anyway because that's the first thing that happens when you initiate: you feel frightened. Fortunately, I had a few tools—the things I needed to do, the inner work that allowed me to move forward with the project. Even with those tools, though, I must admit that, over the two years that I was working on this book, I constantly had to address the challenges and setbacks that reignited my fears.

That often happens: You don't necessarily get over your fear, but you learn to do what you need to do in spite of it. I've read that David Reynolds, the founder of the constructive living school of psychotherapy, has a fear of flying. But his work often takes him from the United States to Japan, and you can't get there from here quickly and easily unless you fly. His take on dealing with his phobia is to acknowledge it, and then go get on the plane. This can be a helpful approach when you're faced with a situation that needs to be addressed immediately. You may not always have time to make an appointment, see your therapist, work through your issues, and have a breakthrough before you address a crisis or problem. If your plane is leaving, you have to get on it!

In chapter 1, we talked about being conscious of our thoughts. That's an important skill to have when we are dealing with fear, because fear tends to escalate if we don't rein in our thoughts. We can allow our minds to run so far away from us that we become paralyzed by our own imaginings. For example, take the defiant, withdrawn teenager mentioned above. Many parents would think the worst because drug-abuse prevention organizations say noncommunicative behaviors are possible signs of drug use or addiction. Such behavior has also been attributed to young people who go on terrible crime sprees. But this teenager might just be in the funky phase called individuation, which many young people go through as they transition from childhood to adulthood. To find out what's really going on, you have to investigate. And no matter what the situation is, it's a change that you want to be aware of and address.

To take a positive step into the initiation phase of your journey, you need to find a way to approach whatever change you are facing from a position of strength and preparedness. That brings us to the second power choice: the way you address your initiation.

POWER TOOL
THE BEST-CASE SCENARIO

Prepare for the best because your thoughts have power. So choose to play big. This is what Babe Ruth did when he set his records. He held both the home-run record and the strike-out record because he swung with everything he had every single time. When I am facing a potentially troubling or frightening dilemma, I like to perform this mental exercise to help me find my place of power. It's simple.

1 Make a list of the best things that can happen in your given situation or as a result of this situation.

2 Then imagine it with all the details possible: what does it look like, what does it feel like, where are you, what is happening. You may even want to draw a picture, write it down, or create a collage to make it feel more real to you. This allows the right side of your brain the opportunity to put amazing things together, which creates a doorway for the seemingly miraculous synchronicities of life.

Initiation

> **3** We also want to utilize the left side of our brain. Create a list of reasonable action items related to your "best-case scenario" with dates by which you'd like to accomplish them. This helps you move toward your most positive outcome. Then take those steps. A sure way to get those steps accomplished is to have a buddy to check in with. Call your buddy before and after you take each step; cheer one another on.
>
> **4** Last, at least twice a day, repeat the following affirmation several times out loud and with power: "I expect the best. I am bigger than any challenge in my life." While stating your affirmation, visualize the final outcome that you desire.

TYPES OF INITIATION

The world is round, and the place which may seem like the end may also be only the beginning. — Ivy Baker Priest

When you're called to initiation, it is always a signal that it's time for you to grow. But I can tell you that in my twenty-five years as a psychologist, I have never had anybody come into my office and say, "My life is just great, but I'm here because I thought I'd like to grow." People come in because they are resisting necessary growth so strongly that they're stuck in a painful place. Or they're already involved in a growth situation, and they're facing the painful feelings that signal that they are about to take an important step on their journey. Either way, they are hurting and need help.

There are many kinds of "normal" life initiations, of course. Marriage is an initiation; so is divorce. Getting promoted or getting fired—both initiations. We tend to put judgments on these things, labeling some "bad" and others "good." But sometimes being fired, for example, is the best thing that can happen to you. This maybe difficult, maybe even devastating at first, but these kinds of experiences open you to new possibilities. I know people who have gotten fired and said, "Well, I hated that job anyway. Now I'm going to do what I really want to do." For them, this was the beginning of a grand new life. Being fired reminded them that the world wouldn't end if that job ended. And it helped them find the strength to do the things they wanted to do—the thing that really made them happy. These kinds of initiations aren't always pleasant, but the end result can be more wonderful than you imagined. This brings to mind the experience of childbirth—another initiation. There's a lot of pressure, pushing, and pain, but in the end there's a wonderful result. I'm extremely grateful for my two daughters, who are the most wonderful results in my life and who have initiated me into the growth of being a mom.

As I look at other initiations in my own life, I think of my very first television job on *AM San Francisco*. I was hired as an on-air psychologist, bringing self-help segments to their viewers. I was severely underpaid because when they asked me how much I wanted, I didn't know the going rate for the kind of thing I was doing. I said, essentially, "Oh, pay me a pittance; that's fine. Just give me the job." The way I saw it, that TV show was going to give me the chance to reach a larger audience with whom I could share my psychological tools, and I was grateful for the opportunity. But after a while, I realized I was actually losing money every time I went to the studio to work. It took three hours of my time, and I was being paid for one. So I talked to my therapist about my problem. (I've always believed in taking my own medicine, of course.) When I told him how badly I felt every time I went there, he said, "Do you realize that every time you go there and let them underpay you, you're hurting your own self-esteem? You're hurting your own sense of self-worth." I thought, "Well, wait a minute. I'd better change this." So I went in to speak with the production executive and told him I needed a raise.

He said, "Sorry."

As if I hadn't heard him, I repeated my request, "I need a raise!"

He said, "Sorry, the budget just won't take it."

Initiation

So then I really, really, really, really scrounged up the courage and I said, "I need a raise, or I'm going have to leave the show."

And he said, in so many words, "Sorry. Good-bye."

I was devastated. I thought, "Oh, no. I stood up for myself, but then I blew it." But guess what? This was my initiation. I had to learn that I was worth more and deserved to be paid more, and I couldn't learn that lesson as long as I was allowing myself to be so terribly underpaid. Indeed, after I got over my shock at "losing" my job, I did notice a positive shift in my self-esteem. And I was able to remind myself that something new and wonderful happens when one door closes. The next door always opens.

I started thinking, "Well, there has got to be a way for me to continue working in television." By then, I'd had a number of people walk up to me and say, "I really learned something from what I heard you say on television. It helped me." Folks needed what I had to offer. And I thought a television show was the ideal way for me to reach the people who watch television, but will never be able to come to my office.

On a hunch, I sent a videotape to the *Oprah Winfrey* show. Within a week, I had my first appearance on the hottest show in the country. The producers invited me to discuss "the other woman," and I talked about how that pattern is a manifestation of low self-esteem. (Talk about teaching what I had just learned.) From there, I was hired as the regular psychologist on *Hour Magazine*. And when it went off the air, I got an offer to host my own national TV show, *Can This Marriage Be Saved?* And wouldn't you know, the night before I signed the contracts, the executive at *AM San Francisco*, now my good friend, called saying, "Our budget has changed. Could you come back?" Guess what I said.

> **POWER TOOL**
> **ASK THE RIGHT QUESTIONS**
>
> *This tool involves altering your perspective on life. Most people, without meaning to, have a victim mentality. Have you*

noticed that when something comes along in life, there's a tendency for people to ask questions like "Why do the bad things always happen to me?" Or "Why would God let this happen to me?" People seem to like blaming God for something. It is equally popular to blame somebody else for issues in our life. But when we start asking questions like "Why me?" we are embracing a victim's position. We're saying that we are powerless to do anything other than respond to the (bad) things that happen to us. (And we're asking a futile question to boot-because no one can really explain why things happen to us.)

We have to learn to ask empowering questions. No matter what happens-no matter how bad or difficult the situations we face in life-we have to train ourselves to think about them from the perspective that we are in charge of our lives. We may not be able to control everything that happens, but we can certainly respond to them effectively.

There are four very important questions to consider when you are faced with a challenge in life.

1 *What is this situation here to teach?* What am I supposed to learn from this?

2 *What in me might need to grow?* Do I need to be more loving, more patient, more open? Is there something in me that needs to improve in order to meet this situation or challenge?

3 *Do I need to ask for help or support to get through this?* For most people it is much easier to give help than it is to receive it. It seems that our culture encourages people to adopt a self-serving approach to life, but when it comes to asking for help, pride rules. When you are faced with a challenge, asking for help might be the only way you'll get through. In fact, you may be faced with the challenge just so you can learn to ask for aid.

Initiation

4

How can I help someone else in the same situation? This is crucial. Buddhist teachings say that if you're suffering, you're never suffering alone. There are a million other people having that same experience right now! Think about that. First of all, it tells us that our suffering is not special, nor does it make us special. The narcissist in us thinks, "Oh, nobody's ever suffered like I've suffered," but everybody gets their share of pain, grief, and suffering. The good news is that, if you can learn something from your experience or even simply be open to sharing your experience, you have the opportunity to help someone else by sharing resources, offering a listening ear, or coming up with some creative way to help end the suffering for everyone who is experiencing it. And the realization that you're not alone in your experiences might be just what you need to hit the ground running toward a less self-involved view of yourself and your life.

Think about the founder of Mothers Against Drunk Driving, MADD. There's a woman who transformed a terrible tragedy in her life—the death of her child—into a way to help ensure that other mothers don't have the same experience she had. Here's a case of someone saying, "Something painful happened to me; how can I help other people as a result of it?"

And didn't she make us conscious? Did she not change our culture? MADD originated the concept of a "designated driver," a phrase that is so commonly used these days that we even see it on beer commercials. When we face a challenge, we want to get to the point where we immediately access our feelings about what is happening, work them through (in our next chapter, "Insight," I'll show you how), and as quickly as possible begin to look for the lessons and possibilities in the situation. These lessons keep repeating until we master them.

WHAT ARE YOU CHOOSING?

The thing always happens that you really believe in; and the belief in a thing makes it happen.
— Frank Lloyd Wright

Have you noticed that we all have patterns in our lives? Something happens and you find yourself thinking, "Wait a minute, haven't I seen that issue before? I thought I worked through that one, but here it comes again." If you want to know why you're creating certain patterns, you are going to have to look very deeply and ask, "What am I choosing? Do I have a subconscious pattern that causes me to choose this way of being?" You're going to have to look very deeply at where you learned that pattern. Ask yourself, "What part of me is programmed to do this?"

The easiest way to discover what you're choosing is to look—honestly and consciously—at your life. I remember once asking a woman sitting in a workshop I was teaching, "By looking at your life, can you tell what choices you've been making?" She said, "Yeah. Apparently, what I have been choosing is to spend every penny my husband makes as fast as he can possibly make it." Her husband, of course, wasn't all that happy about this, and it created some conflict in their marriage. Once his wife got in touch with her choice, she then had the power to change it. How do you know that you are stuck in a patterned response loop? Simple, you keep repeating the same behaviors over and over and producing the same results.

In her research, pharmacologist Candace Pert has found that many of us are programmed to do the things we do. Literally. We have little receptor sites in our brain that make us crave certain kinds of feelings and certain ways of doing things, and we create situations to satisfy those cravings. But we can break those negative patterns by becoming conscious, by paying attention, by using some focused energy and changing our interpretation of events.

My client Molly, for instance, a gorgeous style diva with a mild couch-potato streak, made the astonishing choice to get on a bike and ride in the AIDS Ride Europe hundred-mile trip from Amsterdam to Paris. This choice transformed her life in ways that made her want to click her Jimmy Choo high heels together. She came back from the journey more self-confident, better able to speak up for herself, and able to set boundaries with family and friends who used to damage her self-worth. Molly made a choice and carried out her own initiation.

REFUSING THE CALL

Of course, the person I was fleeing most fearfully was myself...
— Bill McKibbon

There's a running joke among therapists that most men enter therapy when they are ushered in by a woman holding a weapon in her hand. This was true for Alberto. His wife Celia's weapon was the divorce papers she'd filed. She had actually already moved out, and she refused to consider reconciliation until he stopped his philandering behavior, but she was willing to come to therapy with him. This split was especially painful for Alberto who was a devoted father to their three young children. He and Celia were very involved in their church and, as a devout Christian, he felt deeply ashamed that the church community was aware of his transgressions. In their first session Alberto told his wife, "I'm here for myself as much as for you and our family. I have got to change." Turning to me, he related the story of his first marriage, which ended in the same way and caused him to lose contact with his firstborn child when the child's mother moved three thousand miles away. Though this hurt him deeply, Alberto didn't make the effort to change when his first wife left him; instead, he ignored his problem, perhaps hoping it would go away when he entered a new relationship. This is a classic example of a phenomenon that mythologists term "refusing the call." The heat is on the hero; he knows he needs to do something about a problem, but balks instead.

This jibes with the findings reported in the *Change or Die* article we discussed earlier. If your cardiologist says you must make lifestyle changes to survive, that is as strong a call as you're likely to get. But people refuse to change every day. In fact, refusal seems to be part of almost every wisdom story in mythology and in everyday life. Think of Lucy refusing to go down the hole after that poor old man's bag. Think about the number of people you know whose behaviors—be it their uncontrolled anger, their alcoholism, their poor health habits—are ruining their lives, but who haven't chosen to do a thing about it. We see this in the people who could evacuate their homes in the certain threat of some natural disaster, but refuse to do so. Why would someone risk life, family, and what is most precious rather than get up and get moving down the road? In psychology we call it denial; our subconscious is protecting us from something that we are not ready to face.

And what wakes a person from their denial? The answer can be seen clearly in our myths: the hero usually suffers some loss. The Native warrior above loses his friend when White Buffalo Calf Woman appears. In *Star Wars*, Luke Skywalker loses his family. Dorothy is taken from her home in Kansas and plopped down in the strange land of Oz. My client Alberto had lost one family and was on the verge of losing a second one. Such loss acts as a sign that it is critical to address an issue rather than deny it further. Because the hero has paid such a high cost for ignoring, delaying, or denying the call, he understands the importance of the change that he is to face. Loss often provokes a sincere effort from the hero, because the pain of any further loss she may face is greater than the pain of facing the thing she fears. She tells herself, *I will no longer sit by and simply let things happen. I will accept the call.* Thus, she seizes her power and initiates a quest.

I am happy to report that when Alberto answered the call, he acquitted himself as a true hero by going the distance in both couples therapy and group therapy, breaking through with the help of his wife and the members of their church community who stood by them and offered encouragement. His wife, inspired by the example of Jesus who protected and forgave the adulterous woman, forgave Alberto after he completed his transformation, and she remarried him in a ceremony that they both reported had much deeper meaning for them than their first wedding.

The Birth of the Buddha

When Prince Siddhartha was but twelve years old, a prophesy declared that should the prince ever encounter old age, illness, suffering, or death, then he would forsake his royal birthright to embark on a life of spiritual seeking. Upon hearing this, his father the king, fearing the loss of his son, did everything in his power to circumvent the prophecy. He used all his wealth and power to keep his son from seeing any of these realities. But to do so, he essentially had to make Siddhartha a prisoner within the palace. Destiny, however, could not be avoided. One day, as a young man, Siddhartha, desiring more freedom, slipped by his father's guards and ventured into the world. Almost immediately he saw each of the fateful sights his father sought to censor. Of course, having been so sheltered from the world, Siddhartha was extraordinarily shocked when he saw people who were ill, old, and dying. But, true to the prophesy, his internal struggle with what he had seen set him squarely on the path of a spiritual quest.

In this case, as in many, refusing the call heightens the call's urgency in the end. In fact, it is first his father who refuses. His father's attempt to have Siddhartha avoid his fate sealed it instead. Never having seen any suffering, the young man was probably even more sensitive to it. His father unwittingly played a part in the prince's eventual need to completely cut himself off from the royal life and cleave to his spiritual aspirations. Had the king succeeded, his son may have become a king, but certainly an inexperienced, unwise one. As it was, Siddhartha came to have even more power and influence than the ruler of any kingdom. Known as Buddha, his journey and teachings have uplifted millions of people all over the world. ೨

LIFE'S CHALLENGES ARE LESSONS

I am the North Wind. I am very impatient.... To meet me you have to be strong.
— Carlos Castaneda

A marriage crisis is often a way that modern heroines and heroes are called to the quest for personal development. As the host of *Can This Marriage Be Saved?*, I had the good fortune to work with one of my own heroes, Dr. Aaron Beck, who is famous for his research in the area of depression and thought by many to be the father of cognitive psychology. He assisted me in counseling a couple whose marriage was shattered by the wife's infidelity. The couple wanted to continue their marriage, but the husband was haunted by recurring dreams and flashbacks of finding his wife with her lover when he came home early from a business trip. He was despondent and anxious, and he suffered from classic symptoms of depression. Dr. Beck explained that depression is triggered by a downward spiral of negative thinking; by changing your thinking, you can lift your depression. He intervened with this troubled man by asking him to imagine a beautiful, safe place—embellishing the mental image not only with sights, but with sounds and smells, so it became as vivid as possible. He then instructed the man to visualize a red stop sign every time the flashbacks began, and then to switch to the beautiful scene he'd practiced visualizing. The exercise is completed by repeating a positive phrase over and over; this husband repeated, "I am peaceful." In his fifty years of research at the University of Pennsylvania, Dr. Beck has found that this cognitive technique is an effective treatment for mild to moderate depression. Why does this work? Because through repetitive practice, we reinforce our positive thinking, and that changes our emotions, which in turn shift our behavior.

Yemaya's Ocean

The idea of "reframing cognition"—changing our minds—is not new. Many ancient stories point to this process of coping with life's vicissitudes. We find Dr. Beck's ideas embedded in the tale of the goddess Yemaya, which originated with the Yoruba people in Nigeria. As the story goes, *Yemaya was raped by her brother and was so infuriated by the act that she cursed him, and he died. She'd taken her revenge, but eventually her sorrow at the loss of her sibling threatened to take her life as well. She made her way to a mountaintop where she chose to die, and as she took her last breaths, fourteen Yoruba gods and goddesses came forth from her womb. When her uterine waters broke, they caused the great flood that created the oceans. And from her bones came the first human woman and man, who became the parents of all humans on earth.*

During the slave trade, when Yoruba people were taken from their home on long, dismal ocean voyages, they believed that Yemaya, showing compassion for her people, went with them. She was their comforter and protector as they traveled to distant lands.

Today, Yoruba believers honor Yemaya as a mother goddess—the deity of family, home, fertility, and love. Like water, she embodies both change and constancy, creating life, protecting it, and changing it as needed. The goddess of comfort and inspiration, she reminds us that the worst catastrophes can be endured and that good can come from them. She teaches us to be like a leaf floating on the water, adjusting to the ebbs and flows of change that occur in our lives and flowing along with grace, wisdom, and courage. This idea of nonresistance, or flow, is very Eastern. It gives additional credence to Dr. Beck's findings that our thoughts about our situation determine how we feel. Clearly if we choose to look for the good and "reframe" a situation, we meet it with more power. As Buddhist teacher and author Sylvia Boorstein said, "It's not that spiritual people have fewer problems, it's just that they meet them with more grace."

Leaving Home

The longest part of the journey is said to be the passing of the gate.
— Marcus Terentius Varro

In classical mythology, the call prompted by adversity or crisis takes the protagonist somewhere he or she has never been before. We might call this leaving home. Remember, home represents what's comfortable and familiar. Change—an initiation—disrupts that, so we don't want change. Our initiation might take us away from our physical birthplace. It may take us from the home embodied in our parents and other caretakers. Leaving home may be more spiritual or psychological—a situation wherein we have to leave behind the thoughts and beliefs that don't serve us and embrace something new. The first day of kindergarten, the first day of college, the day you cross the threshold with your spouse, are all moments of stepping off of an old path to embark on a new journey.

Even if your leave-taking is physical, such as moving out of your parents' home into a place of your own, it's likely to be accompanied by spiritual, emotional, and mental shifts as well. Take, for instance, the familiar story of that young girl from Kansas who was carried away in a tornado. Dorothy and her trusted companion Toto are forced to leave home and want nothing more than to return. But in seeking to find a way back to her physical home, Dorothy faces tests, finds friends, discovers truths, and, in the end, finds within herself strength she didn't know she had, including the power to get home. We don't know what happened to Dorothy after she "comes home"—literally wakes from her unconsciousness—but I'd be willing to bet that she was not the same timid country girl she had been because even though she seems to have been dreaming or hallucinating, the messages she received and the lessons she learned were real.

The Faith of Ruth

The biblical story of Ruth touches on many themes that

we find in the hero's journey—leaving home, making choices, accepting challenges, and dealing with family inheritance.

During the time of the judges of Israel, a great famine struck the land. In order to find food, Elimelech moved with his wife, Naomi, and their two sons from Bethlehem to Moab. In those days, it was considered treacherous for an Israelite family to move to another country. Each country had its own gods, so moving was the equivalent of leaving your god and accepting another. In the minds of many Israelites, Mohabites were pagans, and Elimelech's family risked facing the wrath of their own god for associating with those idol worshippers.

But a man has to feed his family so they went. Elimelech did not live long after the move, leaving Naomi in the care of the sons, who eventually took wives of their own. For ten years, they all lived happily until tragically both sons died leaving the wives, Ruth and Orpah, childless, and all three women without a man's protection.

In the intervening years, rain had returned to Israel, and the famine had ended. Word spread that food was abundant. Naomi decided to return to her homeland, but when she was about to leave, Ruth and Orpah asked to go with her. Naomi knew that since the young women were from Moab, they would be better off (that is, more eligible to marry again) if they stayed with their relatives. Orpah agreed with her mother-in-law's reasoning, but Ruth insisted on staying with Naomi, saying, "Your people will be my people, and your God will be my God."

The two widowed women arrived at Bethlehem at the time of the barley and grain harvest. Since they had little money and Naomi was too old to work, Ruth offered to go and glean in the grain fields. In those days, the poorest people followed the field workers to pick up whatever grain was left, trying to gather enough to sustain their families. Ruth gleaned in a field belonging to a man named Boaz, whom she learned later was Naomi's close relative.

Boaz had heard of his relative's arrival with her foreign daughter-in-law. Impressed with Ruth's loyalty, and probably pitying the lone women, he encouraged Naomi to continue to glean from his fields where he could offer some protection.

With no husband and no sons, Naomi had no one to carry on her husband's name or to inherit his land. But in order to keep land ownership within families, it was a custom that the closest relative could buy the property if the owner had died without direct heirs. Boaz was close enough. Knowing this, and seeing that Boaz held affection for Ruth, Naomi encouraged her daughter-in-law to keep gleaning Boaz's fields and devised a plan to get them together.

One night, after everyone had fallen asleep, Ruth, following Naomi's instructions, went to where Boaz lay, uncovered his feet, and lay down. When he awoke, they spoke of how they felt for one another, and Boaz promised to marry her. But first he would have to negotiate with the one relative who was closer to Elimelech and who held the customary claim to the land and the daughter-in-law's hand. The next morning, Boaz gathered the town leaders as witnesses and asked the relative if he would buy the land and take Ruth as his wife. The man declined, and Boaz announced his intention to do both. Later, Ruth had children and became King David's great-grandmother and thereby Jesus' ancestor.

The young woman's sense of loyalty and self-sacrifice led her to fulfill her destiny. Ruth's initiation began as a series of profound losses—extremely severe tests of her strength, her faith, and her sense of purpose. In those days, a woman without a husband or some male protector was like a baby bird without a nest. Many of us, if put in Ruth's position, might have scrambled to find some man to turn to. (Many of us are doing that anyway!) Her challenges were strong, but her call to follow and serve Naomi was stronger. Perhaps because of the severity of her loss, Ruth was no longer tied to her native country and felt free to follow the call that took her to a new land and a new life. In the end, her character, supported by Naomi's wise mentoring, brought triumph to all. ✤

Initiation

Take the Hero's Plunge

A hero is no braver than an ordinary man, but he is braver five minutes longer.
— Ralph Waldo Emerson

When we look at the nature of initiation—the fact that it is the first *action* step on the hero's journey—it can seem like the most difficult power choice. If investigation is standing on the diving board contemplating the sparkling water in the pool below, initiation is the leap, the fall, the plunge into the chilly depths. It takes courage to step off the board into the abyss, to hold yourself together as you dive, and to face the sudden shock of the cold water. It's not easy, which is why so many people don't dive. Some of us sit on our lounge chairs beside the pool, slathered in protective sunscreen, sunshades dimming our vision, far enough from the edge that we don't even get splashed. There are those who will float on the surface, never getting our faces wet. Others of us dabble in the shallow end, sticking a tentative foot in now and again, allowing ourselves to be drenched by the boisterous play of others. And then there is the diver.

I don't mean to judge the sunbather more harshly than the swimmer. In reality, we are all at the same pool because we know it offers us something that we need. And somewhere in each of us is that diver—the hero—who is ready to take the plunge and will dare to do so. Is it your turn on the diving board? If not now, your turn is certainly coming. Having read this chapter and practiced using the power tools, you are ready to take the initiation plunge. Yes, you are.

Questions

1. What is this situation here to teach me?
2. What in me needs to grow and change?
3. Do I need to ask for help or support to get through this?
4. How can I help someone else in the same situation?

Power Tools

1 **Best-Case Scenario**
Design a best-case scenario for each of the areas you chose to work on during chapter 1.

2 **Ask the Right Questions**
Change your perspectives; ask questions that empower you rather than cast you as the victim.

3 **Invite Initiation**
Invite initiation by writing down the areas in which you'd like to grow as you travel your life journey. Then paint, write, sing, dance, plant seeds or otherwise use your creativity to make something to symbolize that growth area.

Power Decree
I Am a Door Opener.

> *Change has a considerable psychological impact on the human mind. To the fearful it is threatening because it means that things may get worse. To the hopeful it is encouraging because things may get better. To the confident it is inspiring because the challenge exists to make things better.*
> — King Whitney, Jr.

Chapter Three

Insight
Crossing the Threshold to the Inner World

As long as you are running away from your problem, you will continue to meet it in a new guise in every turn in the road.
— Emmet Fox

"Holy crap!" Lucy explodes as she stands frozen for a couple of heartbeats. Then a corner of her brain processes a metallic glint in the hand of the skateboarder rushing toward her. Without thinking, she eases backward, tripping over the elderly man who is still scrambling toward the open hole that swallowed his bag.

Hearing Lucy's shout, the old man twists around, throwing up his hand. Suddenly the skateboarder catapults backward, slamming into a wall and crumpling like an old tin can. His comrade, lined up behind him, is now on a collision course with Lucy. Before she knows what is happening, the elderly man pushes Lucy into the hole.

She falls into the darkness with a piercing shriek. It is a longer fall than she imagined, giving her just enough time to mentally note how endlessly she seems to be falling. Then she lands in water, sinking, then scrambling to surface. The water is deep and fast enough for the current to pull her along. As she gasps for breath and tries to stay afloat, all she can think is, "Hell!" quickly followed by, "Mother of God, help me!" Her flailing hands hit a piece of metal. She grasps it and tries to pull herself out of the water. Her wet hands slip on the railing of what seems to be a ladder. It suddenly gives way, and Lucy realizes it's a hatch door. For the second time, she falls into a void.

When she opens her eyes, she is lying on a mat with a dim light flickering overhead. She tries to move, but feels stiff and numb; she realizes that her head and her arm are bandaged. She turns her head to discover that someone is crouching next to her. She shrinks away, and then sees that it is the old man, looking extremely grim.

"Well, Lucy," he says crisply, "This is a life-or-death situation. You have a lot to learn and fast, or we are all lost."

"Where am I? Who the hell are you?" she rasps, realizing that her throat is sore, too.

"No," he counters. "The real question is: Who are you?"

"I don't know who you are, Pops, and I don't know where you've taken me, but you need to get me out of here."

"You can call me the Bag Man."

"Whatever," she snaps, fresh out of patience with all this. "Hey, you pushed me. What the hell was that all about? No never mind; I don't want to know. Just show me the door. And by the way, I know who I am."

"Do you?" he responds as he gets up "And by the way, there is no door," he says cryptically as he heads for a window. Without hesitating, he jumps out, yelling, "You had better follow me."

Lucy can't stop herself as a force she can't resist pulls her off the mat, aching bones and all; then screaming with terror, she jumps out of the window. She's kind of falling, but kind of flying too. Outside, colors flash by—red, orange, yellow, green, blue. When she sees violet, Lucy sees an image of herself—her seven-year-old self, standing beside her Aunt Mary (her mother's twin sister) and Uncle Bill as they wave good-bye to Lucy's mother and father. Her mommy and daddy are waving back at them through the tiny window of a plane headed for Bermuda. She couldn't know it then, but her parents wouldn't make it back. Their plane would go down in a storm off the island's coast. But for now, young Lucy waves good-bye with one small hand; in the other, she's clutching a bag....

Lucy is lost, hurt, and probably in danger. She has no idea what's going on, and as far as she's concerned, there are a lot of questions that need to be answered. But the most significant question, as the Bag Man said, is: Who is she? Not name, rank, and serial number. Not where she's from or what she does for a living.

Insight

Not where she goes to church, not who she's related to, not what clubs she's a member of, nor anything else. But who is she *really* at the core of her being?

Interestingly, the answer to that crucial question often makes itself clear—at least in part—when we are in a severe crisis. All the affectations, the pretenses, and the politeness falls away; we don't have time for prettying things up or being nice because we're in survival mode. If you've ever been in a highly threatening situation, you may remember acting quite differently than you do under normal circumstances. That's often the time we hear people say things like, "I've never seen this side of you" and "I didn't know you had it in you."

We're wired that way. We all have a place in our body that responds when we register a threat. The neurological response follows one of two pathways. First, we have emotional routes to the higher cortex of the brain, and second, there are other routes that skirt the cortex. In the first case, we have time to think and adjust our responses to the feelings of those around us and to the situation. In the second case, a signal flows directly from the eye to the thalamus (the sensory decoder) then to the amygdala (two emotional "speakers" in the primitive brain). When the amygdala broadcasts the signal, the brain responds without thought occurring. The result? We respond to the situation instinctively. Years ago, a dog threatened my then-one-year-old daughter as we were relaxing at a friend's pool party. Before I knew what I had done, the baby was in my arms, the dog landed in the pool, and my heart was pounding so fast it seemed ready to leave my body to orbit the moon. When our neural circuitry combines with social and familial conditioning, we respond like Pavlov's dogs—physically first.

The threat you face can be physical—say, you're trying to evacuate from a house on fire. But emotional, mental, or spiritual catastrophes can strip us to our core as well; they send us to the place within us that is the most basic, the most primal. How we respond when we find ourselves in these inner crises shows us what we're made of.

In this chapter, we're going to work on developing insight. This will help you get to know your inner self and have a good idea of your strengths, abilities, and core beliefs without having to discover them in the midst of a hurricane, a blackout, or any other sudden crisis.

Insight means just what it says: looking in; it's inner sight. Insight is important knowledge to have as you travel on your journey because it enables you to better understand what tools exist in your repertoire that you can employ when you do face a life challenge. For example, it's helpful to know that when it's called for, you will stand your ground. Conversely, if you're the type to turn and run, knowing that about yourself gives you the opportunity to choose to empower yourself. I'm not judging what you have inside you, but I will be asking a variation of Dr. Phil McGraw's signature question: "Is that working for you?"

Recognizing your inner tendencies will also help understand your responses and behaviors in relationships at work, at home, and in social situations. It will give you a lead on your insecurities, and other emotional and mental blocks. Wherever you are, whatever you're doing, you remain the same person and likely to respond in the same way. As the Buddhist teacher Thich Nhat Hanh put it, "Wherever you go, there you are." Removing interior blocks is the bread and butter of all professional psychologists, but my approach is different in that I combine spiritual teachings, philosophies, theories, and techniques that allow you to go beyond traditional psychology. (And, by the way, I don't think you'll discover anything that you don't already know. That's the good thing about insight—all the information you need is already within you. This chapter will help you tap into what you know, make sense of it, and put it to positive use in your life.) The idea is that the better you understand yourself—all aspects of yourself—the better you're able to handle any situation you find yourself facing.

Having conducted an investigation of our lives, we've faced some truths, and we have a better idea of what is working well and what isn't. We have embraced initiation and accepted the call to meet the challenge of life. Now it is time to see exactly what tools we packed in the bag we are taking on our journey.

Insight

The King's Man

The Arthurian legend of Igraine illustrates a quest for insight. In King Arthur's court, one knight—Igraine—was chief among all the knights and Arthur's right hand. He was strong, honorable, bold, and a great problem solver often called upon to settle disputes in the king's absence. An uncommonly well-proportioned physique, a handsome face, and a gallant manner made him a favorite with the ladies of the court as well. All in all, Igraine had a good thing going.

One day a stranger came to court telling a tale of a magical fountain in a far distant land. Igraine, gripped by a profound desire to see the fountain for himself and to experience its magic, decided to leave the prestige and comfort of his position at court and set out on a quest to find the fountain. He packed all the things he thought he'd need—though not too much because it was a long journey, and he could move along faster if he traveled light. He bade farewell to his beloved king and fellow knights who implored him to stay. Quite determined, he left.

Igraine had been traveling three days when he came to a dark wood guarded by a giant who wore severed human heads strung across his chest and wrapped around his neck. There were even disembodied heads on the massive club he wielded. The giant stood ready to challenge the knight, but Igraine rode up to the giant and said, "Good evening, sir. You are actually just the person I was looking for. Do you know the way to the magical fountain said to be beyond the mountains?" The giant, accustomed to people either fleeing in terror or violently attacking him, was quite surprised by this display of civility. Instead of turning Igraine's knightly skull into another gruesome ornament, he simply pointed the man on his way.

A few days later, Igraine found himself in a dry wasteland that went on and on for miles. He became desperately hungry and so thirsty he felt crazed. Seeing no end in sight, his determination to complete the journey began to waver; he considered turning back. Suddenly, seemingly out of nowhere, three extraordinarily beautiful women appeared, each richly attired and each holding a tray of refreshments. The weary warrior was grateful, but too weak even to lift a cup of cool water. They fed him sips bit by bit. When he'd revived a bit, they took him to their luxurious castle in the desert oasis where they nursed him back to his full strength and made him so welcome that he forgot his quest for some time. At last, reluctantly, he decided he had to go. To ensure he would keep his resolve to leave, he slipped away at dawn, knowing he could not otherwise resist their charms.

Igraine continued on his travels, confronting other horrors, tests, and temptations and at times barely managing to move forward to attain his goal. In the end, however, his determination and commitment led him to achieve his quest. He found the fabled fountain and drank of its magical waters, which opened to him a new life as the husband of an extraordinary queen. This happy ending was later marred through carelessness on Igraine's part, and he had to once again face severe tests to regain his queen and join her in ruling their realm.

KNOWLEDGE IS POWER

For now we see through a glass, darkly; but then face to face: now I know in part; but then shall I know even as also I am known.
— I Corinthians 13:12 (King James Version)

To succeed in our quest for insight, we require the courage to look within and to face the real monster that lives inside us: our fears. We need the persistence to cross the desert of losses and emotional pain. We need the strength to resist the temptation of what seems like instant pleasure, but that beckons us to give up the quest. And in the final leg of the journey, we break patterns that can lead to self-sabotage, learn to forgive ourselves and others, and gain the ultimate prize—an open heart capable of love and service to others.

Just as we tend to register fear when we're faced with initiation—we don't want to commit to the hard work that initiation requires—we also tend to be afraid at the beginning of the

Insight

insight phase of our journey. In this case, we're not afraid of what we have to do; we're afraid of what we'll learn. For some reason, we never assume that when we look at our most basic self, we're going to find, at our core, a good, kind, wonderful person. We believe that we're unworthy imposters and that, as so many of my clients have said to me: "It's just a matter of time before I'm found out." We'll examine the reasons for this negative self-assessment shortly. But I find that, more often than not, when people use the power choice of insight, they discover the cause of and the means to heal the wounds that caused them to regard themselves as less than lovable. They then can access the ability to fulfill their good intentions and the desire to do what's good and right, which was there all along. Most often, when my clients complete their insight work, just like Igraine, they tap into strengths and gifts they didn't know they had. The demon they were so sure was lurking in the farthest corner of their heart was just an illusion.

We also don't want to wake up those feelings that gnaw at us just beneath the surface of our lives. However, when we inquire within, we must cross the threshold to the inner world of emotions. We have to awaken our feelings and deal with them. No matter how hard we have tried to suppress or avoid our inner selves, especially our feelings, they are alive, if not well, within us. Feelings are never dormant. Let me repeat that: *feelings are never dormant*, no matter how much resistance we put up. They come out somewhere, either through physical ailments or when you covertly express feelings through passive-aggressive, self-destructive, or numbing-out behaviors. And those behaviors impede your ability to move effectively in the world.

In order to gain insight, you have to get past your fear of yourself and your feelings. Believe me, after twenty-five years of helping people move through resistance, I know that it's easier said than done. But this is what I've learned that can help you:

First, remember that resistance and fear are normal; they are actually a signal that something important is taking place. Let yourself feel the fear and anxiety and the resistance. Dare I say, don't resist the resistance?

Next, ask yourself, "Would I let my roof leak, my car break down, or the heel of my shoe come off without repairing them or replacing them?" Then ask, "Aren't my feelings and needs at least as important as my material possessions?"

Now for the big one, the final question; ask yourself, "Where did I learn not to value my emotions and not to take care of myself?" So, which of your parents modeled that behavior? Both of mine did; they worked and worked to provide for my six siblings and me, but they also had the profound wounds of growing up in Louisiana under Jim Crow. Those painful experiences never got resolved, and they came out in the form of rages that were directed toward their children. No wonder gaining insight can be scary; it usually means going back into a tunnel of hurts and traumas before we can come out on the other side, to more freedom and joy. But thinking about it is usually more difficult than doing it, and the reward in the end is tremendous.

So we must recognize our resistance and make friends with it. We have to learn to acknowledge how our fears and resistance are in themselves teachers. By examining our fear, we learn more about ourselves. Remember the old adage "Any fear we face disappears." Fear derives its power by skulking in the dark, so let the light in! Now you're primed to ask more insight-oriented questions that lead deeper into self-knowledge.

- *Where am I along the road to achieving the goals I've set?* If you find that you are working toward a goal but keep stumbling over roadblocks, it's a sign that there's something inside that you need to examine.

- *How well can I express my feelings?* When we think of suppressing feelings, we tend to think of controlling angry outbursts, resentments, and tears—the feelings we consider negative. But many of us also have difficulty expressing positive emotions—love, pride and gratitude, for example.

- *What am I feeling?* That's a tough question for many of us, since the message that we receive from society, from our upbringing, and even from our own experiences is: "At all costs,

Insight

avoid those pesky feelings. They'll only make me feel bad and make it harder to survive." We get so good at burying our feelings that we don't know what we're feeling. Something happens, and a feeling doesn't readily pop up on our emotional radar or "emodar," as I like to call it. Those feelings that we fail to pick up on our emodar are the ones that often manifest as physical symptoms. Tension in our necks or stomachs, migraine headaches, backaches are often experienced when we face an emotionally challenging situation but lack the skill or the time to process our feelings.

• *Do I manifest any physical symptoms that may be the result of suppressing my feelings?* Carolyn Myss, Louise Hay, and Joan Borseynko, among many other mind-body healers and researchers, emphasize the importance of examining the connection between physical ailments and their mental and emotional correspondents. An illness that is rooted in the emotions is no less real so it is best to have a trained medical professional diagnose and recommend a treatment strategy. But don't fail to do some self-examination as well. The following exercise can help.

POWER TOOL
LISTEN TO YOUR BODY AND YOUR EMOTIONS

ASK YOURSELF

What physical symptoms do I tend to get on a recurring basis (for example, headache, sore throat, or stomach issues)? Notice when these symptoms tend to occur. Is it when you are under stress at work, in a conflict with your spouse, or worried about finances? Note the patterns and take the time to identify your feelings. Trace them to their source, and then sit down and talk it out with a confidant. Getting the feelings moving is the key.

2

> **ASK YOURSELF**
> Where do my feelings and patterns originate? Take an even deeper look and examine the origins of your emotions. Look at both family and cultural patterns.
>
> *As we proceed through this chapter, you will examine these questions in more depth, and do some practices that will help you open up your secret vault of feelings, see what's hidden there, and examine how you can transform those feelings so you can put them to positive use.*

EMPTYING THE SACK

It's not the mountain we conquer, but ourselves.
— Sir Edmund Hilary, first to scale Mount Everest, 1953

Sir Edmund Hilary, a sort of modern-day Igraine, scaled the highest mountain in the world after many people had died attempting the same feat. It was an impressive display of will, determination, and physical strength. We all have our mountains to climb. The quest for insight is about climbing the mountain inside. In order to reach your highest self, what do you need to conquer inside yourself? What do you want to grow within you? What internal issues or possibilities have you ignored although confronting them might help you to achieve true power?

One of the best metaphors for the process of personal growth, one employed in both Eastern and Western philosophies, depicts life as high winding road leading to the top of a high mountain. This steep and arduous climb becomes even more grueling as we drag extra baggage with us in the form of a knapsack filled with rocks. The rocks are the beliefs and assumptions we hold about ourselves and about our world. We've inherited some of this weight by accepting unconditionally what others have told us. Many of these rocks have been in the bag since we were children.

Insight

But we are still carrying the rocks in our sack today *because we have made the choice to hang on to them*, whether we made that choice consciously or unconsciously.

If you want to know why you respond the way you do, and if you want to know why you ask the questions you ask, the answer is in the thousand-pound sack full of rocks on your shoulder. Are you dragging through life wondering, "Why isn't my life working better? Why aren't my relationships working? Why aren't I getting promoted?" It's because you need to unload the sack of rocks on your back. Now here's the kicker. Many of us don't know what's in the sack—we don't even know we have the sack—but everybody around us can see it.

I had a friend once (notice I said *had* a friend, as in past tense), who had some very hot rocks in her sack. One of her hugest boulders was anger. She had a very abrasive way of saying things, and she was alienating even those who were close to her. A group of her friends got together. "Susie's wonderful; she's brilliant and beautiful," we agreed, "but her anger is really a issue." We decided to talk to her and do an intervention.

We sat down with her and said, "Susie, we're talking to you because we love you. We've noticed that you have an issue with anger."

She said, "Anger?" She was clearly defensive.

We said, "Yes. You scream and yell at people for no reason; you curse at strangers for bumping into you on the street. It gets pretty hard to take."

Well, she couldn't take it, so she began to scream and yell at *us*. "I am not angry!" she shouted angrily. Obviously, she didn't get it.

Susie had no idea how she was coming across to people. And she couldn't see her anger even when the mirror was held that close. Her thousand-pound sack was invisible to her. She couldn't see it, but everyone else could. It's pretty unfortunate when you're the last one to know about your own sack because by the time you discover it, you've done damage to yourself, your relationships, and your life.

I've had a similar experience myself. Years ago, I went away for a month-long residential training with Virginia Satir, founding member and later president of the World Humanistic Psychology Association and one of my personal mentors and sheroes. For four weeks, I lived and studied with great therapists from all over the world learning to communicate and work through family issues. I came back home after that month profoundly changed. I'd been dating a very nice man—smart and kind—but we were mismatched. I'd known for a long time that it wasn't working, but I was too afraid to confront the problem and end it. When I came back from the training with all my new skills and my confidence boosted, I broached the subject. "I'm feeling a bit suffocated and unfulfilled," I told him. "It's not you. You're a lovely person, but this relationship really isn't working for me, and I need to move on."

And do you know what he said? He said, "Yeah, I know. I've known it for a long time. I just figured since I liked you, I'd stay as long as you stayed."

If I'd been honest with him and with myself, we could have moved on with our lives months sooner, rather than wandering along in a relationship that we both knew had no future. It was an unforgettable lesson.

Transforming Childhood Pain

What do we do when bad things happen to good people?
— Rabbi Kushner

If you are questing for insight and really want to understand why you feel, respond, and act as you do, then you are going to have to ask yourself those hard questions about the patterns in your family—not just your immediate family, but all the generations in your family that you can possibly examine. You're going have to look at what you learned in childhood.

Let's be clear. This is not about pointing fingers at your parents. One reason people avoid therapy is because it has gotten the

Insight

reputation of being a forum for blaming our neurotic mothers and overbearing fathers for our own internal issues. We all love our parents no matter how neurotic, overbearing, or otherwise damaged they may be, and it's uncomfortable and even painful to admit that they weren't perfect. I don't want you to blame them for your "stuff." I want you to take responsibility for what's going on in your life now, but also to understand that your patterns came from *somewhere*. Your parents, as your first and most influential teachers, contributed *something, in some way*—consciously or unconsciously—to your behavior. In order to learn as much as possible about yourself, you have to look at what you learned from them. Note that I didn't say "what they taught you," but "what you learned," because we pick up things from the actions and behaviors of the people in our lives as much as from what they deliberately teach us. You also learn a lot from a parent who abandoned you at (or even before!) birth—someone you've never even seen. This process is about becoming aware of what you experienced and how you felt as a young person, how you may be holding those feelings in your thousand-pound sack and, most importantly, how you can take them out of the sack and get rid of them once and for all.

What happened to you in childhood gives rise to the behaviors and choices that may later lead you to create self-defeating roadblocks. For example, I worked with a man who founded an innovative company. Given the potential market for his product, his company should have been hugely successful. It did fairly well, but never more than that. Why? The man sabotaged it himself. His self-defeating behavior consisted of having martini lunches. After 1:00 p.m. each day, he got nothing done. When he did make it back from lunch, he was surly and abrasive, alienating his customers and his employees so his turnover was too high and business was too slow. I called him on his drinking problem and suggested AA. He said, "Why? I'm already a success! This is just the way I am! It doesn't matter if I like to relax at lunch. These are business lunches."

My response was, "I wonder what kind of success you would have if you were functioning at your peak in the afternoon?"

Did I mention that his father was an alcoholic? This illness isn't just inherited genetically; it is also an emotional, mental, and behavioral bequest. Young children learn through imitation, so they will copy a parent's behavior (Dad always had a glass in his hand), including their emotional coping mechanisms, for example saying, "I've had a hard day. I deserve to relax."

Research conducted at the University of California, Berkeley examined international patterns of alcohol use and revealed strong cultural norms that support the behavioral inheritance model. The researchers found that alcohol is used in a functional way in the cold, damp climate of the U.K. It's cold out so you're more likely to go down to the pub to socialize and warm yourself with a pint. Unfortunately, alcohol is an addictive substance—so in the process of socializing and warming up, people may become alcoholics. This behavioral inheritance applies to many different behaviors. People with angry parents tend to imitate their angry response; those whose parents ate or shopped or gambled compulsively are going to lean toward those behaviors. I and many other researchers and practitioners have observed that addictive behavior can skip a generation or one person in a family while it strikes down others.

Our parents and those who came before us weren't passing down unworkable patterns to punish us; they just didn't know any better. So we have to forgive them. But we also have to excise the negative lessons they taught us. Insight is about looking at these patterns in order to understand them and change them. I can't change what's in my past, but I can change how I respond to it and then only if I begin to see it clearly.

We repeat what we've learned. That early childhood template is all we've got to work with. That's what we've "inherited," so to speak, and if we don't initiate the quest for insight, we're going to be stuck with what we learned as children as our only means of moving through the world as adults. Think about it this way: When you were in first grade, you could only read the most basic Dick-and-Jane-type books and do the most basic addition and subtraction. That's as far as your learning had taken you. But as you got older, you learned more and were able to do more. It's the same with your emotional patterns. If you rely only on what you learned as a child,

Insight

you're not working with all the tools that are available to you.

One of the jumping-off points for the insight process is identifying what your parents' choices were. It's easy to identify their choices if you take a moment and look at your life. You'll probably find your parents' choices mirrored in how you are living your life. Some of us, in an attempt to break free of our family dysfunction, tend to "overcorrect." For example, many of those who grew up with rigid, domineering, or punitive parents swing to the opposite extreme. In an attempt to be "free," they become unable to set appropriate boundaries or clearly express their needs and feelings. As John Bradshaw, author of *Bradshaw on the Family*, a groundbreaking book on family dysfunction, once quipped, "One hundred and eighty degrees from sick is still sick." Overcompensating just puts us in another rigidly polarized position where we are acting out of fear, not real healing. Even if you say you are nothing like your parents, you can bet that it's because of their influence. You came from them. You're connected to them even if it's ironically, in opposite behavior. If you understand this, you can make different decisions that will lead you to more flexible and workable ways of responding.

POWER TOOL
FAMILY *PATTERNS*

1. Go through your genogram, and circle all the people who exhibit compulsive behavior of some kind or the one hundred and eighty-degree "correction" for a family pattern.

2. Identify any other patterns you see, such as divorces, children being abandoned, philandering, financial losses or instability, and so on.

3. Note any family pattern that you can see creeping into your life.

BREAKING THE CHAINS OF FAMILY PATTERNS

By allowing expression of your true feelings and releasing emotional scars, you will open the flow for your power to return.
— Unknown

Family patterns manifest in many forms. We often hear people say, "The apple doesn't fall far from the tree." That's true, even when you're talking about a big tree with lots of branches. You may see an abandoned son who abandons his own children, or the child of a divorce who can't seem to keep her relationships afloat. Unplanned pregnancies and people putting children up for adoption can become a pattern. Sexual, emotional, or physical abuse can all become repeating cycles. Addictive illness certainly is one of the easiest patterns to spot. Harder to see are the patterns that skip a generation or that manifest in extended family. I've heard of odd situations, including ones in which an uncle goes missing, then, in the next generation, another brother or uncle goes missing.

Patterns in families run the gamut. I liken it to relay racers running with a baton. It gets handed off. It's your turn; you've got the baton. Now what are you going to do with it? If you don't change it, you're going hand it off to the people who come after you. Your children or grandchildren or your nieces, nephews, or cousins—somebody near you is going to get that baton.

When a pattern shows up and something happens in a family again, again, and again, it's because nobody had the time or the tools to shatter the pattern. To break those patterns, somebody has to feel the emotions embedded in the pattern and be willing to admit the issue, take it out of the closet, look at it, really deal with it, and then get rid of it once and for all.

You can learn to recognize familial precedents by looking at the events and behaviors that recur in your family. Not to mention the self-defeating behaviors that arise from unmitigated family dysfunction. If you don't have any models of success in your family, and if, as in most dysfunctional families, love was scarce, then no matter what opportunities may come your way, you will

Insight

sabotage yourself. At least until you work through the issue and break the family pattern.

Ancient wisdom says it takes seven generations for a pattern to dissipate. Over that time, people gradually begin to figure out that they have to make different choices. But seven generations is a long time. Think about it: A Jewish adult today may only be two generations removed from the experiences of the Holocaust. An African-American adult may be only three or four generations from slavery. If you don't work out the deep emotional scars from the losses or issues related to your family experiences, you could potentially pass them on to your children, your grandchildren, your great-grandchildren, and beyond.

Don't Fight the Feeling

With my poems I know that I have shot a lot of arrows, but the hand that drew back the bow was always placed over my heart.
— Ana Castillo

I've seen mothers who, because of their emotional blocks and baggage, couldn't tell or show their children that they loved them or that they were proud of them. Their hearts might have been cold or they might have been swelling; either way the child lost out because the mothers couldn't express their feelings. Men aren't allowed to cry in our society no matter how terrible a situation they face. (I think here of a professional baseball player who played a game the day after his mother died. That man should have been encouraged to be at home supporting and being supported by his grieving family. Instead he was praised for his "strength" in being out on the ball field.) There's even a trend among some young people to avoid smiling for their school pictures. They want to look cool and unimpressed, instead of looking happy.

For most of us, it's a real challenge to change old emotional patterns because we live in a culture that does not encourage us to deal with feelings. Our anti-feeling culture encourages us to "keep a stiff upper lip" and "stay strong" in the face of emotional situations. We aren't supposed to "break." We avoid emotion through all kinds of distractions. We obsess about having the biggest, newest television, and then we glue ourselves to it and its million channels. Or we go shopping for the newest, the brightest, the most expensive—and more, more, more of it. Our culture says that if you smell better, have brighter teeth, wear the latest jeans, and drink the hippest soda then you are going to feel better about yourself. And if that's not good enough, have this nice,tasty, new, supersized something. Better yet, get a new (larger) car!

Or maybe you could just work more. You're not going to feel anything if you're working, and this approach to avoiding your emotional life has the added benefit of making you look dedicated, earnest, and responsible—a virtual martyr with a perfect excuse for being distant. "See how hard I'm working? Sorry, but I don't have time to feel." It's become a cliché, but it's true: we become human *doings* instead of human beings. Friedman sounded the alarm thirty years ago in the classic book, *The Type A Personality*. He outlined the health costs associated with overworking, as well as the "emotional blunting" that leads to depression and poor relationships. Working hard is one thing; our motivation for working may be something else.

If you're waiting for our culture to say, "All right everybody, it's okay to feel; we want you to feel feelings," you'll be waiting a long time. The sad news is that our culture does not want us to feel because if we feel our emotions and express them, what might happen? We might get powerful! We might wake up with enough energy to make a difference in the world in ways that are important to us. We might change the status quo.

Emotion is power. As long as we're numbed out and disconnected emotionally, there's a lot of power we're not going to use because we don't have access to it. The insight power choice—like each one of the power choices—frees up energy. If you have more energy, you have more power.

Insight

> **POWER TOOL**
> *THE FEELING JOURNAL*
>
> This simple but powerful exercise increases emotional awareness.
>
> Buy a notebook that you can use as a "feeling journal," and use it to write down what you are feeling every day. At the end of the day-or even at different moments throughout the day-take a moment to reflect on your day and then jot down how you felt during different conversations, encounters and experiences. It could be as seemingly minor as the slight annoyance you felt when the cashier at your favorite coffee shop was short with you. Or it might be the range of emotions you felt when your estranged sister called.
>
> Just make the list short and sweet and don't judge the emotions. But do look at patterns that develop. Are you always offended by something? Does any little thing bring you to tears? Do you lash out in anger before you can catch yourself? Being aware of your feelings begins the process of healing and caring for yourself.

CREATING CONGRUENCE

I want all of my senses engaged.
— Maya Angelou

My mentor, Virginia Satir, introduced me to the concept of congruence in my first training with her. In order to achieve the goal of being "more fully human," she said, we need to bring our feelings, thoughts, words, and actions into alignment so they all match. In other words, what we say should reflect what we think and feel; what we do should align as well. Like many before her, Dr. Satir pointed out that when we don't do this, we suffer.

It sounds simple, and it certainly would simplify our lives and our relationships if we all did it. But it's almost as if our society encourages us to do the exact opposite. We often see this in large corporations and other bureaucracies, often with devastating results. We say what we think the boss wants to hear. We think something may be dangerous or illegal or ineffective, but we keep our thoughts to ourselves and do it anyway. We sit at our desks, collecting our paychecks, saying and doing what's expedient, and moving ourselves further and further from the reality of our feelings and the link they provide to our principles and our integrity. The folks who *don't* do this—the whistle blowers—are often ostracized, attacked, and pushed out of the fold. They may receive their fifteen minutes of fame, but I wonder how long it takes them to find another job.

Making power choices—choices that allow us to be true to ourselves—leads us to create personal alignment. When we choose initiation, we become more congruent in our openness to life; when we make the choice to pursue and master insight, we become more congruent in our openheartedness. Openheartedness comes about through removing emotional blocks that cause us to close our hearts.

Many of us are so used to saying one thing and thinking another (can you say, *politicians*?) that we don't even know we're out of congruence. To get into alignment and to maintain it, practice listening to your body when you are making a decision; if you feel comfortable physically and emotionally, you are on the right track. If you experience "a disturbance in the force" as they say in the *Star Wars* movies—something that doesn't feel quite right inside you—then you may need to sit down and talk over your concerns with a trusted friend. When I was working at the television station where I was being so grossly underpaid, I had a knot in my stomach whenever I thought about it.

SAM AND ROCHELLE

Sam and Rochelle came to me at Rochelle's insistence. The couple sought marital therapy because she felt that they were headed for divorce, and she wanted to save their marriage. Unfortunately, they were worlds apart emotionally. She was a warm expressive person who affirmed her love for her husband even as she wept over the state of their marriage.

He had constructed a lot of rationalizations and clichés: "Well, you know, you're dealt a hand of cards, and you make the best of it." He related his sad family history matter-of-factly. His father was an alcoholic who abused his mother. Eventually his dad left the family, leaving Sam's mother with three boys to raise. Instead of expressing sadness, resentment, anger, or any emotion at all, Sam was stoic. "This is just how life is," he said. "Things happen. Everyone has something. You just carry on. It doesn't have to hold you back."

But it was holding him back, particularly in his marriage. For years, Sam's approach to Rochelle was, "I need to do things for myself. I don't care what you think or feel; I've got to do what I need to do. You don't have the right to interfere with anything I do because it's my life." You would have thought he was talking to a stranger on the street instead of to his wife of twenty years. He couldn't say, "I love you"; he could only manage, "You know I care." He didn't have the skills to be compassionate or loving with Rochelle because he didn't learn them at home; he *couldn't* have learned them in a home where his father abused and then abandoned his mother. He had yet to learn that his history made him fear the vulnerability of love. It was too threatening for him because it was associated with his childhood fear of abandonment.

Rochelle was understandably feeling that she couldn't go on without a change in their relationship. Aside from the trouble he faced in his marriage, Sam's business was flagging; he was perpetually in financial trouble that Rochelle was constantly working to pull them out of. Yet he couldn't accept his emotional problems. He couldn't even see them.

Sam constructed so many rationalizations because he didn't realize that he was deeply wounded by his father's behavior, and that it had left a deep mark on him. This man walked into my office manifesting so many obvious symptoms of depression that it was actually shocking. When I asked if he'd been feeling depressed, he said, "No, I'm just very irritable because I've gained weight, and I'm so tired. I want to sleep all the time." When I told him that these are classic symptoms of depression, he shrugged and insisted, "I'm just tired from working long hours and not getting ahead."

This ignorance of his own condition is what created the roadblock in his marriage. He was truly out of touch with his own feelings, and he didn't seem to believe that he could do something about it. Sam kept repeating, "Well, you know, that's how life is." All his rationalizations amounted to, "I'm stuck, and there's nothing I can do about this."

When we're in denial, we need a breakthrough to open the door. Sometimes I use stories as a tool to help people break through their denial. So I told Sam about another person with a similar family history and similar symptoms who also initially felt it was impossible to change. But when this man began a closer examination, he realized that he had brought a lot of his parents' neglectful behavior into his marriage and that he could in fact heal and learn new skills. That's when his marriage started to improve. "Maybe that's possible for you too, Sam. Would you like that?" Again, he gave his defeated shrug.

Sam had emotionally shut down years earlier in response to his father's abuse and abandonment. As an adult, even with the threat of losing his wife, he clearly chose to stay closed down. He was too entrenched to change or even to give therapy an honest effort. He stopped coming. Rochelle eventually filed for divorce but continued in therapy to understand her part in the problems they had encountered. After all, she reasoned correctly, "I picked him, had a daughter with him, and stayed with him for twenty years."

Like Sam, most of us can't change by ourselves. We can't always be open to feedback from others, especially, if like Sam, we grew up with a parent we couldn't trust. So how do we begin to break through the denial and lack of understanding surrounding our own emotional wounds? Look for patterns—incidents or behavior that you see repeating over and over in your life or in your family from generation to generation.

> **POWER TOOL**
> **CONNECTING THE DOTS**
>
> *If you completed the earlier genogram power tool, you now have a picture of the patterns in your family. Hopefully you could see a connection with the generations that came before you and how much of an impact those patterns may have on you. Now look over the list of patterns you are exhibiting in your life and notice how they get in your way. Maybe, like Sam, you don't trust and push people away, or maybe, like Rochelle, you put up with mistreatment without speaking up and insisting that you be treated with respect.*
>
> *Write down your observations or talk them out with your confidant. This deeper self-discovery assists in breaking your patterns.*

One of the things we must clarify is: being victimized doesn't make you a victim. The classic example of this is Dr. Victor Frankl, the psychiatrist who was imprisoned in a Nazi concentration camp. He was in the midst of the most horrific situation we have seen in modern times. Did he say, "Ah, I'm a victim...." No! He started asking the right questions. "How can I make meaning out of this nightmare? How can I help other people, in the midst of all this?" He began to offer support and counseling to his fellow prisoners, even to the Nazi guards. The right questions opened possibilities for him. He developed his concept of "transpersonal psychology" in his book *Man's Search for Meaning*. That took a lot of power, but he wasn't willing to see himself as someone who was powerless. He made an extraordinary choice to gain more insight into his experience and the experiences of the people around him. He made a true power choice.

NEGATIVE TO POSITIVE LOVE

Love is the flowing, the rendering, and the outpouring of the heart and soul of emotional goodness, to yourself and to those around you.
— The Hoffman Institute, The Negative Love Syndrome

Bob Hoffman speaks of a concept he calls the Negative Love Syndrome. "The Negative Love Syndrome is the adoption of the negative behaviors, moods, attitudes, and admonitions (overt and silent) of our parents in order to secure their love. It includes the subsequent compulsive acting out or rebellion against those negative traits throughout our adult lives," according to the literature at the Hoffman institute.

I experienced this when I gave a talk on family dynamics to a group of college students. I pointed out the damaging impact of parental abuse and neglect and the long-term effect this could have on self-esteem, among other things. During the question-and-answer period, a lovely young woman raised her hand and stood up to declare emphatically that corporal punishment was not damaging, that her parents had followed a spare-the-rod-spoil-the-child philosophy, that she felt she deserved the beatings she got, and that the beatings were good for her. When she was done, I went on to explain that the biblical reference to the "rod" meant the rod that shepherds used to guide their sheep, not to beat them, and

Insight

that it had nothing whatsoever to do with children. After my talk, this same young woman asked if she could speak to me privately. When we stepped aside to do so, she asked what I thought might be the cause of her never feeling she was good enough. I gently pointed out that the beatings had contributed to those feelings.

In childhood we are literally programmed—physically, emotionally, and mentally. On the physical level, we actually develop neural receptors sites for the emotional states that we experience repeatedly. Candace Pert through her research in neurochemistry discovered that certain coded proteins (peptides) carry a particular emotional state that fits into a receptor in the brain like a nut and bolt. Thus, the repetition of any thought or experience programs the mind. This is literally how brainwashing occurs, and this explains physiologically why we re-create the patterns we grow up with.

In order to transcend my own negative love syndrome, I long ago made a pact with myself that I would create initiation and seek insight through personal growth experiences. My husband and I made a similar pact to annually attend a class or workshop or marital therapy to keep our love strong. One of the most intensive and transforming experiences I've undergone in recent years was my week at the Hoffman Institute. (I've done many growth processes, and I love doing them, approaching them with real excitement because I know my life is going to move to the next level, whatever form that may take.) I especially wanted to do this work because it was holistic in nature and used many of the same principles and techniques that I had been utilizing in my private practice and my writing.

The results were immediate and uplifting. I became more sensitive to the messages from my body and my "emotional child," which allowed me to break even more old childhood patterns and then to substitute new, healthier ways of caring for myself.

One of the most important breakthroughs for me was noticing that I was so busy that I often had little time for my friends. I was mortified because I always thought of myself as a good friend. Guess what? I was smack in the middle of a negative love syndrome without realizing it. It turns out I talked to my friends on the phone but rarely saw them in person. This was a pattern I learned from my mother. We used to joke in the family that she would talk on the phone for hours with her best friend, but they hardly ever got together physically. I wrote a new declaration for myself, one that granted me permission to have more balance in my life and to spend more face time with my friends. In chapter five, "Intention," I will share with you a tool for making new declarations.

Charlotte

Charlotte came to my office wearing one of the cute hats that hid her baldness, the result of her chemotherapy. She had two more chemotherapy treatments to endure. These last ones were the roughest because now her body had to fight the accumulation of the chemicals in her bloodstream as well as the cancer itself.

We'd talked about having her join an emotional support group, but she repeatedly rejected the idea. I wondered why so we delved deeper into her life.

She had grown up in a rigid and restrictive family, cast in the role of caretaker for her disabled mother. The message she received was, "Your needs and feelings don't matter. You don't even need to think at all; we'll do all the thinking for you." When she married, she let her husband do the thinking, as so many women do in traditional marriages.

Her husband died suddenly of a rare illness when he was only thirty-three, leaving her a widow at twenty-eight with a two-year-old son and another baby on the way. Her husband, a very high-functioning and responsible guy, had left retirement money and life insurance to provide for his young family. She was grateful he had taken care of them, but her money didn't ease her devastation. Then his parents and siblings started to call her, claiming they were entitled to his life insurance money. She said, "I don't understand how you can think that under the circumstances. And frankly, I can't afford to give any to you. I have two children to care for alone." When she refused their claims for the insurance, they launched a campaign against her, calling child protective services to investigate supposed abuses and claiming the second child wasn't his.

With this stress added to her grief, she began to ask, "Why did they do this to me? Why did my husband have to die?" These are almost irresistible questions—totally understandable that she'd ask them—but I explained to her that they weren't productive or helpful. "Instead, ask, what's the benefit of this experience?" I told her. "Ask yourself, how did you learn or grow? How were you changed for the better by this tragedy?"

After some reflection, she started to talk about how this suffering brought out a resourcefulness that she'd never had to use before. Her solution to the in-laws' attacks was to pack up and move to South America for five years; by the time she returned, they had given up. She settled in a new area of the country and started over.

The new resourceful streak was wonderful, but she took it too far; she overcorrected. She actually developed an allergy to depending on anyone for anything. She had gone from being too dependent to becoming radically independent. That's why she kept rejecting the idea of going to a cancer support group. But now that she was forty-five and facing the terrifying lesson of leukemia, she had to learn to accept help and support in caring for herself. When she began to recognize her patterns, she looked at being more *inter*dependent—a balanced place between being totally dependant on someone else and being so independent that you shut other people out of your life. She said, "I'm fighting for my life. If I lose this inner battle, I lose my life. I have to listen to my feelings, talk about them, and let people in." She's learning to set healthy boundaries—ones that nurture her, and she finally joined a support group.

The Faery Flag of Dunvegan

The Faery Flag of Dunvegan came to the McCleods of McCleod, who for a thousand years lived at Dunvegan Castle in the west of Syke in Scotland. Chieftain Malcome fell in love with a beautiful maid of the faery people. They wed and she bore a son, but she could not tolerate the life of humans and in the end left her husband and baby to return to her own people, who lived across the faery bridge, which no human could cross.

Even though he was heartbroken by his loss, Malcome carried on with the ceremony that initiated his son into the clan. The revelry and celebration were in full swing while the babe slept under the watch of his young nurse. Tempted by the sound of merriment, the nurse crept down to the hall, leaving the child unattended in the tower. When he awoke alone, he was frightened and wailed frantically. His mother heard him in the land of the faeries and magically sent a beautiful green flag of silk to soothe him. The nurse, sent back to fetch the baby, brought him into the hall with the flag wrapped around him to the accompaniment of faery voices who foretold that the flag would save the McCleods from dire circumstance three times if it were waved in a time of desperate need. The voices went on to warn, however, that the flag was never to be waved in a casual way or it would bring about the McCleods's destruction.

Indeed as the generations passed, the story of the flag was passed down, and the flag itself was kept in a chest to which only the chieftain himself had the key. Twice in a time of dire need the current chieftain, after carefully reviewing the faery instructions mentally, unlocked the chest and waved the flag. Immediately, circumstances for clan McCleod changed for the better. As generations came and went the chest grew dusty, as did the memory of the faery legacy. The day came when a servant found the chest and, scoffing at the dimly recalled legend, waved the flag in sport and caused the death and destruction of almost the entire clan McCleod.

The legend of *The Faery Flag of Dunvegan*, like the story of Igraine, originates in the U.K. It points to the power of the feminine magic given to Chieftain Malcome by the faery woman he loved, showing how love can be a grace and protection in our lives. But this tale also illustrates the importance of understanding and valuing our legacy and the magic in understanding who we are and where we come from. What a creative way to view the gift of the generations who have gone before us and their message to us. ∞

Mind and Body

Life is rather like a can of sardines: we're, all of us, looking for the key.
— Alan Bennett

How do you know if you're under stress? You don't have to look too far. Check your own shoulders. Are they knotted and tight? What about your heart? Is it pounding or palpitating? Maybe you feel breathless or have trouble sleeping. Maybe you're craving cigarettes or mocha fudge ice cream or a slab of steak. When you're under stress, a physiological syndrome clicks into place. Before we are aware of it, the brain sends a signal to the adrenal cortex, which begins to dump cortical hormones into the bloodstream, thus putting the body into fight or flight readiness and also creating the emotional sensations of fear and anxiety.

Sometimes we know we're stressed, and we notice that it's manifesting in some physical way—tension, sleeplessness, appetite changes, headaches, and so on. In other cases, the physical signs are practically hitting us over the head before we realize that stress must be causing them. When we're really distracted and busy, moving fast and juggling too many things, we don't always recognize our stress level right away—not until someone pulls us aside and questions us: "Darling, what are you doing?" Or until something happens in our bodies. I find that women have an especially hard time knowing when they're overstressed. We often struggle to fit together the puzzle of attending the needs of children and partner, careers and social activities, perhaps even the care of elderly parents or a sideline job. To paraphrase an old perfume jingle, we bring home the bacon, fry it up in a pan...then we help our kids with homework, share work woes with our husband, check e-mails, tidy up the house, and wonder why we fall into bed exhausted but unable to sleep. It sometimes takes a major health scare to wake us up to the simple fact that we're trying to *do too much*.

It's not always about how many items you have on your plate. If you're single, childless, and responsible for no one but yourself, but have a highly stressful job, that alone may be enough to give you stress-related health concerns. The point is, when you're hit over the head by a major illness, as in Charlotte's case, it's a wake-up call that you need to pay more attention to and find more balance in your life.

Knowing how much stress you're under is a very important insight to have. It can clue you in as to why you're snappish with your colleagues or unresponsive to your partner, which can, in turn, give you an indication as to why those relationships aren't working very well. Having such insight can help you figure out why you're not feeling as creative, as resourceful, as able to handle the everyday challenges that come up and explain why you aren't getting promoted at work or developing the love relationship you want.

People who have been victimized by racism or sexism literally become ill unless they express their feelings. When you start to open up about how you feel about what's going on, it brings about a sense of release that is healing. For one thing, talking about what's happening opens the door for you to get the support you may need. It also gives your body a release; the tension and stress can abate. But opening up doesn't mean explosively taking out your frustrations on others; it means venting in an appropriate setting and in the right way. It has been proven again and again that if we express our feelings, even just by writing them down, we can relieve stress and pressure.

Many new-thought leaders, those on the forefront of advancing our view of human potential, among them people like Deepak Chopra and Joan Borysenko who have made specific connections between our ailments and the fears and stresses we cope with in daily life. Louise Hay, a metaphysical teacher and author of books such as *Heal Your Body*, believes that whatever is happening in your body—from a pimple to a stroke—is caused by something that we're thinking, some belief we hold or some pattern we're repeating. Some of her books include charts that list dozens of physical ailments, the corresponding thought, and an affirmation to help you replace that negative thinking with something positive, thus getting rid of the physical problem as well.

Some of these mind-body connections may be very directly correlated. Back problems have to do with feeling overburdened and unsupported. Ulcers may reflect something eating away at you. Urinary infections may be a sign that you're angry about something. ("Pissed off." Get it?)

All this may sound a little New Agey to you, but the link between feelings and health has been scientifically validated. In the early 1950s, a sample of healthy, undergraduate Harvard men participated in the Harvard Mastery of Stress Study, answering questions about their feelings of warmth and closeness with parents. Thirty-five years later, the researchers obtained detailed medical and psychological histories from this group of men. According to L.G. Russek and G. E. Schwartz, in the *Journal of Behavioral Medicine*, 91 percent of participants who had not perceived themselves to have a warm relationship with their mothers had diagnosed diseases in midlife—including coronary artery disease, hypertension, ulcers, and alcoholism—as compared to 45 percent of participants who had a warm relationship with their mom. When researchers looked at participants' relationships with their fathers, the results were similar. Since parents are usually the most meaningful source of social support in early life, the perception of parental love and caring may have important effects on biological and psychological health and illness throughout life.

You don't always need a book, a chart, or a scientific study to tell you what's going on in your life. Often, if you get quiet, really sit still, and take a close look at what's going on in your life, you can determine for yourself what emotional or mental issue is exacerbating a physical problem.

It can't hurt to adopt a practice that helps you get still and centered so you can be in better touch with your mind and your body. A practice like yoga can help you notice where your body is stiff or hurting or out of balance. If you follow such a practice with meditation or some kind of quiet reflection, you will often be able to open yourself to the insight that indicates where that physical discomfort comes from. You must start asking good, productive questions once again, such as: "Exactly what am I feeling? What emotion does the physical feeling relate to? Where did it come from?"

Of course, if your physical problem is more serious, you may need more than just a half-hour meditation to get at the root of it. Many times, the stress of coping with major physical problems is what brings clients to my office. And when we get at the root of some of their psychological issues, the physical symptoms dissipate as well.

Finding the Balance

For the first time, women are asking their partners to access the very skills—emotional sensitivity, expressiveness, responsibility—that most men have stamped out of them as boys. — Terrence Real

One of the primary reasons we don't express our feelings is that we live in an antifeminine culture. But it's too simple to say that things that are considered feminine, like emotions, sensitivity, softness, and nurturing, aren't valued as much as are so-called masculine traits. In fact, male traits—strength, aggressiveness, and a firmly cerebral approach to life—are valued *in men*. If a man speaks up and expresses his anger, that's power; it's manly. When a woman gets angry, we label her with the "b" word. Conversely, men who cry are deemed weak. Women who cry are considered weak, too, but it's acceptable; it's "feminine." In our culture, weak and feminine have long been synonymous and, despite advances women have made, that's still the case.

In other parts of the world, men can freely express their joy, sorrow, and affection for other men without the same kind of severe censure that they would get in a largely homophobic culture like ours. (Interestingly, in many of the cultures where men can express their emotions, there is a high reverence for the feminine in spirituality. In India, Saraswati and Lakshmi are honored goddesses. In Tibet and China, Tara and Quan Yin are revered. Khadesja is respected in Islamic countries, as is Shekinah in Judaic societies. Even in Italy, one finds a Madonna on almost every corner.)

Where "female" and "feelings" have become synonymous (read "bad"), we perpetuate the belief that the more masculine power you have, the better. When women began to say, "I want to be more masculine because I want the power that men have," we began to see more female heart attack patients. I am by no means saying that women shouldn't pursue power. I'm suggesting that our idea of power should include more so-called feminine strengths. We should see the ability to nurture as powerful. We should see the ability to express feelings as strength.

This is important for men, too, because they actually have these kinds of "feminine" emotional skills in their repertoire—skills that would be useful to them in relationships, parenting, even in work situations—but they are tamped down or stamped out, leaving men out of balance and forced to function with only half of their emotional resources. In *How Can I Get Through to You?* Terrence Real writes, "A generation ago, women united to support one another in reclaiming the half of their humanity—assertion, public competence, independence—that patriarchy denied them. Now, empowered, they are insisting on levels of relational skill from their spouses that men have in no way been prepared to deliver. They are also concerned for their sons—desperately wishing for means to help keep them intact. It is men's turn to recapture that half of our humanity—receptivity, emotional expressiveness, dependency—that has been denied to us."

A letter that Real received from a reader illustrates the need men feel to process their repressed emotions. "Terry, I want to heal. I am scared about entering the process because I gather that I may have to live through some significant pain to get there. But I'm even more scared of what will happen to me if I don't. I'm writing to you—please take this the right way—because in your book, you don't seem so nice. I mean, you have a lot of heart, but I want someone to grab me by the throat. I don't really need more understanding; I need help. Throw me a lifeline, man. Everything's fine here—the house, the cars, the kids, the marriage. Everything's really, really fine—except that I'm drowning. I look forward to hearing from you. Bob"

When we demean the ability to nurture, support, and express feeling, we promote a disconnect from the feminine within each of us. It becomes easier to shut down and harder to achieve insight, and both men and women lose something vital. We have cut off the parts of ourselves that might be points of connection between us so it's harder for us to relate to one another, particularly in love relationships. We begin to fear one another even as we long to make meaningful connections. The result is that our attempts to get together are clumsy and ineffective at best, dehumanizing and objectifying at worst. Think about the men you know who are constantly pursuing women—who claim to love women—but who lie and cheat and run from commitment. Or the women who say they want a man, but who bury themselves in work, their hobbies, their shopping excursions and never make time for a guy. No wonder love relationships are so difficult.

Expressing emotion is vital to physical health, emotional well-being, the health of relationships, success in one's career, and to transmitting healthy intergenerational patterns. How do we go about expressing feelings?

POWER TOOL
EXPRESSING EMOTIONS

You can learn to express emotions. There is a right way for you.

1 **EXPRESS EMOTIONS PHYSICALLY**
Find a physical motion that helps you to get it out. This

Insight

> can be beating pillows, hitting tennis balls, jumping up and down, and so on.
>
> **2**   **EXPRESS EMOTIONS VERBALLY**
> Talk it out. Write it out.
>
> **3**   **EXPRESS EMOTIONS MENTALLY**
> Examine your thoughts. Do you recognize the thought pattern from anyone in the generations who have come before you? For example, my mother used to say, "It's a wicked world." Then ask whether your thoughts are positive or negative.
>
> **4**   **EXPRESS EMOTIONS SPIRITUALLY**
> Do the relaxation exercise in chapter 1 and then quietly carry on a dialogue in your own heart about your feelings, listening for responses that may come.

MARCIE

Marcie was a bride-to-be who wanted to heal the family pattern that threatened to crush her union with her fiancé Paul. The couple fought all the time. They'd go away for a romantic weekend and have ferocious arguments the entire time. They would meet friends for an evening out and fight all the way there and all the way home. The seemed to love each other, but they couldn't get along.

When they came in for couples therapy, it was clear that Marcie had a severe case of low self-esteem that caused her to torpedo the relationship. She felt terrified that Paul would not view her feelings and needs as being important so she often anticipated this and become angry without giving him a chance to respond to her needs. She imagined that Paul was not as in love with her as he had been with other

Power Choices

women, and she became quite distraught at the thought. This was far from the truth as she was the only woman he had ever been deeply in love with.

Using the Jaffe Remembrance Exercise (developed by Robert Jaffe, MD, and John Laird, MD) to open her heart and tap the wisdom of her intuition, she got in touch with the hidden history of her behavior. She relaxed deeply and focused on her heart, asking for answers to specific questions, such as: "Where in my body am I experiencing an emotional block? What color is it? What feelings are there? At what age did I first experience these feelings, and what happened to create them?"

POWER TOOL
REMEMBRANCE EXERCISE

To tap the power of your heart, do the Jaffe Remembrance Exercise daily.

1 Do your remembrance for twenty to sixty minutes daily. The Sufis believe that the best time to do this exercise is in the middle of the night, typically between 2:00 a.m. and 5:00 a.m. God has said: "This is the time of our –nearness." The veils between the material and divine worlds are thinnest at this time. The second "best" times to do a remembrance are either upon awakening or before retiring. All other times during the day are thought to be approximately of equal value.

2 Place your hand over your heart.

3 Picture your heart as a rose-choose the color you feel that you need today.

4 Choose your favorite name for the divine (God, Allah, Jesus, the Most High, Krishna, and so on), and picture this name written in your heart as you begin to repeat it over and over. When you say the name, say it quietly on your tongue-barely audible or just inaudible. This allows the name to travel deeper into your being. Eventually, your heart begins to repeat the name spontaneously, without conscious effort.

As you repeat the name, allow your heart to open gently, so you can "place" the name more and more deeply into your heart. Allow your heart to be moved, washed, and "structured" by the name. In other words, give the divine your consent to be cleaned and changed. Trust what the divine brings for you.

Let the emphasis of the practice be on *receiving* the name, the presence, and the light of God. It is a gentle relaxing, a letting go. Let the petals of your heart open to the name as the petals of a flower open to the rays of the sun.

Everyone has moments of drifting off, thinking of something else, or "going unconscious." No big deal. When you notice this, simply return gently to repeating the name.

The content and quality of your experience is not necessarily so important in this practice. Having a "Wow!" experience is not the goal. No matter what you experience, whether it's a flashy vision or a negative reaction, simply continue to say the name and go deeper.

If you are unsure or uncomfortable in any manner with the remembrance, be sure to ask inwardly for guidance. Feel free to ask for help in working through

> your concerns. In time, you will gain comfort and confidence with this practice.
>
> *As your practice of remembrance deepens, your being will transform in beautiful and holy ways. This is a vehicle for returning to the divine. As all the blood flows to and from the heart, so the mentioning of the Divine in the heart begins to spread through the body and all the being. Then every action becomes an expression of the remembrance of the divine. And so, starting from the tongue, it goes to the heart, and through the heart it spreads to all your body.*

The process helped her remember the chaotic year when she was five and her parents separated. Her father moved across the country, taking Marcie and her three-year-old sister with him. He took them, but he acted as if he didn't want them. He often berated Marcie, calling her stupid, magnifying any perceived fault or infraction and using it as an excuse to hit her and yell at her. This verbal, emotional, and physical abuse continued throughout her entire tenure with her father.

Marcie felt a surge of energy as she awakened these emotions in her heart. I guided her through a Gestalt process, which encouraged direct dialogue with the person one has issues with. Rather than talking about it, imagine the person in front of you and tell him or her your feelings so the release is more immediate and real. "Who do you need to express these feelings to, Marcie?" I asked. "Both my dad and my mom," she responded. I asked her to envision her parents sitting on the empty chairs in front of her. "Tell them what you are feeling," I coached. She started sobbing as she confronted her virtual parents. "How could you treat me like that, you fucker? You never had anything positive to say

Insight

to me or about me. It was constant drama. I hate you. I hate you, too, Mom because you left me with him. You've never given me your time or stood up for me."

I also guided her through some Reichian work, which allows the physical release of emotional pain, asking her to hit the chair with a rolled-up towel, as I instructed her. She hit as hard as she could, sobbing out her rage, grief, and feeling of worthlessness. When she felt it was all out, she collapsed and sighed, "I feel so much lighter."

After doing the release work, Marcie no longer rushed into fights with Paul. She began to practice checking in with her feelings regularly. The release tools helped to clear feelings; the remembrance tools helped to heal her heart. She began to look for ways to nurture and care for herself and to treat herself like the lovable and loving person she is. This reconnection with her feelings, her feminine self, also ignited her creativity, and she took up sculpting. She and Paul also spend time mastering good, solid communication skills. I recommended materials on effective communication (see *Love Lessons: A Guide to Transforming Relationships*, my first book, coauthored with Brenda Lane Richardson). Marcie tapped her heart's wisdom, and today she's a more contented person. She says, "I know what it means now to be more feminine, and Paul knows what it means to be a healthy man. Neither of us gets our dukes up the way we used to. When there's an upset, we access our feelings, look at childhood stuff to see what's been triggered, share it, and get to forgiveness as quick as we can."

NOTHING TO FEAR

Fear is the main source of superstition, and one of the main sources of cruelty. To conquer fear is the beginning of wisdom.
— Bertrand Russell

The feelings that seem a constant challenge for most of us are fear and anger. We have all these "isms"—sexism, ageism, racism and homophobia—because we have not worked through our fears. We don't connect enough with anyone or anything different from ourselves so we don't know the truth about other people and other experiences. That lack of understanding makes us suspicious and fearful. Our hearts slam shut when we find ourselves gripped by fear. Often an angry response becomes a defense against the feeling of fear. Take Lucy's response to Bag Man in the beginning of this chapter. It seems that, being hurt and helpless, she would have been kinder to him. In fact, it was because she was hurt and helpless that she was so rude and short with him.

In *The Dance of Anger*, Harriet Lerner broke new ground as she followed the trail of repressed emotion in families that had suffered tragic losses—in one case, the loss of a child—identifying the fear and anger that marred interactions between family members. There were so many areas this family could not talk about. Fear infected the bereft mother's behavior toward the child she had left. Terrified of losing her remaining child, she became overly controlling. At the same time, she was cold and distant from her child because she couldn't tolerate feeling love and vulnerability again. So imagine that—she was too close and too distant at the same time.

Our fears manifest in many different ways. I led a women's group once where a woman complained that she had a very difficult time getting dates. The group, eager to help, suggested she go to singles events. She said, "Oh, I go all the time. But I never meet anybody." This woman was very attractive, smart, and well put together. We couldn't imagine how she could go out and not meet anyone. We pressed her about what happened at the singles events. "Nothing much," she said. "I always take a good book, and I sit there and read." We all wondered how she expected to meet anyone if she wasn't engaging in conversation or interacting in any way. "If someone really wants to meet me, they're going to come over and meet me, even if I'm reading." Talk about making a man jump through hoops. She apparently wanted someone who was going to ignore the obvious message she was sending—"Leave me alone"—and try to engage her anyway.

Insight

Our lovely bookworm grew up with a mother who took great pains to warn her about men. "They will leave you," "You can't count on them," "Always have your own money," and so on, were messages she drummed repeatedly into her daughter. Having been widowed at a young age and scurrying to provide for herself and her three daughters, her mother never had time to grieve. She was caught in a loop of anger and depression of unresolved loss. But it manifested in her daughter as fear of intimacy.

FINDING EMOTIONAL FREEDOM THROUGH FORGIVENESS

Forgiveness is the key to happiness.
— The Course in Miracles

After we get in touch with our feelings, understand the triggers involved, and learn to express our emotions effectively—that is, without blaming or playing victim—we move toward forgiveness. Forgiveness is often difficult for people, mostly because we want to hang on to our sense of self-righteousness, but also because it's hard to forget the hurts that other people have inflicted on us. But we all need to get the point where we can forgive whatever was done to us. Deep down we want to let go of that anger and resentment because we know it's eating us up inside.

Forgiveness frees us from the heavy weights of anger and resentment that impede our ability to love. It is an important goal, an important prize along our quest. It must be significant; every spiritual tradition teaches its importance. In the Christian tradition, Jesus says we must forgive our enemy "seventy times seven." In the Jewish tradition, there's a story about a rabbi who forgave a man who spread vicious lies about him. "Those lies can not be retracted. Trying to repair the damage your lies have done is like trying to pick up feathers that have been scattered to the wind." But he still forgave.

In the Muslim tradition, there's a story of Mohammed walking through a city. Each time he passed a certain house, the old woman who lived there cursed him and threw garbage on his head. Every single time he passed her way, she attacked him. And every time, he just greeted her, offered her blessings, and kept on his way. Then one day, he passed by her window and there were no curses; no garbage was thrown. Curious, he went to see what had happened. The woman was lying in bed, weak and sick. She told him that she had no one to care for her. Though she had done nothing but curse him time and again, he offered to take care of her and nurse her back to health.

First, let's define what forgiveness is not. Forgiving the person who hurt you—whoever it was and whatever they did—doesn't mean what they did was okay. It hurt you; it left you with scars and damage. It wasn't okay, but you want to forgive because anger and resentment and unforgiveness are big boulders weighing down that thousand-pound sack you carry. If you don't forgive, who is carrying that sack around? The person who hurt you? No. You are. You don't deserve to have been hurt *and* have to carry around a bunch of baggage.

Don't try to fake forgiveness. You can't. One of the things that makes me crazy is people who say, "I've forgiven that. I don't have any feeling about that. I forgave it all" when they haven't gone through the process of expressing and examining their feelings about the hurt. Saying you forgive someone without working through feelings is like putting sugar on garbage. It's still going to stink. Real forgiveness requires some work. We'll get to that in detail in chapter 7; for now just hold it as one of the goals of emotional healing.

I got a letter from a woman who told me the most wonderful story about forgiveness. She wrote: "Dear Doc Wade, I'm writing to let you know that I read your book, *What Mama Didn't Tell Us About Love*, and I realized for the first time that there wasn't a single woman in my family who had a relationship. No love relationships. None! And I thought, I'm forty years old. I'm following the same pattern." She went on to tell the story about how her father had died, and her mother had said, "That's why you should never trust men. They'll leave you. You better get a good education and have your own money because you see what can happen to

Insight

you." She was just a little girl at the time, but she took it in. Mom must be right, she thought. And she said, "I'm writing this letter to you because today is my first wedding anniversary, and I want you to know I broke the chain! I found greater freedom and success and love afterward."

CONTINUE THE JOURNEY

If I told patients to raise their blood levels of immune globulins or killer T cells, no one would know how. But if I can teach them to love themselves and others fully, the same change happens automatically. The truth is: Love heals.
— Bernie Siegel, MD

We've all broken chains in our lives. We've come to a point where we've realized something was not working for us and decided to change it. But there's always more work to do if we're willing to choose to develop our insight and to keep growing. So, you want to know what to do with all that brilliant insight? Well then, like our hero Igraine, we must move on to the next turn in the road, but don't worry. You'll be armed not only with insight, but with our next power choice-intention.

Here are some questions and power tools that will enable you to continue on the journey.

QUESTIONS

1. What am I feeling right now…could it be fear? Now remember, if you have a fear, it will cause you to create the very thing you don't want. I knew a man who was frightened of rejection. He pushed everybody away so they wouldn't reject him, and then he said, "See, I knew you were going to leave me!" That's how fear works. This is the Pygmalion affect. We'll get to know the Greek youth, Pygmalion, in chapter 5.

2. What's triggering this feeling or this fear? An external stimulus can trigger the same feelings we experienced as a child and send us into a trauma trance in which we begin to use the same defensive maneuvers that we developed in childhood.

Power Choices

3. When was the first time I felt this way? Look at your childhood to get the answer.
4. How can I best express these feelings? Talk to a friend or therapist, or write these feelings out in a journal.

Power Tools

1 LISTEN TO YOUR BODY AND YOUR EMOTIONS
Do this exercise.

2 FAMILY PATTERNS
List the family patterns you find within your family genogram and in your life. Look over the list of patterns you are exhibiting in your life. How do they get in your way? Write these down or share with a confidant.

3 THE FEELING JOURNAL
Write in your Feeling Journal every day.

4 CONNECTING THE DOTS
Go over your genogram and identify the patterns in your family and any you can spot in your own life.

5 EXPRESSING EMOTIONS
Explore this exercise.

6 REMEMBRANCE EXERCISE
To tap the power of your heart, do the Jaffe Remembrance Exercise regularly.

Power Decree
I AM FILLED WITH UNDERSTANDING.

Climb the mountains and get their good tidings. Nature's peace will flow into you as sunshine flows into trees. The winds will blow their own freshness into you, and the storms their energy, while cares will drop away from you like the leaves of Autumn. —John Muir

Chapter Four

Intuition
Approaching Our Inmost Being

It's what Goethe said in Faust, *but which George Lucas dressed in modern idiom. The message that technology is not going to save us—our computers, our tools, our machines are not enough. We must rely on our intuition, our true being.* — Joseph Campbell, *The Power of Myth*

"THIS IS TOO FREAKY!" Lucy thinks to herself from the middle of her multicolored fog. "Maybe somebody slipped me some bad drugs the other night at that bar. Walt? Would Walt have done that? He wants me to make up my mind about him, but if this is the way he's going about it, screw him."

"Quiet!" a voice commands. She recognizes it as the Bag Man's, but it seems to be coming from inside her own head. "Yes, I'm speaking inside your head," the voice answers the question she hadn't asked. "Maybe that will get you to listen."

"All right, tell me this," Lucy says, testing the mental communication, "Are we really falling through the air as we are having this insane conversation inside my head?

"You might call it that. I would call it teleportation. It's more like flying."

"Bad drugs," she thinks to her herself. "It's definitely bad drugs."

"Stop blabbing. Go back. Go back to the airport, to the plane and your parents. Look at yourself holding that bag. What's in the bag?"

"You saw it, too?"

The voice ignores her question. "What's in the bag, Lucy?"

Abruptly, they land (if you could call it that. It was more like settling *down somewhere) in a cave—dark, dank, and, to Lucy's way of thinking, ominous. "This is definitely a funky looking spot," Lucy blurts, unconsciously using her usual bravado to cover the chill frisson of fear creeping up her spine.*

Bag Man ignores her and strides briskly—without a walker, Lucy notes—to the back of the cave. Before he reaches the wall, he raises his arm, and, with an imperious wave of his hand, the back of the cave seems to –dissolve. Beyond, Lucy sees the most beautiful place she ever imagined possible. Instinctively, she leaves the cave and follows Bag Man into the scene before her—cascading waterfalls, brilliantly green trees and plants, unusual and stunning flowers of iridescent blue and violet. In some of the trees hung fruit that she would swear looked like gold. After crossing a bridge over a ridiculously blue river, Lucy sees what appears to be a cabana filled with deep, comfortable cushions and a table set with delectable food.

"God, I'm hungry. Aren't you?" she says, examining the spread. When she turns, she finds that she's alone. "Oh, hell no. Don't you dare leave me! Where are you?"

She hears the voice in her head reply, "Sit down. Eat. Relax. And figure out what's in that bag." So Lucy sits down, mostly because she doesn't know what else to do, and she hears the Bag Man's urgent voice again: "Hurry, Lucy. There isn't much time. They'll be here soon." At that very moment a truly stunning man, just her type, walks toward her. "Oooh, I like it here," Lucy purrs, hoping the Bag Man can't read her thoughts....

Has Lucy been drugged? Or is she actually having an out-of-body experience? Is the Bag Man a friend or an enemy? Has she just encountered the man of her dreams? How can she be sure? And what is in that bag? She will find the answers to all of these questions eventually, as the journey she's on plays itself out. What she doesn't realize is that, deep inside, she already knows the answer to these questions—and she could answer them right now if she tapped into her intuition.

Intuition is that much-discussed sixth sense. It's the part of us that clues us in when we need to answer a question like, "Is this my

Intuition

soul mate or an enemy?"—the kind of question that it might take years of evidence to answer objectively. When people talk about the "still small voice in the heart," they're talking about intuition. We all have it, whether it's well developed or not. But how do we access it? And if we can tap into intuitive power, how do we put it to practical use in our lives? These are among the questions we explore as we consider the power choice intuition.

Intuition grants us the ability to plumb the depths of our subconscious to acquire the deeper self-knowledge we need to meet our challenges—especially those we encounter in love relationships, parenting, and collegial relationships. Of course, ultimately, it is our relationship with ourselves and with the divine that we cultivate when we build this seemingly psychic instinct.

When we work toward strengthening our intuition, it isn't enough to simply feel feelings or examine thoughts as we did when we practiced developing insight. (Not that those are simple things!) In delving into intuition, we shift our focus from analyzing what is going on and why to a deeper level of self-awareness that is innate and inborn. This level of awareness can potentially answer questions like those Lucy faces at this juncture of her quest and that you will face in the tests of your life.

Merlin

The story of Merlin the Magician may help us shed some light on the mysterious power of intuition. *As legend goes, Merlin played a pivotal role in shaping the life of sixth-century English King Arthur. First, Merlin stole the babe Arthur away from his birthplace in Tintagel so that he could be reared in a safe foster home, away from the threat of other challengers to the throne who would not have hesitated to end young Arthur's life to further their ends. Over the ensuing years, Merlin served as a great friend, mentor, counselor, and seer for young Arthur. When the time came for Arthur to pull the legendary sword from the stone and claim his true identity and birthright, it was Merlin who assisted with the defeat of Arthur's enemies so the young king might unite the Celts as one kingdom under one banner.*

According to legend, Merlin's powers extended to shape shifting and communing with animals; he was a great bard who often played his harp as he sang ballads recalling the history and deeds of valor of kings and knights for the court; and, as a high priest, he was welcomed at the holy Isle of Avalon, the retreat of priestesses. Throughout his long career, Merlin carefully guarded his powers and the secrets of his magic. Some accounts say he never had a lover for fear of becoming vulnerable and losing his power. But there was his Achilles heel.

Very late in his life, the young priestess Nyneve began to seek Merlin's company, and he fell deeply in love with her. Mad with desire for her, the old sorcerer couldn't see that she coveted his great power. He wanted her, and she promised to make love with him but only after he proved himself by sharing his magic. My grandmother used to say, "There ain't no fool like an old fool." *Merlin was both. Before long, he had divulged many of his secrets in an attempt to win Nyneve's love. In the end she used the very spells he had taught her to imprison him.*

An inglorious end for the mighty magician, but even at its conclusion, his story contains a magic formula. Having devoted himself to making a king and building political power, he had neglected his inner kingdom. His intellect was well developed; his influence at court and beyond was vast. He played beautifully his role in developing a united Britain, and, with loyalty, he always advised and assisted the king with the utmost wisdom. But his final test was a test of the heart—a realm he hadn't developed. The surrender and vulnerability required to pass this test were foreign to Merlin. He didn't know himself well enough—hadn't developed his insight—and he lacked the skill of listening to his own guidance, his feelings and intuition in matters of love. In the end, when it was too late, he saw how he'd been trapped not so much by his unslaked thirst for Nyneve as by an unwise and an unschooled heart. Had Merlin paused to access the

Intuition

inner knowledge that he used so effectively for others, he may have been able to preserve himself. This tale also contains the idea of partaking of the lessons that only an open heart can yield. His story cautions us to beware a life devoted to external pursuits at the expense of inner development. ᛜ

HEART POWER

The good neighbor looks beyond the external accidents and discerns those inner qualities that make all men human and, therefore, brothers.
— Martin Luther King, Jr.

Let's take a moment and really think (as oxymoronic as it sounds), think about love. What is the impact of actually wielding heart power? Or of not using it at all? In the new biography *Hans Paache Militant and Pacifist in Imperial Germany* by Werner Lange, the early twentieth-century German writer and activist, Hans Paasche, in a letter is quoted: "What is to become of us Germans when we are raising generation after generation without love?" He was commenting on the predilection of German parents to prize obedience and performance in their children while showing them little sensitivity or love. He predicted the rise of fascism and the deadly turn it would take in the form of the Nazi regime. He understood that these loveless children would grow up to be adults who had no access to their own heart. He knew that, with a desire to win the parental love they craved, they would follow a parent figure who was just like the parents who had raised them, doing anything to please him. (The late Bob Hoffman, of the Hoffman Institute, calls it the Negative Love Syndrome.) But people didn't want to listen to Paasche's predictions; they didn't want to face what they and their culture had become. Hans Paasche was assassinated early in the Nazi's rise to power by the very fascists he sought to restrain. But killing him didn't change the accuracy of his perceptions or his predictions. He was one more casualty in the horror story that would forever mark Germany's history.

Intuition can be thought of as tapping a kind of latent inner sense, using subtle sensory input to understand the environment and people around us, or it can mean understanding the link between the information available from an open heart and the subsequent decisions we make in the world. Merlin with his closed heart lacked necessary information to choose wisely in love. Paasche correctly predicted that loveless children would grow up with closed hearts and do worse than just make unwise political choices. What does the heart teach us when we develop the skill to listen? The ultimate lessons: compassion, wisdom, truth, and love.

Bart

Tall, dark, and handsome with sparkling green eyes, Bart was an enviably successful property developer with a mega-figure salary and piles of expensive boy toys (including three luxury cars). In college, he'd earned the title ULM, the Ultimate Ladies Man. He was now forty-four, and the label still fit. But Bart wanted to retire the title. "I want to have a permanent home, marry a good woman, and have a family," he told me emphatically the first time he came in for psychotherapy. "I'm getting too old for this."

Though his outer life was going on "business as usual," he kept feeling that something wasn't right. He'd recently lost a cherished development project. He'd been ditched by yet another girlfriend, and the passing of his father made his need to mend his life feel more urgent. He'd screwed up the courage to face himself head on. It was courage he was going to need.

He began his investigation by admitting that his selfishness doomed his romantic relationships. "That's hard to admit," he said softly, "but it's true. I lose interest and start looking for the next conquest after about six months. Most of the time, I've already got somebody else waiting in the wings."

"You mean you cheat?" I asked. He nodded sheepishly.

It was a major blow to Bart to realize that his self-centeredness extended into his work life. He looked out for number one first and foremost, ignoring the needs and contributions of his team members. Undoubtedly, his me-me-me attitude caused him to lose what he described as the biggest opportunity of his life.

"Maybe, healing the cause of that selfish streak will be the most rewarding opportunity of your life," I suggested.

Fearlessly proceeding, Bart faced his emotional numbness and his recurring feelings of depression. "I never called it that. I just thought of it as feeling burned out. I would think I just needed a change of scene so I would go looking for the next project in a new locale. Or I would get on to the next sexual conquest. I loved the feeling of falling in love. Well, it was more falling in lust, if I'm really being honest." Yes, I affirmed, sexual intrigue can be a powerful mind-altering, mood-altering experience; it can even become addictive.

The last blow to Bart's ULM image came when he had to admit that his "attitude adjustment hour" each night actually translated to an addiction to marijuana.

"Ouch!" He said, "What am I going to have left?"

"You get to choose the answer to that question," I told him. Bart's quest to address the dilemmas that he hadn't been able to resolve began with deep soul searching. He developed the habit of sitting down each day and asking his inner guidance for help and support. If he hadn't been able to face the truth and utilize its bracing, clarifying light, he would have continued on a road of self-destruction similar to the one that claimed Merlin. They were opposite sides of the same coin—one a womanizer, the other a virtual celibate—both afraid of real intimacy. The cost in Bart's case was clear: personal loneliness and detachment edged him toward depression; and his ever-worsening addiction, lack of a spiritual outlet, and negative thinking pushed him further into a clearly destructive spiral. While his life still appeared exciting and successful from the outside, Bart knew it was crumbling at its foundation. Fortunately, he took the step to seek help and healing before he took a more serious fall.

Despite the fact that his life was successful on the surface, he knew in his heart something was wrong. He had just never been willing to listen to that gentle instructor before.

THE FREEDOM WITHIN

There is a brokenness out of which comes the unbroken.
— Rashani, Cofounder of Earthsong Holistic Healing Institute

Here in America, we worship efficiency and individualism because we firmly believe they contribute to our freedom. And they do. But there is a deeper meaning in freedom that can actually bring about personal transformation and that frees us to be our authentic selves. This authentic way of being is captured in a concept created by Dr. Virginia Satir. She named it the Five Freedoms. Briefly they are:

1. *The freedom to say what I think and feel.*
2. *The freedom to reach out for what I want.*
3. *The freedom to take risks on my own behalf.*
4. *The freedom to see what is really here right now without illusion.*
5. *The freedom to be fully present.*

These freedoms essentially empower us to create the necessary conditions to maximize our intuition. The ability to be fully present, to witness what we can see and hear, in order to sift through that information for clues provides invaluable fodder for intuitive awareness.

In a dramatic demonstration of these freedoms, Virginia Satir worked with a teenage girl who was suicidal and suffering from grand mal seizures. As was her wont, Satir called the entire family to the hospital for a meeting with herself, the patient, and the hospital staff. As she began to talk with the family about the girl's disturbance, she realized that the father who was present was not the biological father of the children in the family. She looked around at them all and said, "Well, what happened to the biological father?" At that moment the girl who had been sitting with her head down with her long black hair acting as a curtain over her face suddenly began to have a seizure and fell to the floor convulsing wildly. The medical staff rushed to her aid as Satir got down on the floor next to her and, speaking directly into her ear, said, "I noticed that you started having this seizure when I mentioned your biological father. When your seizure is over, we'll have to talk about that." Indeed she used what she could hear and see and risked speaking about it even in the midst of a seizure. They went on to heal the loss of the missing father, which had been a taboo subject for the family. That was the last seizure that young girl had, and an epilogue about her was videotaped a year later. She appeared radiant as she sang a song of her own composition while playing her guitar.

To attain the inner freedom that leads to self-mastery, each of us has a soul lesson that is part of our life work. In *The Tenth Insight*, James Redfield emphasizes the importance of examining where your parents left off in their work because what they have left incomplete is something we must either repeat or complete. For example, if your father never dealt with the deep shame he felt as a child growing up in poverty, the issue of shame is going to come up in your own life as a soul lesson.

My spiritual teacher, Chow Chow Imamoto, always said, "I was born Japanese to get over embarrassment." She believed embarrassment was a soul lesson that she needed to heal. She had an extraordinarily opportunity to face embarrassment when, as a teenager during World War II, she was placed in an internment camp. Embarrassed, ashamed, and deeply pained by the experience, she didn't speak of it for forty years. But she was eventually able to bring the wound to light—a process that was crucial to her healing and that released her bondage to embarrassment, which allowed her to make even greater progress on her spiritual path. Author Tian Dayton calls this kind of inner pain a "heartwound," and she states, "The power of intuition greatly enhances our healing by giving us the vital insight we need to understand what is blocking us and what to do to facilitate healing." In her book *Heartwounds*, Dayton goes on to say that in healing childhood trauma, the process of psychotherapy where we connect a person with their own intuitive wisdom dismantles the traumatic reaction and rebuilds an awareness of sources of strength and support in childhood.

AVERY AND MARGARET

Avery and Margaret are an excellent illustration of intuition's power to help in healing a childhood trauma that creates heartbreak in a marriage. This couple, now in their late forties, had married the day after they graduated from college and started their family a year later. Avery soon left his job at a brokerage firm to go out on his own, and Margaret worked in his office part-time and raised their twin sons. Avery had the golden touch; his business took off. Margaret, responding to the boys' increasing need for her involvement in their lives, chose to be a full-time homemaker and mother. Everything looked good. With a beautiful family, beautiful home, wealth, and an excellent standing in their community, they were fit subjects for a Norman Rockwell painting.

But behind the frame of that perfect picture, Avery and Margaret had frequent communication breakdowns that led to terrible fights. Their dark secret was that they were so alienated from one another that they didn't touch one another sexually for months at a time. When it got to the point that they hadn't made love in two years, they came to see me.

"I just don't understand it," Margaret lamented. "We are two good, well-educated people. Why can't we just sit down and talk to one another? I can talk to anyone except Avery."

I asked each of them to describe the situation from his or her own perspective.

"Margaret just wants me to agree with whatever she says. She wants me to feel her feelings. I just can't do that. I

Intuition

feel trapped and suffocated. There's no room for my feelings. She just won't listen to me," Avery recounted angrily.

Margaret shook her head, visibly upset. "I see it so differently," she said. "All I want is to share what I'm feeling. But it's as if I'm waving a red flag in front of a bull. I say the word 'feeling' and you charge."

After a round of blaming one another—"It's you!" "No, it's you!"—I blew the time-out whistle. I asked them each to sit back, relax, and close their eyes. Then I led them through the Jaffe Remembrance Exercise described in chapter 3. Using that powerful technique, they moved through a series of questions through which their intuition drew them to the childhood memories that contained long-buried hurtful experiences, which had triggered dysfunctional reactions in both members of this couple.

They were each able to bring forth their inner guidance with results that startled them.

"I see myself at age five. My mother is leaving me to move to another town for school. She's leaving me with my grandparents," Avery said quietly.

"How long did you stay with them?" I asked.

"I'm not sure," he said. "Maybe a year, maybe two, I lived with her for awhile but after that she left me with an uncle, then I went to live with her and then back to my grandparents again".

"Ask your intuition what you decided about yourself as a result of these experiences."

"That my feelings don't matter and that I'm not important."

"And what did you decide about relationships?"

"That I can't trust them; they hurt."

"And women?"

"I can't trust them either. They go away in the end, and I just have to start over again."

Then it was Margaret's turn. Her intuitive guidance reminded that when she was seven, her father had beat her severely for something she hadn't done. She had decided that no matter what she did, she would be punished and that she couldn't trust that a man would really love her enough to listen to her. For each of them, just knowing the source of their original pain was a big step toward healing it.

They also intuitively knew how to find a solution to their communication problems. When they asked their deep wisdom what to do, it suggested first comforting their frightened inner child, then helping the child to understand that they were no longer at home at the mercy of their abusive and abandoning parents. Using self-talk (more in chapter 5), they learned to stop and get clear before they reacted to one another—to notice whether the reaction was a result of childhood beliefs or related to a real present—time issue.

They completed their work by asking their inner guidance what color light or energy would clear this old pattern. I taught them how to visualize this color and wash away the stuck energy of these deep cellular memories. The use of light energy is the oldest form of healing on the planet. Many records from early healing by the Greeks, Egyptians, and indigenous healers indicate the discovery of the efficacy of letting ailing patients sit in bright sunlight, especially by the seashore or another body of water. Many modern holistic therapies include visualizations and meditations on light, and people who make use of them report that a feeling of calm and peace comes over them, and they find it easier to respond in a peaceful way to external situations. I have found that this is true for my clients also, and this is exactly what happened for Margaret and Avery. They made an agreement to call a halt for intuitive work whenever they noticed their interactions going south. It made all of the difference for them; this couple was finally able to stop fighting and start talking.

Intuition

> **POWER TOOL**
> **LISTENING TO YOUR INTUITION EXERCISE**
>
> *Listening to your inner self will help you work through strong trauma reactions or feelings. Begin by placing your hand over your heart and taking three deep relaxing breaths. Ask your inner guidance to give you the message that you need right now in order to deal with what is in front of you. Listen quietly for a few moments and focus on your heart. Accept the first thing that comes to mind even is it doesn't make complete sense. I've found that the more practice you have with this exercise the easier it is to access the intuition so be patient and keep working with it. Use a tool like the power choices meditation kit to assist you.*

LEARNING YOUR SOUL LESSONS

The real enemy that destroys peace is our internal enemy.
— The Dalai Lama

Emotion that rages out of control destroys the possibility of achieving contact with the more subtle information of intuitive power. A peaceful mind leads to peaceful feelings, which allows the revelation of the quiet whisper of the inner voice. This makes it vitally important that we learn to gauge our emotional reactions. An additional yardstick by which to determine whether you are dealing with feelings that are trauma reactions or feelings that are current is what I call the Emotional Intensity Scale.

I have learned to ask my clients to gauge on a scale of one to ten, (ten, the upper end, means you've gone over the edge and are having a tantrum) the intensity of their emotion. If it's more than a five, as it clearly was in the case of Avery and Margaret, then a

Power Choices

cellular memory is being triggered, a painful experience or trauma from our childhood. The thing we're responding to in the here and now as a rule isn't likely to rile us up to a seven or eight, unless something deeper is exacerbating our feelings. Road rage isn't about the guy who just cut you off in traffic. That would only rate a two on the scale. But if you find yourself screaming and cursing, there's something deeper going on. The rude driver triggered it, but your old issues escalated it to a ten. After you've calmed down, do some deep breathing and some writing or talking to get the feelings out. The Listening to Your Intuition Exercise we just went through will help sort it out.

POWER TOOL
EMOTIONAL INTENSITY SCALE

When you are experiencing a big emotional reaction, determine whether you are experiencing a trauma reaction or feeling by using the Emotional Intensity Scale.

On a scale of one to ten, rate the intensity of your emotion. If it's more than a five, then cellular memory may be triggered, and the following process may help.

1 Close your eyes and use the relaxation exercise in chapter 1, then, call upon your inner guidance. Ask inwardly:
- How old was I when I first experienced this feeling?
- What was happening?
- Ask any other questions that help you to see what was really going on at the time.

2 Ask your intuition what you decided about yourself as a result of this experience.

3 Then ask your intuition what you decided about [name the

Intuition

> relevant experience or circumstance, such as relationships, men, women, or work] as a result of this experience.
>
> Ask your intuition what color light or energy would clear this old pattern. Then visualize this color light washing away the pattern from every cell of your being.   **4**
>
> After you are done asking your intuition questions, open your eyes and write down the key points so that you can use them to change the patterns that need changing by tearing up and throwing away the old dysfunctional patterns.   **5**

Discovering the emotional patterns in your life will help you to discover your soul lesson. You'll know what the lesson is by how intensely you respond when it's triggered. The thing that upsets you the most or gets the highest score on your Emotional Intensity Scale is going to be related to your soul lesson. My own soul lesson is clearly forgiveness. Repeatedly in my life, I've found that the only way to restore myself to the sanity level on my Emotional Intensity Scale is to practice forgiveness. Until I release my feelings, examine the underlying triggers with the help of my intuitive strength, and then practice forgiveness exercises (yes, they're coming), I feel miserable. I am happy to report to you that it takes less and less time to get the forgiveness done because I've come to believe so firmly that most often when someone does something hurtful its because they are emotionally triggered and unaware of the damage and harm that they are causing to me or to anyone else. This does not mean that hurtful behavior is okay or that people are not responsible for their unconscious behavior.

We will work on mastering soul lessons when we get to the chapter on inspiration. Here we want to use the power of looking deeply within to discover the lesson.

Trusting Your Vision

No bird soars too high if he soars on his own wings.
— William Blake

Hildegard of Bingen was born in 1098 to a German family of wealth and nobility. At birth, she was dedicated to the church, as was customary for the tenth child of every family. At age three, she began to have visions, but she hid this gift for many years. By the time she was five, Hildegard was already launched on her life as a nun when she was sent to live with her aunt, an anchoress named Jutta, who began her religious education. Hildegard was devastated by her parents' decision, though in spite of her emotional pain or because of it, she studied and practiced her faith with fervor and devotion. Her devotion was rewarded when, at thirty-eight, she became mother superior of the convent.

Throughout her life, her visions had never ceased. At age forty-two, Hildegard had a commanding revelation that compelled her to break her silence and instructed her to share her visions at last. She painted her visions, which she called illuminations, which depicted the sacred feminine arrayed in white flowing garments with brilliant jewels in the same positions as the eastern chakras. Wary of the impact her visions could have, she first consulted with Pope Eugenius for advice before she made them public, but when he had heard what she had to say, he encouraged her to have her visions written down and circulated. She soon was heralded throughout Europe.

Hildegard wasn't just a spiritual prodigy. She wrote on philosophy, science, and the curative value of herbs. She also wrote songs, a biography, a history book, and a drama and carried on an extensive correspondence that included royalty and three popes. She is possibly best known for the chants she wrote as means of expressing devotion. In fact, she said, "All the arts serving human desires and needs are derived from the breath that God sent into the human body." The bishop of Mainz declared her works divine, and, during a time when few women dreamed of earning such respect, she was consulted by and advised bishops, popes, and kings.

Many of Hildegard's revelations echo those of mystics the world over. Clearly she had tapped some deep vein—that thing Carl Jung called the universal unconscious. Hildegard of Bingen's story is a prime example of listening to one's inner vision and following its wisdom. In her case, she spoke up, even to criticize the Church and the pope for the greater good—admonishing the pope to reform the monasteries and to put an end to their abuses of power and in some cases blatant greed. Hildegard's works, considered archetypal in nature, speak to balancing humans in the spiritual as well as the material world. She is now recognized as a great mystic within and without the Catholic Church. Matthew Fox related in his commentary on Hildegard's life that whenever he reads Hildegard's words to Native American students, they respond that it's like hearing the voice of their ancestors. It seems clear that through her illuminations, Hildegard did tap into a universal consciousness that touches many hearts even eight hundred years later.

TRUSTING YOUR FEELINGS

Force is experienced through the senses; power can only be recognized through inner awareness. — David Hawkins, MD

We are taught at an early age not to trust our feelings, not to trust our inner wisdom, not to trust ourselves. Think about it. You skin your knee and someone tells you, "Oh, that didn't hurt." Or you don't want to give old Mrs. Jones a big kiss, but you're made to embrace her anyway. And you hear "no, no, no" perhaps more than any other single word. That kind of upbringing makes it hard for many of us to use our intuitive power because we are being taught to deny our true feelings.

Children know more than we give them credit. Research tells us that children have some amazing, innate capacities from birth. During my first couple of years at the University of Washington, I studied and conducted research on child development. Among the findings we reviewed were the following. Newborn infants already showed a preference for faces or face-like stimuli, rather than inanimate objects. They could smell well enough to identify their mother. (Even if they were hungry, they would turn away from another woman's breast, preferring to nurse with mama.) They could also see quite well, but had a field of vision of about eight to twelve inches—perfect for looking into your mother's eyes if you're nursing at her breast.

Personality and temperament seem to be inherent at birth as well. Some children have easy temperaments, some are highly sensitive, and others are spirited. You can guess which child might have the most challenging time. Yes, the highly sensitive child. Yet these children are most likely to grow up to be good scientists, therapists, or artists because their temperament gives them the ability to see deeply into their work—whether it is a painting, a patient, or a scientific problem. Sensitive children are also likely to be the first to notice danger because they cautiously scan the environment for clues. Parents of these children report that they're able to pick up on subtle cues in other people's feelings and responses. This kind of child seems most likely to respond in an intuitive way...if their intuition isn't pressed out of them.

A former client told me about the childhood discovery that ended his parents' marriage. He remembers hearing his mother's voice as she spoke on the phone, immediately sensing that something wasn't quite right. He was present when his father angrily confronted his mother, accusing her of having a lover. He was only four years old at the time; he didn't know what a lover was, but he piped up. "Yes, Daddy," he said. "I heard her talking to another man like she loved him." His mother turned to him and screamed, "You are a liar! A liar!"

It's easy to see why he hasn't forgotten that incident—what a terrible trauma for a child. And it's easy to see why he may have begun to mistrust his intuition. First of all, his mother negated it; by calling him a liar, she made him question his own senses. But even if she hadn't, he would pick up the message that his intuition was a bad thing since nothing good could be related to seeing your parents argue so bitterly. For this man, his mother's betrayal and

Intuition

her negation of his awareness created a tremendous amount of self doubt and mistrust that he carried into adulthood, though it cost him jobs and relationships. It took two years of intensive therapy for him to begin to trust himself and his awareness again.

What is harder to understand is how this little boy knew what was going on just from overhearing one side of a conversation. Is such intuition an inborn trait? Does it occur in all of us or just a few? Is it something that we can learn, practice, or enhance? And do some people automatically have more of it than others (such as women's intuition)? Does it ebb and flow according to one's life circumstances—which would explain the development of "motherly instinct"?

Research bears out the idea that at times we actually know more than we know that we know—that there is a part of our brains that works as a kind of automatic pilot sifting through environmental stimuli for any hint of a threat. Before we are consciously aware of danger, the brain highjacks the body and moves it out of harm's way. Indeed, evidence of intuition has been scientifically demonstrated. David G. Myers, author of the beautifully researched and written book *Intuition*, sets the gold standard for the scientific approach to intuition and summarizes these aspects of intuition:

Everyday Perception

Research shows that we instantly process and integrate complex information streams even though they may be coming in simultaneously on parallel sensory channels. For example, a broker friend of mine told about an occasion when she was sitting in her office where she keeps as many as twenty screens going simultaneously—including news feeds on televisions and financial information on computers. She was sitting there, talking on the phone and sifting data from the screens when a news story suddenly jumped out at her. The report showed executives from a major corporation at a meeting in Los Angeles. Despite the many sensory inputs, her mind grabbed this piece of information. She thought, "Why would all those executives be having dinner in Los Angeles? Something is up." She arranged to acquire stock in that company. Two weeks later she heard the announcement that the company was being bought by a major Fortune 100 company. Her intuition led to great financial rewards.

Implicit Memory

This form of memory involves unconscious learning in which we know something without realizing we have learned it or being able to say, "I remember it." Yet when tested, the results of unconscious learning reveal themselves. A common example that most of us have experienced is learning to walk in childhood, though we have no conscious memory of having learned to walk.

Thin Slices

Research by Nalini Ambady and Robert Rosenthal indicates that, based on a ten-second clip of someone's behavior, we can effectively predict various personality traits in that person. Another researcher in this field, John Bargh, flashed an image for a mere two hundred milliseconds before his research subjects—barely time for them to decipher the picture—but he found that they still had strong feelings, either loathing or liking the image. David Meyers says that forming snap judgments of people or events is a biological adaptation that assists in our survival.

I had a firsthand test of this early-warning system one midnight on a dark street in downtown San Francisco. A colleague and I had just presented a paper at the American Psychiatric Convention. (It was on domestic violence, so maybe my radar was up already.) As we walked down the street on our way home, my colleague whispered, "I think that man is following us." I turned and saw a man stop and pretend to look in a window. I said, "Let's cross the street." When the man crossed behind us, I turned and started screaming every expletive I've ever heard—and some I must have acquired through implicit memory! He turned and walked away. My friend asked, "Is that what you are supposed to do?" I said, "I don't know. That just came out of me." We'll never know whether that man intended us harm or not; I certainly scared him as much as he'd frightened us. But my instinctive, if not unusual, behavior definitely moved him away from our safety zone.

Emotional Intelligence

Emotionally intelligent people are self-aware.
— David G. Meyers

Intuition—or lack thereof—reveals itself most strongly in social situations. We intuitively pick up cues that allow us to negotiate social situations and respond appropriately to people's emotions. This skill is best known as emotional intelligence—sometimes called our "EQ."

Peter Salovey and John Mayer refined Daniel Goleman's original idea of emotional intelligence by defining it as "the ability to perceive, express, understand and manage emotions." People with emotional intelligence experience life without dysfunctional depression, anxiety, or anger. They are also able to delay gratification and express an empathic ability to decipher other people's emotions, offering encouraging responses. No surprise that these people frequently garner more success in their professional and personal lives.

A high emotional intelligence has to do with empathic accuracy and the ability to interpret moods. If you lack these aspects of intuition, you may have a very difficult time in personal or work relationships; conversely, people endowed with high levels of emotional sensitivity excel in management and human relations. I've seen this play out in the workplace as people whose emotional intelligence is most suited for isolated and intensely focused work are promoted to management positions in which they need to manage and interact effectively with a team of other people. Too often, the result is that the new manager is ineffective and out of his or her element, their team feels mismanaged, and everyone is unhappy and frustrated. This is more than just the Peter Principle at work—the idea that you rise to the level of your incompetence. This has to do with our very personalities.

The first step in avoiding this kind of scenario is to measure where you are on the emotional intelligence scale. The Multifactor Emotional Intelligence Scale (MEIS), developed by Peter Salovey, John Mayer, and David Caruso, measures the three components of emotional intelligence and gives an overall score. The three components are as follows:

1. **EMOTION REGULATION**
   Emotional regulation assesses your ability to rate strategies that you or someone else might use when facing various dilemmas.

2. **EMOTION PERCEPTION**
   Emotional perception evaluates your ability to perceive emotion transmitted through stories, music, faces, and so on.

3. **EMOTION UNDERSTANDING**
   Emotion Understanding rates your ease in predicting emotions, recognizing emotional fluctuations over time, and understanding how emotions blend (that is, knowing that someone might laugh if they're nervous or cry when they're happy).

The EQ concept isn't just some self-help buzzword. Research using the MEIS has established emotional intelligence as reliable, coherent, and age linked (meaning we develop more of it as we mature)—solidifying it as an authentic type of human intelligence. Interestingly, the data has shown that women have a greater awareness of emotional cues and a generally higher level of emotional intelligence. It would seem, then, that women are in fact predisposed to intuitive strength. (Another argument for men to tap into their feminine side.)

Intuition

Based on his research, David Myers offers some cautions against depending too much on intuition, pointing out that there are studies showing that our memories can be influenced by our moods, we can exaggerate our actual knowledge, and we can hold on to beliefs even after they've been proven false. These are among other flaws science has found in the use of intuition. Excellent cautions—and I advise that we take them to heart—but I'm afraid that science does not get the last word when it comes to intuition because there are phenomena that science simply cannot explain, like Hildegard's visions or numerous flashes of revelation that have led to everything from problem solving to Nobel Prize-winning research.

INCREASING YOUR INTUITION

Gently, gently I trained my mind...to let go of thoughts, then a flickering lamp shining brighter and steadier illuminated who I am. — Lalleshwari

Here's some good news. We can increase our levels of sensitivity, intuition, and emotional intelligence. You've heard the Native American saying, "If you want to understand a person, walk a mile in his moccasins." For many years, I've used that adage as a jumping-off point to assist clients in building emotional sensitivity: I help them walk in someone else's shoes.

My client May had been a successful software engineer—so good at her job that she was promoted to project manager for a new major product line. Her shy, introverted personality made her a good fit as an engineer, but posed real difficulties in her new role as a manager. She found herself in uncomfortable conflict with her former colleagues—now working under her—and unable to find balanced ways of managing them. She not only felt like a failure at her new job, but she also didn't have anyone to vent with since it would have been inappropriate to complain to her former friends. To assist her, I asked her to do the following:

- Do the breathing and relaxation exercise (Meditation) in chapter.
- After we'd practiced relaxing her mind and body to lower her

Power Choices

anxiety level (anxiety interferes with sensitivity), I asked her to envision one of her "difficult" team members sitting in an empty chair across from her. She pictured a man with whom she'd recently had a discussion that had disintegrated into a still-unresolved argument.

- I then had May literally switch seats—to physically sit where her imagined colleague had been. I asked her to imagine what her team member was likely to be feeling. After some exploration, she came to realize that he was feeling the project's time pressure, was having some difficulty in his personal life, and needed support rather than criticism to help him work effectively.
- Then I had her return to her original seat. With her newfound awareness, she practiced relating to him in a more supportive manner.

I am happy to say that her next interaction with her team member went more smoothly. He felt supported, preparation for the product release went much more smoothly, and they were more harmonious throughout the process.

POWER TOOL
EMOTIONAL SENSITIVITY EXERCISE

This exercise will help to increase your level of emotional intelligence.

1. Meditation. Do the breathing and relaxation exercise in chapter 1.

2. Envision sitting in an empty chair across from someone with whom you are having difficulty, and then imagine that you are having a difficult discussion with that person that reflects the current problematic circumstance.

3. Switch seats, and imagine what the other person is likely to be feeling.

4. Return to your original seat, and practice a new response based on what you have learned.

Esther

The story of Queen Esther gives us another look at aspects of intuition. *In the day when the Persian Empire stretched from India to Ethiopia, King Ahasuerus put out the call for the most beautiful women in his kingdom to come to his palace so that he could choose a wife. Mordecai, who worked in the king's palace, immediately thought of his lovely cousin Esther. He encouraged her to present herself to the king, but he warned her to not tell anyone of their relationship or that they were Jews. Esther followed her cousin's advice. When King Ahasuerus saw her, he fell in love with her and made her his queen.*

Some time later, Mordecai overheard a plot to kill the king. He quickly got word to Esther, who warned the king and foiled the plot, and Mordecai's bravery was recorded in the king's official records.

Since the empire was so vast, the king had many princes who helped him rule the land, but Prince Haman was promoted above all other princes in the kingdom. The king issued an order that people must bow down before Haman and pay him respect. Mordecai refused to bow down before Haman because he believed that, as a Jew, he shouldn't bow down before anyone except God.

When Haman heard of Mordecai's refusal, he was furious—so furious that he developed a plot to not only punish Mordecai, but all the Jews: He would have them all put to death. Haman went to King Ahasuerus and proclaimed that there were some people living in the kingdom who were different from them and who refused to listen to the king's laws. He proposed that since this disrespect was not good for the kingdom, the king should issue a law that all the troublemakers should be put to death. The king agreed, not knowing the scope of Haman's plan. With the royal seal, Haman issued an order that on the thirteenth day of the twelfth month all Jews in the land were to be killed.

The community of Jews was shocked and thought their plight was hopeless. But when Mordecai heard about the plan, he knew there was one last hope. He went to Esther and pleaded for her to go to the king and try to get the edict reversed. It was punishable by death to go before the king without his request and permission, but

Esther presented herself before Ahasuerus anyway. He was delighted to see her and handed her the golden scepter, which signified that her life was to be spared. He asked what he could do for her; he would give her half his kingdom if that was what she wanted. Esther replied that she wanted the king and Haman to attend a banquet that she would prepare the next night. Ahasuerus agreed.

During the banquet, the king again asked about what he could do for her. Esther said that she wanted to prepare another banquet for both the king and Haman the next night; there she would tell him her request. The king and Haman accepted this second invitation. Haman left the palace that night so confident in his standing with the king that he was sure the king would allow him to hang Mordecai. So Haman ordered that a gallows be built.

The king was restless. He called for his official records to be read to him so that he could more easily fall asleep. When the reader got to the part where Mordecai had prevented the king's assassination, Ahasuerus asked how Mordecai had been honored and recognized. He discovered to his dismay that Mordecai had not received just appreciation.

At the banquet the following night, King Ahasuerus again asked Esther about her request. She said that if he had found favor with her as his queen, she would ask that he spare her life and spare her people who were going to be killed. The king asked who would do such a thing; Esther pointed at Haman. The king was furious. When his guards told him about the gallows Haman had had built for Mordecai, he ordered that Haman be immediately hung.

It was against custom and law to change any law so even the king could not reverse the edict that Jews be killed. Instead he permitted all Jews to defend themselves with lethal force as needed on the scheduled day. Many died, but the community wasn't wiped out entirely. Esther is still honored for saving her people.

Esther displayed enormous courage in the face of possible death by appearing before the king unbidden. Perhaps she had an inkling that his feelings for her were strong enough that he would spare her and grant her

Intuition

request. It's possible that her woman's intuition told her when to approach him, what to say, and which dress and jewels were most likely to get his attention. The idea of plying him with two days of good food and drink was an intuitive stroke of genius.

It also seems that the king picked up that something unusual was going on, which would explain his sleeplessness. He didn't ask for warm milk or a sedating tea to help him sleep. Intuitively, he asked that his records be read to him. Intuitively, he was struck by the Mordecai story in the records and asked about Mordecai's reward. What are the chances of this happening out of the blue? Clearly something was at work. Maybe the hand of the divine was stretched over the Jews, made the king restless, and directed him to the records. That would mean that the spiritual teachers of the world are correct that intuition or the "still, small voice within" are divine promptings. In any case, Queen Esther richly deserves to be honored for saving her people. ✾

TAPPING YOUR FEMININE INTUITION
God ain't a he or a she.
— Alice Walker, *The Color Purple*

It's interesting to me that intuition and sensitivity are generally thought of as feminine traits and, as such, are often demeaned. But intuition is, in fact, so powerful that it can make or break our relationships, our careers, our health, or even our very self-worth. Our society values intellect highly, but even the smartest leader— whether he's president of a club, a company, or a country—will fail if he can't sense how his constituents feel and what they need emotionally. Almost all Nobel Prize-winning scientists have attributed their greatest findings to leaps of intuition. We admire our sports stars for their physical strength, but athletes will tell you that along with their athletic prowess, they develop an inner sense that guides their competitive strategies.

Consider the power of intuition from the vantage point of our holistic model. Intuition can help us meet out bodies' needs—telling us when to eat less, sleep more, start an exercise program, have sex, or plan a vacation so that we keep our bodies in balance. I know of a woman who realized she was overdue for her annual checkup with her OB/GYN. Her doctor's busy schedule meant she had to make an appointment months ahead, but she was in no particular rush; it was just a checkup. When her appointment rolled around, her doctor told her she was pregnant. She had barely missed her period.

In earlier chapters, we reviewed the Glaser's work dealing with the effects of stress hormones in the bloodstream so we know that our bodies have physical responses to our mental and emotional stress. That chronic headache or backache is sending us a strong signal that something is going on in our lives that needs to be attended to. So why do we keep popping painkillers, but don't address the stress? It can only be because we lack sensitivity to our feelings and bodies, and we are not paying attention to the messages from either.

We can develop greater intuition by checking in with our feelings and our bodies, our mental, emotional, and spiritual states, and looking for connections among them. The more we pay attention and notice things that are happening in our lives—like, "Whenever my neck gets stiff, I realize I haven't been paying enough attention to the children" or "Whenever my skin starts to break out, I notice I've taken on too much responsibility at work"—the better able we are to address issues before they become chronic and damaging.

You also have to acknowledge your intuition when it kicks in. We tend to dismiss our hunches and premonitions, rather than really paying attention to *how* that process works and being grateful that it *does* work. When we ignore our feelings, we aren't allowing ourselves the power that intuition holds for us.

Intuition

Becoming self-aware through checking in with our feelings and our bodies puts us in a position to share our feelings. That, in turn, leads to increased emotional connection between ourselves and others and allows us to cultivate compassion.

OPEN A DOORWAY FOR MIRACLES

The sixth sense: the door to the temple of wisdom
— Napoleon Hill

When I lived with the Wilhelm and Samuels family, I heard their son, Helmut, tell many stories, folktales, and myths from almost every culture and country around the world. But it was Helmut Wilhelm's wife, Erica, who told one of the most interesting stories I've ever heard about the power of intuition. Her story provided one of my first adult opportunities to see that a force was at work in our lives that could intervene at the right moment if use our intuition as a channel for communication.

Erica's family escaped the Nazi regime by way of an unlikely emigration to America. Erica's father, Arthur Samuels, was a physician whom the Nazis had imprisoned. They refused to release him unless the family produced an affidavit proving they were emigrating elsewhere. The Samuels's only chance was to get an American medical school to admit Arthur. But at this time, medical schools had quotas on Jews. In fact, the United States had a quota on Jewish immigrants and was turning away Jewish refugees on the now infamous "ships of doom." Samuels's wife, Hilde, wrote desperately to a former student of Arthur's who had returned to the U.S. under Albert Einstein's sponsorship. She explained their dire situation, asking if he could find their cousin Cornell, who was in the U.S. and who might be able to help them. The student didn't know where to begin looking for this cousin. Despondent, he went to synagogue to pray. While he was there, he was moved to share the letter with a stranger sitting next to him. When the student mentioned that the letter came from Arthur Samuels's wife, the man he was talking to looked up in surprise. "I am Cousin Cornell," he said. "I am Cousin Cornell."

I have gotten a case of goose bumps every time I have heard that story; I have them even now as I write about it. What prompted these two to sit next to one another? What made the student engage Cornell in conversation? What forces were at work that led to the salvation of the Samuels family's lives? That is the power of intuition, the inner sense through which providence creates miracles.

The preservation of my friends' lives is but one of many strange-but-true accounts I've heard over the years. My friend Jim was led to collect such stories after receiving a phone call from his aunt who lived a couple of states away. When he picked up the phone, she asked, without any prelude, "What's wrong?" She had no way of knowing he'd just been about to leave for the hospital with his son. And neither of them knew at the time, but his son had a fatal illness. Jim once asked a class full of graduate students whether they happened to have any such stories and everyone had something to share. What is at work here?

Based on my background in science and psychology combined with my many years of spiritual study around the world, I will offer my opinion. There is something we can access and even cultivate that yields enhanced sensitivity to emotional states—our own and those of others. This inner knowing extends to promptings that can carry us where we need to go to help preserve life or offer support. Our own receiving system picks up signals not just from others but, it seems, from other metaphysical sources as well. But it best picks up these signals when we have quieted our minds and placed ourselves in a contemplative state. The inmost cave is a place to shine the light of self-reflection onto the subconscious. It is also the place to hone our magic and discover the soul work and life purpose we are here to fulfill. Intuitive power can be cultivated, and it definitely has a practical role to play in human relations as we learn the value of being sensitive to ourselves and to one another. In the next to chapters on intention and inspiration, we'll take an even closer look at the intellectual and spiritual workings of the power of intuition.

Intuition

QUESTIONS

1. What part of my body is most likely to register feelings?
2. How can I calm and release my feelings so that my mind, emotions, and body become still?
3. What tips me off when my inner guidance is trying to give me a message?
4. How can I best implement my inner wisdom?

POWER TOOLS

1. LISTENING TO YOUR INTUITION EXERCISE
To work through strong trauma reactions or feelings, do the Listening to Your Intuition Exercise.

2. EMOTIONAL INTENSITY SCALE
Determine whether you are experiencing a trauma reaction or feeling by using the Emotional Intensity Scale. On a scale of one to ten, rate the intensity of your emotion. If it's more than a five, then cellular memory may be triggered, and a relaxation process may help.

3. MEDITATION
Do the breathing and relaxation exercise in chapter 1.

4. EMOTIONAL SENSITIVITY EXERCISE
To increase your level of emotional intelligence, do the Emotional Sensitivity Exercise.

POWER DECREE

I AM LISTENING TO THE VOICE OF THE DIVINE IN MY HEART.

The creative is the place where no one else has ever been. You have to leave the city of your comfort and go into the wilderness of your intuition. What you'll discover will be wonderful. What you'll discover will be yourself.

— Alan Alda

Chapter Five

Intention
Facing the Test

The person who makes formal [their] intent will be sustained and supported by life. — Dr. Howard Thurman

LUCY IS DUMBSTRUCK. Mr. Gorgeous, as Lucy is already calling him, walks over to her smiling, "Please don't be frightened," he says. "I'm a friend. My name is Theodore."

Lucy immediately thinks, "Teddy Bear! That's perfect." She mentally compares Theodore and her erstwhile boyfriend, the long-suffering Walt. "Sorry Walter, no contest," she thinks, mentally drawing an X in bright red lipstick through his image.

She welcomes her new Teddy with a smile, and he sits down next to her. But just as she's about to lean in and turn on her best flirting technique, strong hands grab her from behind, pulling her down and placing some kind of blinder over her eyes. Instinctively she reaches for Teddy, only to hear his voice croon, "Sorry, baby," Then, "Okay guys, take her to the cave."

"Stop!" Lucy screams and flails, knowing it's futile—there's no one there to help her. In another part of her mind, she thinks: "I'm tired of this shit."

"You'll want to be quiet now," Teddy says in a dangerous tone of voice. Then she feels herself being dragged away by four strong hands.

Soon, Lucy is roughly tossed down on what turns out to be a very soft sofa. The blindfold is removed, and she looks up to see who had grabbed her. The skateboarders she'd encountered this morning are standing next to a smug Teddy, who is reclined on a chaise a few feet from her. She smirks

Intention

at him and blurts out the most hurtful thing she can think of at the moment: "You're not that good looking." He throws back his head and laughs.

"All I want to know," he says, "is..."

She finishes his sentence: "What's in the bag?"

"Right. And you are the only one who can answer that question."

"Look, I don't know what's in the bag or where the bag is. I don't know anything about the bag!" she yells. "What I want to know is why, all of a sudden, everybody is worried about bags."

"Well, Lucinda, you don't get to leave here until I get the bag, and my friends are here to encourage you to figure out where it is and what's in it. And they aren't nearly as nice as they look..."

Before he can continue, one of the skateboarders throws a flashing metal object at Lucinda; she is engulfed in dark, acrid smoke, and vermin swarm all over her.

She screams and tries to run, but the smoke and the parasites only grow thicker. She thinks, "Bag Man, where are you? Help me! You got me into this. Help!"

Suddenly in her head she hears the Bag Man speak to her calmly, "Take a deep breath, Lucy. Keep your eyes closed and take a deep breath."

"Where have you been?" she snaps back mentally.

"You've got to break through the illusion so I can help you. Stop screaming. Try to be still and listen. This is going to take all the concentration you can muster. Focus on your own heart, and envision it filled with light." Desperate, Lucy tries to calm down. It's easy to focus on her heart because it's practically beating out of her chest, but she has to struggle to keep herself calm enough to envision light.

"Now see that light becoming so intense and so bright that you are engulfed by it." Surprisingly, as Lucy accomplishes this mental feat, the crawling feeling of vermin disappears. "Keep it up, Lucy," the Bag Man says. "Keep it up—more light, more light. I'm helping you as much as I can."

Suddenly, it's as if the light explodes gloriously inside and all around her, and Lucy realizes what's in the bag and where it is.

At that moment, she hears Theodore and the skateboarders yelling, "Stop her! Get her!" ....

Power Choices

Lucy has had an interesting morning. She's tumbled into a hole, found herself wounded and in a strange place, and been lured by something that seemed lovely only to find it was danger incarnate. Finally, now, with the guidance of a voice in her own mind, she is learning to focus. And as she focuses on light, her situation seems to be changing.

That is the power of intention. It is key to affecting an actual transformation in your life. You have already learned about initiating—accepting a call and stepping into something new. Through gaining insight you have done the hard work of taking the thousand-pound sack off your back and sifting through it. You've examined some very difficult experiences and recalled some difficult feelings. You may have more feelings and behaviors to process (the journey can be circuitous), but you have already acquired deeper insight into why you are making the choices that you're making and why you may be behaving in a way that does not serve you. So you've learned a lot about yourself. Now what are you going to do with this knowledge? What are your intentions? Intention is an important point on the hero's journey in that it is a turning point—the point at which you face the ordeal that will turn the tide. It's the day you *decide*. Decide what? Decide what you're going to do with all the information you've acquired about yourself, your history, your journey, and your purpose.

Our approach to intention isn't just about deciding what you want and willing it into being. Intention is built on insight, intuition, and understanding—a foundation of wisdom that ensures that what you intend to do, be, say, or have is the best thing. The work we've done prior to getting to this point gives you the tools you need to set your intention into motion. You must have access to your emotions—and to the tools you'll need to work with those emotions—to effectively achieve the goal of your new intention.

So what's next? What do we have to do if we really want to take the work we have done and create change? How do we implement our fifth power choice, intention? If we think of insight as opening our heart and intuition as opening our soul, then intention opens our mind. It means choosing a point of focus for the mind. This

Intention

power choice sets the foundation for understanding the tremendous power of focused, heartfelt attention.

STERLING

I once worked with a young man named Sterling who was living with his girlfriend; then his mother and sister moved in, too. The three women were constantly bickering, and they blamed him for the things they didn't have or that weren't going right in their own lives. It seemed that he could do no right in their eyes. But they continued to depend on him to support all three of them financially and emotionally. Meanwhile, Sterling was drowning trying to take care of these demanding women. Though he was bright, he had never managed to get a job at which he could earn a decent living. He came in to see me because he felt unfulfilled and very depressed. He was clearly emotionally blocked so we started by clearing his emotional blocks and drawing the connections between his family patterns and his current life. His father had abandoned the family when Sterling was a child, so the boy had taken on the role of family savior, taking care of his mother and siblings. Even after he left home, Sterling couldn't escape the pattern. First, his girlfriend wanted to be taken care of. Then here came his mother and sister, needing him again. Their need became a trap.

In order to escape the negative cycle, Sterling worked with an important tool: intention. He worked on creating a new intention to take care of himself rather than playing rescuer with his entire family. In the rescue triangle, rescuers usually find themselves trapped, constantly trying to pull a supposed victim out of trouble. (And the victim's troubles never seem to end because she hasn't done anything to change her own life; she's depending on a rescuer.) Inevitably, the rescuer ends up feeling like a victim—beleaguered, attacked, and drained; that makes the original victim a persecutor. Now the new victim (formerly known as a rescuer) looks for someone to rescue him. He's invested in the idea that people can't help themselves or in the thought that "It's my turn to sit back and let someone else take care of me." Or he becomes angry enough to turn on the one currently playing the victim role, thus transforming himself from rescuer/victim to persecutor. It only takes two to play this complicated three-part game—and in the end, the rescuer, victim, and persecutor all lose because none of these roles empowers the player.

As we worked through Sterling's issues, he began to feel better about himself. His depression lifted, and he had the energy to change his life. That's when he began to put his intention into action. He wanted a love relationship that felt balanced and fulfilling. Not seeing a future for that with his girlfriend, he left his unhealthy relationship. He set his mother and sister up in their own apartment (because he didn't intend to just put them out on the street), but he insisted that they be responsible for themselves. Eventually, he went back to school and got a doctorate in a field that he always wanted to work in, and he's now in a relationship with a woman he is very happy with.

Sterling actually wrote out a new script in which he resigned from the role of family savior. He "cast" himself in a starring role in his life where he felt worthy of receiving as well as giving. He demonstrated his intention by setting clear boundaries and resisting the urge to rescue.

POWER TOOL
ACTIVE VISUALIZATION

1. *Cast yourself in the role you want.*
   Write out your new intention.

2. Create an action plan to carry out your intention.

3. Enhance your action plan using the tool of active visualization.

Intention

MINDING THE MIND
The mind ought sometimes to be diverted that it may return the better to thinking. — Phaedrus

The first time we went to India, my younger daughter, who was six at the time, was absolutely fascinated by the monkeys. In India and other Eastern countries where monkeys live, you see the frisky animals running all over the road, along the rooftops, and through the trees. They were everywhere, and my daughter would sit all day and watch them. And they'd watch her, waiting for a chance to grab a toy, some food, or whatever she was holding. One day when we were visiting the Red Fort in Agra in Northern India, near the Taj Mahal, all the tourists were looking at the monkeys, exclaiming, "Oh, aren't the monkeys cute." Among us was a little boy licking an ice cream cone. Suddenly, before anyone could think to move, one of the largest monkeys leapt down off a wall, slapped the cone out of the boy's hand, and was back up the wall in a flash, devouring it. The little boy was traumatized; in fact, it was pretty unsettling for everyone. Those cute little monkeys could be aggressively mischievous.

In Eastern cultures, the saying goes that the mind is like a drunken monkey. Imagine those fast, frisky, smart, mischievous creatures having had a few too many drinks. Think about just how troublesome and destructive a drunken monkey would be. That's what I'd call out of control. But the mind is often that way—flitting about constantly, looking for things to get into, wreaking havoc, and sometimes not even stopping to sleep.

This is what people mean when they say, "I let my mind run away with me." But think about the wording there, especially "let" and "my" and "with me." Whose mind is it? If we can say, "It's my mind," that implies that we're the owners and masters of it, doesn't it? And if we're in charge, we don't let things happen that we don't want. Nothing that you're in control of is going to do anything with you that you don't want. Would you have a servant in your house that went through destroying the house? Hardly. Your mind is your servant. It serves you, not the other way around, but you have to learn how to manage it and bring it under your control.

We can learn something about mental control by examining how monkeys are caught in India. A monkey trap is a glass bottle with a long skinny neck. The bottle is secured to something stable, and in the bottom, there's a little bowl filled with a few trinkets or bits of food—something that will catch the monkey's eye. The little primate puts his hand into the bottle and makes a fist around the goodies. But then he can't get his hand out of the bottle unless he opens his hand and lets it go. In the monkey's mind, this is hardly possible, because letting go would mean giving up what's in his hand. For his fear of losing his trinkets, the monkey loses his freedom.

To tame your monkey mind, you've got to give it something to hold onto. Something that it won't let go of easily. But trapping the mind won't trap us; rather, it frees us because when the mind is focused we have access to one of the most powerful and intricate instruments on the planet. Once we've stopped the mind, we can begin to examine it.

BELIEVING IS SEEING. OR IS IT THE OTHER WAY AROUND?

God has illuminated me in both my eyes...through them I can choose the path I am to travel. — Hildegard of Bingen

Einstein said that we only use 10 percent of our mental power at any given time—because we don't focus it. That means that 90 percent of the time, the mind is in mischievous monkey mode. But what would happen in we tapped into some of that other 90 percent? A Yale University study conducted over a twenty-year period showed that the 3 percent of graduates who had a clear, specific set of goals written down, with a plan for achieving those goals, were worth more financially than the other 97 percent of their class combined. They were also more successful in other areas of their lives, such as relationships and community service.

Einstein himself seems to have tapped into at least some of that

Intention

extra 90 percent of his mental capacity. You've probably known people who seemed to be able to accomplish all sorts of positive things, seemingly through the sheer force of their will. (I think of people like Oprah Winfrey, who seems to have tapped all her creative and mental power to do amazing things.) How do they do it? How can you?

The sages, the teachers, and the scientists all believe that you can accomplish what you want in life a long as you put the right thought energy behind it. "As a man thinketh, so is he," goes the passage in the Bhagavad-Gita. The idea is that where your thoughts are focused, your energy will be focused; and if you put positive mental energy behind something, you can expect a positive manifestation.

You have to pay attention to where your thoughts are focused—and that may take some digging. When we worked on insight, we took an honest look at the emotional rocks that were in that proverbial sack on our backs. We uncovered a lot of *feelings* from childhood in the sack. Well, there are also a lot of *thoughts and choices* in the sack, which we made based on what happened to us in childhood. A young child whose parents yell and criticize her wouldn't think, "Clearly Mom and Dad have an issue that prevents them from being loving and accepting." Her neural structure is incomplete, and she can't do that kind of advanced, abstract thinking. Plus, her thinking is egocentric, so as a result she always imagines that whatever happens is about her. Faced with angry parents, this child is likely to decide, "The reason my parents are behaving in this angry way is because they don't love me. And if they don't love me, then that means I'm not loveable." Beliefs about self, relationships, gender roles, money, and sex all find their origins in the egocentric decisions of early life. Then, as adults, we can't conceive of ourselves as magnificent beings who can do magnificent things because, secretly, the child-self decided we are not good enough.

Whatever you decided in your childhood is now hardwired into your mind. Like a computer expertly programmed, the mind now runs its encoded thoughts over and over: *I know there is something wrong with me, and if anyone gets close to me, they'll figure it out. I can't have the job, the relationship, the salary, the house, or whatever it is that I want because I don't deserve it.* Once we decide that something is wrong with us, we spend the rest of our lives acting out those secret beliefs. As long as our attention is focused on our beliefs as they were shaped during childhood, our intentions are shaped by those beliefs. So your work on the journey is, first, to uncover those beliefs and then to shift them around or change them to something positive—something that works in our favor.

The Folk Fable of Moses

In *The Fable: Moses, Man of the Mountain,* writer, anthropologist Zora Neal Hurston retells the biblical story of Moses and Aaron using carefully researched southern slave dialect. *In Hurston's version, Moses tells Aaron to take off his high priest's robes. Aaron responds, "I ain't going to do it, Moses. God put these robes on me, and he'll have to be the one to take 'em off. I know you been begrudging 'em to me for a powerful long time. I just wouldn't step down for you."*

"God didn't put no robe on you, Aaron. I put 'em on you, and I'm taking them off because they don't fit you...I thought I needed you for the big job I had to do because you were [one] of the Hebrews. I did need you, too, but you didn't do the job I picked out for you."

"You always held me back. You..." Aaron complained. But Moses wouldn't let him finish.

"No, you held yourself back. You didn't think about service half as much as you did about getting served, Aaron. Your tiny horizon never did get no bigger, so you mistook a spotlight for the sun."

In this excerpt, Aaron is a classic victim—he blames Moses and even holds God accountable, but he never takes responsibility for his actions. Moses, not buying into his victim act, nails Aaron on his self-serving intentions. ൦

Intention

From Victim to Victory

Free your mind, and the rest will follow.
— En Vogue, *Free Your Mind*

When you decide to select a new intention for your life, you have to make sure you are conscious of what you're choosing. You must look at what you're thinking and how you're thinking. Ask yourself: What are the habitual thoughts that my mind entertains? Are these the best use of my mental energy? Are they helping me manifest what is good and positive in my life?

For example, do you intend to be a victim or a victor? To answer that question, look at how you respond to the things that happen to you every day. Do you say, "Poor me," "My life never works," "It's not fair," "It's not my fault," and "See what they did to me?" Victims are always blaming. You can easily identify blaming because its starts with the word "you": "You did it." "You always..." "You never...." Most of us were programmed as children to feel like victims. It's the predictable result of not being able to express our feelings of hurt and anger.

To be a victim, I have to blame someone. It follows that if I am running around blaming people or creating dramas, it is my underlying template or intention to make myself a victim. Naturally, it sometimes is difficult to see that we are actually doing it to ourselves. We tend to think, "That couldn't possibly be of my doing. The market just went down." Or, "It's not me because this random act just happened in my life." The way that you know it is you, is when there is a pattern. Just as you identified them when you worked to increase your insight, look for your thought patterns. In your thinking, if your intention is to be a victim, I don't care how things may come to you, you'll turn it, you'll drop it, you'll misinterpret it. You will see it as being victimized. It's like wearing a set of glasses that has "victim" stamped right on the front so everything looks that way.

Clearly, we want to take those glasses off, stop the train of twisting thought from old negative patterns, and put on a new set of glasses that states our new intention: we are the victor in our own life. If we start from the idea that we are the victor, then whatever it is we want—a relationship, money, a career, the opportunity to make a difference in the world—we expect to have. And because we believe in our own victory we're much more likely to create positive outcomes. Then, on whatever path you choose, you will start out with some victory energy to get you there.

Dr. Aaron Beck, recognized as the founder of the field of cognitive psychology, studied depression for more than fifty years. He is credited with discovering the devastating impact of what he called "negative self-talk"—the ideas you repeat about yourself in your own mind. Beck concluded that depression results from the downward spiral of negative thoughts. Such a spiral inevitably leads to feelings of helplessness, then hopelessness—the kind of thinking found in depression. Once you're in that frame of mind, you have neither the energy nor inclination to produce positive results. Instead, because your thoughts generate behaviors that reinforce your expectations and beliefs, you have created a self-fulfilling prophecy: you've thought the worst, and because you can't muster enough energy to do any better, the worst is what you get. And the cycle repeats.

The process works in the opposite way as well. When you think positive thoughts, you have more energy to contribute toward productive behaviors. We see the impact of beliefs and expectations, for example, in the field of education. You may have heard of the California teacher who was told that the students in her class that year were above-average achievers. Even though her class was actually made up of average students, by the end of the year, they were all performing above average. She believed in them and obviously communicated that belief to them. Without a doubt, our beliefs change our behaviors. This education study is now known as the Pygmalion effect, based on lessons learned from the mythic story of Pygmalion.

After comparing treatments for depression, including exercise, talk therapy, group therapy, and medication, Beck and fellow researchers at the University of Pennsylvania found that for mild to moderate depression, self-talk therapy yielded the greatest benefits. If patients could be coached to tell themselves something positive, they developed a better outlook on life—even if nothing had actually changed in their lives. Thus, modern science proved what the ancients taught: thoughts have power.

Changing your mind, in the sense of really shifting your thoughts, takes practice. The power tools in this chapter will show you how.

Pygmalion

Our beliefs lead to behaviors that create expectations. And our expectations create our reality. The youth Pygmalion in the Greek myth provides a wonderful example of this principle. (You may know the gist of the story from films such as *Pretty Woman* and *My Fair Lady*.) *An arrogant, cold-hearted young man from Cyprus, Pygmalion was a gifted sculptor. He had no interest in the local women, deeming them immoral and frivolous. He even neglected the love goddess Aphrodite, who captured the hearts and minds of everyone else—especially those who wanted to ensure love in their lives. Instead, Pygmalion focused on his art. Then one day, finding a flawless piece of ivory, he carved a beautiful woman from it. When the statue was finished, Pygmalion realized that this was his ideal woman. He dressed the statue and adorned it with jewels. He even offered it flowers and kissed its cold lips, calling his creation Galatea, "sleeping love."*

He became consumed with longing and desire for this ideal woman; he loved her and wanted to feel that love in return. In desperation he went, at last, to Aphrodite's temple. He implored the previously neglected goddess to forgive him for all the years he had shunned her. Then he begged the goddess of love for a wife who would be as perfect as his statue. Aphrodite was moved by his pleas and she wanted to see this perfect statue, so she visited his studio while he was away. She was flattered to find that Pygmalion had carved his woman in her image. Feeling appropriately honored,

Aphrodite brought the statue to life. When Pygmalion returned to his studio, he kissed Galatea as usual. But now her lips were warm, and she responded to his touch. Seeing Galatea was indeed alive, he knelt at her feet. They were wed, and he never forgot to thank Aphrodite for her gifts to him.

Pygmalion transformed the statue into the woman of his dreams by focused intention, and she transformed him by opening his heart to Aphrodite, the divine feminine, who through compassion and mercy blessed the union. ∾

CREATING REALITY FROM YOUR BELIEFS

Where your attention is, there you are. What your attention is on, that you become. — St. Germaine

How can we use the Pygmalion effect—the idea that we create reality from our beliefs—to our advantage? Let's first see how the concept came into being. In 1904, two researchers, Stumpt and Pfungst, began an investigation of a stallion named Clever Hans, who was world-renowned as an equine mathematical genius. The horse's owner, Von-Osten, had decided to teach Clever Hans as though he were a human, so he schooled the horse in basic arithmetic, rewarding Hans with carrots when answers were correct. After two years, Clever Hans could add, subtract, multiply, and divide by tapping out the solutions with his hoof. Many animals have been trained to perform tricks for their owners, but Clever Hans seemed to do math even in Von-Osten's absence—something quite unexpected. After studying Clever Hans, the researchers found that the horse was quite clever—not in math, but in reading people. Stumpt and Pfungst noticed that when a questioner's head inclined slightly, Hans would start tapping. As the questioner's head straightened, Clever Hans stopped. The horse would also react to slight arches of the researchers eyebrows—changes in facial expression so subtle that the researchers didn't realize they had made them. But the horse noticed. Basically, Clever Han was only clever when people

Intention

expected him to be; he delivered to their expectations. Since then, myriad animal and human studies have shown this behavior to be consistent.

The Pygmalion effect can work to our advantage when we are choosing a new intention. We have to shift our expectations from the negative (*I never win anything. I'm not smart enough to start my own business. Guys have never liked me.*) to the positive (*It happens for other people, why not me? I could do that. I've got enough sense to accomplish that goal.*). Just shifting our thinking puts us in a better frame of mind to see our opportunities when they present themselves, to approach them with hopefulness, to put our best effort behind our intentions. You're going to try a little harder and work a little smarter. Your attitude will be better so you'll attract people who will help you. These things alone increase your chance of success.

What if you decided to choose the intention to be victorious? Start by telling yourself, "I'm not a victim; I'm a victor." Give it a little physical effort: Put your arms up in a V, like you just scored a touchdown, and say out loud, "I am victorious!" Keep your arms up, and repeat, "Always Victory; Always Victory." This is a simple but powerful new intention.

Putting positive action behind your intention is a powerful way to achieve your goals and move toward your purpose. One of my favorite examples of this comes from Argentina, where the military once tried to suppress civil society by banning all political activity and by removing all individuals who opposed their agenda. In 1977, a group of women whose children had been kidnapped refused to accept the official response of ignorance. They resolved to discover the truth themselves, through collective action as mothers—and Las Madres de Plaza de Mayo was born. Each Thursday afternoon, the mothers appeared wearing white kerchiefs embroidered with the names of their missing relatives and the dates of their disappearances. In a tight circle and in absolute silence, the group would orbit a monument at the center of the Plaza de Mayo, the center of the military regime's institutions. They didn't speak, shout, or wave banners. They didn't storm the government offices or take hostages or blow anything up. But they didn't just sit at home and worry, either. They simply walked with the intention of getting answers to their question. Through their efforts, which gained international attention, they brought down one of the most repressive regimes in Latin America.

SARA AND JOE

Sara—a thirty-five-year-old mother of two, currently on medical leave from her work due to stress and burnout—came in to see me first. Sara's mother had been very controlling and negative, telling her daughter that she was going to be a failure. Now a mother herself, Sara found herself being controlling and negative with her own daughter. To her credit, she wanted to change for the better and sought help.

Sara was indeed repeating an intergenerational cycle in which she was duplicating her mother's patterns but, ironically, she was also living out the ideas she had formed about herself and her life based on her mom's actions: She was afraid she'd be a failure as a mother.

We looked at Sara's family history. Her father was a compulsive gambler, and her mother, Mary, was a classic codependent who had no boundaries and wrapped her life around scrambling to take care of her gambling husband. Mary was intermittently profoundly depressed and only worked occasionally. She ferociously controlled everyone because, in her mind, every situation was life or death and if she didn't control everything the worst would happen. She had an intense fear that someone would die because when she was eight, her father had died suddenly, causing Mary's mother to go into a profound depression. Mary was left to care for four younger siblings; ultimately all of them were farmed out to relatives.

Mary, playing out the generational patterns, battled her own depression and put all the responsibilities of her own family onto her oldest daughter, Sara. It was Sara's job to steer her father away from the gambling table. She had to clean the house, cook dinner, and take care of her two younger sisters. The most prominent feeling Sara reported was anxiety; she said she woke up in the morning "feeling scared" and had to fight anxiety throughout the day. Trying to keep her fears tamped down interfered with her interactions, especially with her daughter, Zoë.

Once she had looked at this history and untangled and identified her feelings, Sara combined the insight into her mother's difficulties with her new intention.

I taught Sara to use meditation to lower her anxiety because the more anxious she got, the more controlling she became. I also encouraged her to use positive affirmations and decrees, including the denial and affirming technique described below. On my recommendation, Sara also started going to Al-Anon, where she got support with issues of growing up in an addicted family. Sara improved her relationship with her daughter in a wonderful way within a month.

We then invited Joe to join our sessions. Sara's husband also had issues of rage and control. It wasn't surprising that, because of her early belief system, Sara had married someone who mirrored her mother. Joe was so controlling that he would collapse into rage if Sara said hello to a man. He had once had become so angry that he had abusively berated her at a party, accusing her of being unfaithful. Sara was reluctant to invite him to see me because she thought he would clam up.

To her amazement, he talked nonstop for half an hour, finally having an opportunity to release all the negative feelings that had been brewing inside him. It turned out that Joe's early family life proved disruptive also. His mother frequently had epileptic seizures; the family was always afraid and on high alert, wondering when the next seizure would occur. Joe's father, on the other hand, was paranoid and distrustful, constantly looking for signs that his wife was unfaithful. Through our sessions, Joe discovered that his rage and control tendencies had nothing to do with his wife and everything to do with his father. He realized that he'd unfairly laid it all on Sara's doorstep, blaming her for his feelings of jealousy and his abusive behavior.

After he emptied out a lot of the stones in his sack, Joe also started doing meditations and decrees. He now realizes that Sara doesn't trigger his rages; his thoughts do. He has to look inside. To assist him, I drew a picture that helped him see his mind as an iceberg. The conscious mind is like the tip of the iceberg, the one-third that we can see above the water. The two-thirds below the surface of the water is invisible unless we explore it. The part below the water is just like our subconscious mind.

Joe didn't have a case of monkey mind; it was King Kong mind! Joe systematically wrestled with his mind; he had to be quite stringent about his thoughts. Each time he noticed his mind running down the old paranoid track, imagining that his wife was betraying him, he would use some cognitive tools I had given him. First, he envisioned a flashing stoplight and told his mind "STOP!" Then he used a technique called "deny and affirm." He'd tell himself, "That's insane thinking! That's my father's way of thinking. Shut up, Dad! I'm not you, and I'm not going down that path." Then he would affirm, "My wife is a good woman, an honest woman, and she would never betray me. I'm not going to hurt her with these crazy thoughts. She deserves love. I deserve love." Using that for his mental framework, he now resists raging at Sara or anyone else.

This couple literally couldn't sleep in the same bed, never mind have an intimate relationship. After they started their program—following up initiation and insight with mental retraining—they were able to go on a vacation together and are having an intimate marriage again. When Joe lost his job, they faced a new crisis. But they both agreed that with their new tools they could get through the crisis together.

Intention

ALIGNING HEART AND HEAD

Everything that I understand, I understand only because I love."
— Leo Tolstoy

If you are standing with your arms down, when you make your victory declaration, where is your center of gravity? It's somewhere in your abdomen, in your lower energy centers. But if you put your arms up, your center of gravity is at heart level—and if your heart is open and engaged, you will have vastly more power. In the past, we used to think that the physical heart was just a muscle that pumps blood. Anytime we referred to the heart as a center of feeling or sensing—when we talked about someone being "broken hearted" or something being "heartfelt"—we were using the word *heart* metaphorically. Now, however, we know the heart does indeed register emotions.

On the emotional side of the brain, we have neurons that transmit and carry emotional messages. The neural tissue in the brain is identical to that which exists in the heart. Interestingly, the thing that prompted researchers to look into this was the fact that so many people who had heart transplants reported experiencing the feelings and longings and thought patterns they could only attribute to their donors. The heart is an intelligence center, but it is also the center of our emotional intelligence, which we discussed in chapter 4.

We create our highest intention by putting our heart and our head together. The mighty intellect that we tend to glorify doesn't have sufficient power on its own to truly lead to transcendent awareness. Recall the many times you've heard someone say, "Oh, that person is so intelligent!" Yet, if you get the intelligence functioning without the heart, the intellect runs amuck. Without the heart there is no compassion, there's no wisdom. We may have justice but no mercy. In our final chapter we will review some of the extraordinary achievements of women and men who made the marriage of head and heart.

We can make balanced decisions and choices. Remember our

earlier discussion about feminine power? Feminine power, which we all have, regardless of gender, is power of the heart; it's compassion, it's wisdom, and it's love. So we are cultivating a different kind of power with these seven choices. It's the power to be more present, to be more in our hearts, to stand in our own wisdom, our own love, our own truth, and to express from the heart.

In order to keep our thoughts positive, we have to confront fear, which can be a major stumbling block on our path. The fear we face is the fear we can erase. In the field of human potential, fear requires special handling. First we have to realize that fear often wears other guises; anger is a particular favorite, as is control. Virginia Satir names four dysfunctional "styles" as she called them—all manifestations of fear—based communication: blaming, placating, distracting, and being super reasonable. Blamers always point to someone else who in their mind is at fault. Placaters are the codependents of the world. Distractors would rather joke around or get high instead of deal with issues. And the Super Reasonables are the intellectualizers who have a theory about why things are why they are, and God forbid that they should ever feel a feeling. Each of these styles interferes with congruent expression of our needs and feelings.

We find fear messages embedded in media and advertising, in political statements, even in religious services. Fear does have a purpose. Fear is a biologically hardwired response designed to protect the physical body from harm. But our goal is to be prudent rather than fearful. You can tell if you are moving into the realm of fear if you find yourself asking the question, "What if…?" "What if" tends to provoke more "what ifs," which leads to obsessive thinking. Your thoughts begin spinning faster and faster with no place to land. (There's the old monkey mind.) This triggers the stress response, which stimulates the adrenal gland to start dumping norepinephrine into the bloodstream.

Having a plan B and a plan C to back up our plan A takes us down a path to solution-oriented thinking as opposed to obsessing on the possible failure of plan A. If you stop each time you come to a "what if" question and work out a rational answer as to how

Intention

you'd respond "if....," then you will feel more empowered to deal with any situation you're likely to face. When you find yourself speculating, stop and ask yourself, "How likely is it that this would actually happen?" Often we worry about things that have a one-in-a-million chance of happening. Even more powerful is to practice the cognitive technique of stopping the mind chatter by fixing the mind on a positive phrase or image.

My client Sara's fears and anxieties kept her from being in any way centered. She needed spiritual tools to give her an emotional and spiritual anchor. The first step in developing a spiritual anchor is to identify the underlying mental "tape" that we wish to change. Then we find the spiritual tools that we can use as grappling hooks to get up the mountain to realize our intention. We can use such tools as prayer, meditation, chanting, and yoga—all of which increase the energy flow that enhances our vitality and relaxes our entire being.

Ultimately the mountain peak itself helps us get to where we want to be: we see the goal and it inspires us. That mountain peak—our highest goal—awakens spiritual virtues and opens us to the enlightenment that begins to come as we systematically practice new positive thought. As we awaken our consciousness more and more, we find things happening in our lives with an amazing synchronicity. In fact, according to the Hoffman Institute's definition, increased synchronicity indicates inner transformation.

THE POWER OF REPETITION

Your ability to use the principles of auto suggestion will depend very largely upon your capacity to concentrate on a given desire until it becomes a burning desire. — Napoleon Hill and W. Clement Stone, *Success through a Positive Mental Attitude*

The mind is a computer; it is programmable. We can choose the program we want and move it from the conscious into the subconscious mind by using the power of repetition. Autosuggestion, as Napoleon Hill and W. Clement Stone call it in

Success Through a Positive Mental Attitude, consists of repeatedly reading—out loud and with feeling—a list of one's specific goals and desires. Many people who have used these techniques achieved notable results while plenty of others come up empty-handed. The key difference between the two groups lies in the emotional realm. Unhealed, unexpressed childhood trauma blocks the flow of energy. In turn an energy block keeps in place the hidden decisions that essentially counter any new positive thought with Yeah, but you aren't worthy or deserving or lovable. We worked through this in our chapter on insight, but the residue of old beliefs often resurfaces when we rigorously apply our new thoughts.

One of the most effective ways to activate a new thought is through chanting. The rhythm and speed of the chant actually shut down the mind's thought activity, much like the monkey trap. The new intention goes in deeper as we employ repetition, combined with emotional intensity and visual imagery. If you ask Madison Avenue advertising executives about this, they'll tell you that all effective commercials utilize these components. How many times have you found yourself singing the jingle from the ad campaign for a major brand? Marketing research proves that people who are repetitively exposed to the advertisers' message are more likely to buy the product. For example, African Americans are among the largest television viewing groups, and consequently they also are the largest consumers of name-brand products.

Studying the impact of chanting, Dr. Herbert Benson discovered that blood pressure and pulse rates drop, heart rate slows, immune function improves, and depression lifts as a result. Benson's research led to the discovery of the "human relaxation response." Repetition of any spiritual or religious chant—even repeating the words "one," "love," and "ocean"—trigger this response. But Mahatma Gandhi could have told Benson that. Before Gandhi became the deeply spiritual guru leader of India's independence movement, he described himself as an unevolved and ineffectual lawyer. He credits his grandmother's urging him to chant repetitively "Hare Rama Hare Rama" (Rama is the god who

Intention

embodies divine love in the Hindu trinity) with transforming his consciousness, from a lawyer to a guru and world leader.

> **POWER TOOL**
> **DAILY CHANTING**
>
> *Raise your arms in a V (this physical movement encourages the kinesthetic learning) and chant "Always victory! Always victory! Always victory!" Don't be wimpy; speak this with determination and conviction, or as they used to say in the old Baptist churches, "Say it like you mean it!"*

ALEXIS

Alexis is one of the most talented people I've ever met—a born leader, creative, brilliant, and beautiful with a warm, sparkling personality. She claimed that she had few major complaints about her life, but her personal life and business life never took off. She's a career woman, but her career was sluggish; she'd never been the kind of leader she could be. She could easily be a publisher of a major magazine or head of a corporation, but she always sat on the sidelines.

When she was small, Alexis made a decision that she had to go it alone and take care of herself because her father, a significant force in corporate America, was so involved in his career, and her mother was completely overwhelmed supporting her father. The result of her decision was that she never allowed herself to form close alliances with anyone. You can't move forward if you don't know how to form partnerships and allow others to help you.

I led her through a guided meditation that helped her recognize her pattern. She went back to the core moment in her life when she came face to face with herself as a little girl in her crib. That's when she said, "These people are unable to be there for me." She saw herself make a conscious decision to not rely on anyone.

Alexis reversed her childhood decision from "These people aren't able to be there for me" to "I deserve support, and I choose people in my life who are capable of supporting me." She then went on to marry a very devoted man and found her own entrepreneurial venture, which became a major success. This new intention opened the door to the life she had always wanted.

Declare Victory

Victory's impetus is mine this day, for love, wisdom and power in balance!
— Decree from the I AM Mystery School

An easy way to discover your core belief about yourself is to look at your limiting patterns. If you have thought patterns that say you will never win or go past a certain point in life, you may have a core belief that you can't trust other people or can't trust life to deal you a fair hand. Perhaps you won't allow yourself to love or be loved because you believe love causes pain. If you've started over in life four or five times, you have a pattern that allows you to take the exit route rather than doing the learning necessary to see a situation through. For example, a man who grew up with an addicted parent may repeatedly marry women with active addictions. He's subconsciously telling himself, "I always have to start over anyway, so what does it matter." Identifying habitual thoughts, especially fearful thoughts based on childhood experiences, explains why we get stuck in our relationships, our careers, or any other area of our lives. This examination makes it possible to break through our childhood patterns, those we acquired by watching our parents and those we adapted to cope with childhood trauma.

Patterns can work in our favor as well if we establish positive habits, thinking processes, and practices that help us reach our

Intention

goals. Setting clear goals leads to fulfillment and success. Further, increasing our emotional intelligence leads to greater success based on better relational skills. Clearly, choosing to link the power of our mind with the power of our heart creates a transcendent energy—energy we can put to use to become our most evolved and creative selves.

Mystics teach that metaphysical laws govern the invisible world just as the laws of physics govern the material world. With the advent of the field of quantum physics, many of those formerly metaphysical laws make sense in a new way. Five of the metaphysical laws govern manifestation. The first of these laws is *the Law of All Possibility*, which simply states that anything is possible. The second, *the Law of Limitation*, states that anything is possible as long as you choose something specific. Of course the third, fourth, and fifth laws emphasize persistent determination and ultimately allow for divine assistance. Essentially, once we have done everything possible, we declare, "Thank you for this or something even better. Thy will be done!"

In the final chapter of this book, *Power Choices*, you will be surprised, maybe even amazed at the accomplishments—some of them history making—of people who have made the power choice of intention a guide for their lives. But those amazing people had something else working for them because they also interlaced the power choices.

Having broken through emotional blocks, faced our negative thought patterns and fear-inducing questions, and used tools such as positive self-talk and chanting, we've harnessed the energy and thought patterns of victory. The moment has come to select a new intention. Do you want to be loving toward yourself and others? More merciful toward yourself and others? Or maybe your relationship can benefit from your intention to listen deeply to your own feelings or those of others.

This choice employs the universal truth that we are what we think. The Buddha said, "We are what we think, having become what we thought." All the world's teachers teach us that where our intention flows, our energy goes. Pick up a sacred text from anywhere in the world, and it will to tell you that energy follows thought.

QUESTIONS
1. What do I believe about myself and my life?
2. Where did that belief system come from?
3. How do I play it out in my life?
4. What is my new intention?

POWER TOOLS

1 ACTIVE VISUALIZATION
Support your new intention using the tool of active visualization. Picture what you want as already complete.

2 DAILY CHANTING
Chant the Always Victory Chant daily, or more often if you like.

3 WRITE
Write down five things you're grateful for every day.

POWER DECREE
I AM THE MASTER OF MY MIND. MY MIND IS NOT THE MASTER OF ME.

> *The world before me is restored in beauty.*
> *The world behind me is restored in beauty.*
> *The world below me is restored in beauty.*
> *The world above me is restored in beauty.*
> *The world around me is restored in beauty.*
> *My voice is restored in beauty.*
> *It is finished in beauty.*
> —Navajo prayer to the deity Changing Woman

Chapter Six

Inspiration
Traveling the Road Home— Renewal and Resurrection

*They were divine in the transformations they wrought.
They were blessed by heaven.*
— The I Ching

WITH A JOLT, Lucy sits up and finds herself in her bed in her dark apartment. She's clammy with sweat, and her heart is pounding. As she tries to make sense of what's been happening to her, part of her mind tells her she must have been dreaming, but her sense of terror tells her it was real.

Her usual cockiness is gone as she turns on the light with a hand that's shaking. She stares at her bedroom. It's been ransacked. She runs out into the living room; it's been torn apart too. Every part of the apartment is upside down, inside out. This was no dream. "Holy Mother of God. What happened in here?"

Suddenly, someone is pounding on the apartment door. Without thinking, she heads for the back door and, flinging it open, she runs right into Walter. She steps back, wary. "Walt, what are you doing here?" She's not sure whom to trust right now.

He pulls her into his arms, holding her tightly, "Lucy, I've been so scared. I couldn't reach you all day yesterday after the police came."

Power Choices

"The police?"

"Yes, two skateboarders ran down an old man and killed him. Your purse and your lunch were on the ground next to him. Lucy, what happened? You're covered with bruises."

"Killed him?! Are you sure?!" Catching her breath, she says abruptly, "Can I trust you, Walt?"

"Are you kidding?" he asks. "Doesn't your heart tell you anything, Lucy? I've been in love with you for two years, and I have been crazed since you disappeared yesterday."

She pushes him toward the stairs even as her mind flashes back to all the times Walt had been her rock. "Yes, Walt, my heart does tell me that you love me. But right now, I just need you to help me. We need to get out of here—fast." They run down toward Walt's car at the bottom of the steps. But they stop in their tracks when they see the two skateboarders closing in on the car.

"Too late," Lucy thinks. Then she has an idea. She tells Walt they should keep moving toward his car. As they advance, she thinks, "Bag Man, help me," and she begins radiating an intense field of light around herself and Walt. The skateboarders fall back, and the couple gets in the car and speeds away.

"Where are we headed? And what was all that light?" Walt asks, looking at her in amazement. "It was like something out of a science fiction movie."

"I'll try to explain later," Lucy says. "Right now, you've got to get me to Holy Names Cemetery."

There have definitely been some changes in Lucy's life — and not just the incident with the skateboarders and the Bag Man, or even the shift in her relationship with Walt, suddenly recognizing his value in her life. Everything that has been happening to her since she stepped out of her door into Bag Man's path is still something of a mystery, but she's beginning to see farther along the path. She's not resisting, questioning, or fighting as much; she's assessing the situation and acting according to her best intelligence, her intuition, and the insight she's gained during this strange series of events. She has clearly taken in some of what she's learned during this wild whirlwind of a nightmare—at least enough to protect herself from her enemies so she can keep moving toward her goal. Lucy is beginning to use her own power—she's making positive power choices.

The moment that our shero Lucy stops to remember that she can use the light to protect herself and her companion from harm, she is acting on an inspiration. She may be petrified with fear—expecting Walt to save the day, waiting for the worst to happen, or otherwise running scared. And who wouldn't be frightened if they were standing in her shoes? But somehow she is able to call on something that has awakened inside her. She makes a quick, creative decision that saves her neck with the help of what she recognizes as a higher power, the Bag Man—that's the power of inspiration.

Our sixth power choice, inspiration, is the stage during which we begin to make sense of our journey and our experiences so they become a source of enlightenment for us. This stage breathes new life into our journey. (Inspire literally means to "breathe in.") All the things we've learned along the way come together for us and enable us to make leaps that we might not have been able to make otherwise. When you hear someone say, "That was an inspired decision" or "I was inspired to do that," the implication is that the act went beyond everyday activity or mundane decision making; something special was at play.

Inspiration can come from outside of us—from the universe that we live in. For example, studying a hero's path can provide us inspiration for our own journey. But inspiration can also come from within us—when our hearts and minds are open to the universe of possibilities that live in us. When we study and practice the spiritual tools that enhance our capacity to receive light, energy, and guidance from the divine, we are better able to tap into the inspiration we need. In any case, the conduit for inspiration is the marriage of the mind and the heart. When we reach the stage of inspiration, we have the opportunity to solidify our gains, renew ourselves, and step into this new self we have wrought.

Perseus

Perseus, the son of the god Zeus and the mortal woman Danae, began his life adrift in a chest at sea with his mother—cast out by Danae's father, the king, who feared an oracle's prediction, which stated that the boy would one day seize his throne. Guided by Zeus, the chest reaches a distant island where the local ruler rescues the pair and then marries Danae and rears Perseus. When he comes of age, Perseus sets out on a quest seeking glory and to mark his place in the world by finding and destroying the dreaded, fabled Gorgon, Medusa. Instead of skin, it was said that the Gorgons (who were three sisters) had dark, shiny dragon scales; instead of hair, snakes writhed on their heads; and anyone who looked upon them would instantly be turned to stone. Medusa, the only mortal among the three Gorgons, was the most feared. If Perseus could bring back her head, he would be honored as a great hero across the land.

Along his way, Perseus seized magical objects from powerful nymphs that enabled him to fly toward the ocean where the three Gorgons lived. Approaching as they slept, Perseus avoided looking directly at Medusa by using his shield's mirror-like surface so he could see her reflection instead. This simple, clever strategy allowed him to cut off her head. Perseus used the head, along with his wits and valor, to vanquish enemies on the road home and to win the hand and heart of fair Andromeda. At one point, Perseus accidentally killed his grandfather, who had fled to a far land to escape his predicted fate, and the prophecy was fulfilled. After his grief abated, Perseus and Andromeda went on to live gloriously blessed and abundant lives.

Like all myths, this one also has historical roots. Medusa, according to a number of historical references, was an African queen and high priestess of a realm that included north Africa and perhaps Italy and Spain as well. The "snakes," so frightening to Perseus, are described in several accounts as shiny coils on her head—probably the beautiful, traditional braids worn by African queens and holy women. You can see how unusual Medusa's hair and black skin (shiny dragon scales) would seem to her European enemies so it's not hard to imagine that they found her so terrifying that they "turned to stone," most likely frozen by fear. In the end—according to this legend, at least—she met the fate of so many holy women of ancient times (and medicine women in modern times) who were accused of being witches.

The myth of Perseus and Medusa is also rich in archetypal symbols: a lost boy's need to prove himself; a boy who is part human and part divine (like all of us); the need to acquire parental assistance (Zeus's help); and the power of looking into a mirror (facing one's flaws and foibles) in order to wield the sword of truth and thereby escape being frozen in one's life. In the end the scales are balanced as fear leads his grandfather to a distant place where he meets that which he feared and had fled, death at Perseus' hand. It also shows the divine or magical help offered to Perseus, which led to the inspired choices the young man made in his quest to find meaning and love in his life. Each of Perseus' decisions—to answer the call, to ask for help, and to look both within and without for guidance—represents a power choice.

Through employing our power choices, we can mount an investigation to discover what is missing in our lives; we can accept our initiation, the call to set out on a journey to recover what we have lost; we can employ insight to acknowledge the emotional and intergenerational wounds and patterns that affect us; we can tap into our intuition, the deep inner guidance that enables us to recover our personal and spiritual identity; and finally, we can use our intention to rewrite our story and redefine ourselves and our lives to become living inspirations, willing to stand for wholeness and healing for all. Along our way, we use inspiration to create a profound alignment with the truths we have gathered as we've traveled; much like Perseus with the magic objects he took from the nymphs. But unlike Perseus, we don't desire to slay the powerful feminine within us, rather to create a marriage of the masculine and the feminine—to achieve balance within our own nature. ☙

BALANCING ANIMA AND ANIMUS

The meeting of two personalities is like the contact of two chemical substances. If there is any reaction, both are transformed.
— Carl Jung

During the time that I lived with the Wilhelm and Samuels family, Helmut Wilhelm showed me letters that Carl Jung had written to his father, Richard. The two scholars carried on a lively correspondence between Germany and China, where Jung and Wilhelm, respectively, were living, exchanging ideas about symbols and archetypes. Of particular interest was the balancing of masculine traits, which Jung called the animus, and feminine traits, which he called the anima. Not only did he believe that people had both traits within them, he believed that the anima and animus each had a shadow side and a light side. Jung characterized the light side of the anima as love, compassion, and generosity, and the shadow side as passive-aggressiveness, masochism, and cunning. He viewed the light side of the animus as protection, loyalty, and heroism, while the shadow side included bullying, cruelty, and violence. Not only did he believe that humans needed to balance the male and female aspects within them, but also that they needed to pay attention to and transform the shadow sides of each, not allowing the scales to tip in the favor of a less-positive side. Jung noted in his work that the West lacked a symbol to represent the balance of the masculine and feminine, such as the yin yang circle that denotes balance in the East. An interesting point—and, I believe, a quite telling one. No wonder our culture has struggled for so long with balancing masculine and feminine roles.

Whether we have a cultural symbol representing them or not, we have these traits within ourselves, which need to be balanced for us to live as fully and wholly as we can. We have an opportunity to look closely at the relative development of the anima and animus within ourselves, as well as the relationship between the two, and how that plays out within our lives. The goal is to balance the masculine and feminine within ourselves and to increase the light side traits of both. It does no good to cultivate more anima or more animus if you're cultivating the negative aspects of the trait. For example, when women were first beginning to nudge the glass ceiling in male-dominated careers, many felt that they had to act like one of the guys in order to be accepted by their peers and be taken seriously by their subordinates. But in some cases, they took on only the negative traits of their male colleagues, and they didn't temper that with feminine traits or even light-side male traits. They became type A workaholics, leaving the care of home and family to paid caretakers. At work, they were cutthroat with colleagues and hard-nosed with peers. For a time, corporate fashion consisted of tailored pinstriped suits and vests, with little silk corsages made of the same silk and patterns as men's ties. We were mimicking everything that seemed male—as if being more "male" would make us more successful at work. Meanwhile, we were neglecting our feminine power—the special and valuable gifts we have that can be adapted to the conference room or the kitchen.

When we say that we don't like to see these traits in women, it sounds quite sexist. But the reality is, in an ideal world, we wouldn't see these negative traits in men, either. The reality is that men *and* women need to find more balance between home and work. Male managers *and* female managers need to find more constructive ways to motivate the people they work with.

We all need the healing and uplifting power of the healthy feminine, as Jung put it, "light anima," which makes it more possible for men to step into their light, fully developed animus. If motherhood once again becomes a noble and valued profession for those women who choose that path, and if women who choose to work outside the home are equally valued in the workplace alongside men, we will raise generations of children who will get enough love. Hans Paasche's dire predictions, which came true for unloved German children, need not be repeated elsewhere.

To maintain powerful inspiration requires taking time each day to allow your feminine side to balance your masculine side (and vice versa) in order to nurture and support yourself. This leads to creative expression and inner reflection, which then guide you to heartfelt, heart-centered wisdom before you take action. This balance helps you to keep your thoughts free of the web of negative family blueprints and childhood decisions that lead you to fearful thinking. A balanced anima and animus allows you to choose a clear intention to live in the world with compassion and joy and keep your mind stayed on love, to paraphrase an old spiritual hymn.

> ### POWER TOOL
> #### MEASURE YOUR ANIMA AND ANIMUS
>
> *Weigh the balance of your animus and anima in your life.*
>
> *Write down the "light side" traits of the anima and the "light side" traits of the animus. Then count how many times you exercise them on a daily basis.*

MARCUS

Marcus grew up in danger and poverty in the St. Louis projects. His mother, a full-figured, sixteen-year-old, redhead, had run away from a small town in Iowa. Somewhere along her bumpy road, she met Ziggy, a pseudo-Rastafarian from Jamaica. They stayed together long enough for Marcus to reach his third birthday before she took off again, leaving Marcus and his baby brother with their father. The family landed in the projects, where Ziggy would leave the boys for as much as a week at a time while he went on drug binges.

When he came in to see me, Marcus was thirty-eight, struggling with a profound depression, a terrible case of insomnia, and the inability to gain a healthy weight. Despite these symptoms, Marcus had achieved remarkable career success and had managed to hold his family together for ten years. But he'd begun to have serious problems both at work and at home. His relationship with his oldest child was problematic, and he didn't have the parenting skills to turn it around. He found himself repeatedly lashing out with employees but, conversely, failing to speak up with supervisors. Things had reached a crisis point at work, which had prompted him to accept a position with a major software company and move to the San Francisco Bay Area with his wife and two children.

Marcus had never been in therapy before and had never divulged the details of his childhood to anyone—not even to his wife. When he began to tell me one grisly detail after the next, I understood why. His father was a veteran and had received a small disability check each month; he would buy food for the month, which he charged Marcus to prepare and to manage, and then he would sporadically disappear. But the food only lasted two-and-a-half to three weeks. No matter how careful Marcus was, by the end of the month, he and his brother were starving. His father would yell and sometimes hit Marcus, accusing him of stealing the food and eating it all himself.

If it was dodgy for the boys at home, it was even more dangerous outside. Marcus remembered mornings when he would open the door of their ground-floor apartment and have to step over a dead body on the doorstep. Some nights he and his brother huddled under the bed that they shared, with bullets flying through their bedroom, lodging in the wall above the bed. On one particularly awful night, someone broke through the window and crawled over their bed to escape an assailant outside. In the morning, the children found blood everywhere.

Marcus grew up with no model of nurturing, support, or warmth; he had long since inculcated the belief that he was unworthy of such nurturing. Having grown up without a mother, he had almost no feminine traits, and this seemed to be at the root of many of his problems.

Cultivating his inner anima and mobilizing his ability to mother himself became a focus for our work. I encouraged him to purchase a goddess figure that represented the Great Mother to him. He placed it on an altar, where he also put his only photograph of his mother and a photo of his paternal grandmother, who once came from Jamaica and cared for Marcus and his brother for six weeks. These symbols helped him focus on the positive side of the feminine anima.

Marcus wrote out a decree that he practiced every day: "I am worth nurturing and being cared for. I nurture myself and allow myself to be nurtured." He then established a program for himself that included steps he would take *each day* to allow his famished feminine side to grow. He practiced making meals for himself and his family—something he had previously avoided because dealing with food was just too traumatic and painful. For the first time, he told his wife the painful details of his childhood and allowed her to comfort him. I also talked to him about practicing what psychologists call a "reparenting" technique: talking to himself as a loving parent would. He later told me that he had hit on the idea of talking to some of his sales force in this nurturing way and had gotten great results. He went on to craft in-service trainings and bring in consultants to enhance the level of personal growth and interpersonal skills among his team members. He even gained twenty pounds. The quest for balance Marcus so successfully achieved made him an inspiration to his coworkers. Most important to him, he reported success at home as he took down his walls and allowed his marriage to become a source of real joy and intimacy. He said, "I never felt that I could start each day feeling excited instead of scared and depressed." In becoming inspired Marcus became an inspiration. The search for inspiration is a necessary quest for each of us individually and also for society as a whole.

Inspiration

Power Tool
The Loving Mother Exercise

The Loving Mother Exercise focuses on cultivating the nurturing feminine aspect within our consciousness, promoting the emotional relaxation that opens the door for inspiration from within. Even if we were well parented, we can all afford to foster more self-nurturing. This exercise helps us to look at the places in our lives where we are hard on ourselves-where we blame, berate, or hold negative opinions of ourselves. The exercise allows the inner voice we all have to change from a critical or unloving voice to one that is positive and uplifting. Instead of tearing us down further, that voice lifts us up and showers us with the love we have always longed for. This is similar to the emotional intelligence exercise we did in when we explored intuition, where we sat in the other person's seat and envisioned a situation from their perspective. This time, however, the person occupying that chair is your younger self.

1. Choose a period in your life that was particularly painful. Imagine yourself at that age, sitting in a chair.

2. In the opposite chair, picture the most loving, nurturing, supportive mother you can possibly conjure.

3. Take the child's seat and tell the mother how you feel as you describe your traumatic experience.

4. Now take the mother's chair. In this seat, you are the loving, nurturing mother that you imagined. Allow this mother to say to the child all the things that you've longed to hear from your actual mother. Do not say what you think your own mother might say, but what you'd *want* her to say.

Power Choices

5. After the mother is finished, go back to the first seat and tell the mother how you feel hearing her message.

6. Notice if anything feels incomplete. If it does, tell the mother. Then go back to the mother seat and fill in what was missing.

7. Go back and forth as much as you need to in order to feel really heard and understood and to feel nurtured and loved by your "mother."

8. If you had another caretaker in place of your mother, do the same exercise with that person.

9. To extend the benefits of this exercise, take time to speak to yourself lovingly every day, using your newly developed loving mother voice. This is especially soothing when you feel anxious or tired or sad.

10. If you have difficulty coming up with positive, loving things for the mother to say, here are some suggestions to get you started:

- *You have every right to feel angry with me and hurt by me.*
- *I am so sorry I hurt you.*
- *You didn't deserve to be hurt.*
- *You were an innocent child.*
- *You deserve to be loved and supported then and now.*
- *I'm going to do everything I can to make it up to you.*
- *I love you so much.*
- *I'm so proud of you.*

Inspiration

INSPIRATION FROM A HIGHER POWER

Salih always taught his disciples, "Who knocks on the door of someone constantly, one day the door must be opened to him." Rabia one day heard it and said, "Salih, how long will you go on preaching thus, using the future tense, saying, 'will be opened'? Was the door ever closed?" Salih bowed in submission to her. — Attar

There was once a king who, having secured his kingdom and his fortune, loved to go out hunting with his best friend the vizier, the wise counselor of his realm. As they traveled along together, they would engage in rich, philosophical discussions. The king tended to be impatient and negative in his outlook on the world, but the vizier always argued with him that everything in life had a positive outcome in the end. The king should be patient and hold a positive expectation, the vizier advised.

One day while they were hunting, the king had an accident; his toe was cut off. He was furious and in great pain. The vizier said, "Now, now, be patient. Something good will come of this." This was just too much for the king. He flew off the handle and ordered the guards to throw the wise man into prison, which they did.

In time the king's foot healed and he resumed his hunting, though now he had only the guards for company. One day he wandered away from his guards and was captured by a fierce tribe of giants. They practiced human sacrifice and were delighted to have a king to sacrifice to their gods. As the giant's priest prepared the king for death, he inspected him carefully; only perfect sacrifices would please the gods. And lo, a toe was missing. "This is an imperfect offering. Send him away," cried the priest. The king was thrown out into the jungle where at length his guards found him.

When the king returned to the palace, he immediately asked that the vizier be taken from the prison where he'd been languishing and brought before him. He told the vizier the story of his near escape and said, "Please forgive me for throwing you in prison. You were right in the end. Something good did come of me losing my toe. I will now use this experience to be a better king and a better friend."

"Oh, my friend, there is nothing to forgive," said the vizier. "Being in *prison was the best thing for me, for if I had been with you, they would have sacrificed me."*

The king had learned three hard-won lessons. One: accept wisdom and inspiration from his wise advisor. (Like most of us, he had a hard time learning through advice so he had to learn from experience.) Two: the vizier was right about looking for the positive in every situation. And three: the choice to accept inspiration from his friend could make him a better leader because he himself became an inspiring example of enthusiasm rather than pessimism. What if we chose to see life as a series of events that unfold for our highest good? Suppose we were always able to view life's challenges as an opportunity to bring forth good? That mindset actually changes outcomes for the people who are able to maintain it. Thus, two people in the same situation—one with a positive outlook and the other with a pessimistic viewpoint—end up having two very different experiences. The person with the more upbeat approach will expect the best and be open to seeing it when it comes. She won't dwell on what seems not to be going her way, but look for ways in which she can turn the situation in her favor. That person's attitude is also going to bring out the best in the people she interacts with—they'll be more likely to work to make circumstances more favorable. A doubtful, suspicious approach will likely garner the opposite result. Even if the outcome is the same for each person, the optimist is more likely to sleep peacefully at night and wake up hopeful; the pessimist will toss and turn with worry, then dread the next day.

Even in the case of major catastrophes, it is possible to find good. During devastating tragedies such as the terrorist attack of September 11, the tsunami that devastated Asia and Africa, and Hurricane Katrina that demolished so much of the Gulf Coast, we rescued hope and reaffirmed that we are an international community, as the entire world rushed to help the survivors and to assist in rebuilding. Yes, people suffered tremendous mental, emotional, physical, and spiritual devastation. But among their memories of their most trying time, they will recall people who came to their rescue, who lent aid and support, a hand and a

Inspiration

shoulder. Those who helped did so because they realized the truth in what spiritual traditions throughout the ages have taught: what affects one of us, in the end, affects us all. They were inspired to reach out beyond their normal routines, in order to give something to someone who needed it. And their inspiration was likely contagious. We can see from these situations that inspiration doesn't have to come from positive sources. We can be inspired by trauma and tragedy as well. One of the movements ignited by the Katrina disaster seeks to uncover and cure the hidden connections between racism and poverty so clearly revealed in the storm's wake. The people involved in this movement—which Dr. Cornell West, author and professor at Princeton University, has dubbed "Povertrina"—are heroes as much as the people who left homes and jobs to help out in the crises above. When you are reminded of the human kindness to be found in the world, it can inspire you to do things you didn't believe possible.

THE TRANSFORMING POWER OF SPIRIT

I'm saying that everything is a ritual. Just as a great mass is a ritual, composed of various parts, the everyday experience of any person is also.
— Paulo Coelho

When we find that we are having difficulty accessing our power, offering love to ourselves or to another, or growing on our spiritual path, fear is most likely at play. Fear is the primary interference in our personal development. Yet fear is not our enemy. Properly expressed and gently exposed to the healing light of spirit, fear becomes our friend. I'm not saying that fear itself is a good motivator for change. Research and experience has shown that, contrary to the popular belief among educators, health-care givers, business managers, and some parents, trying to frighten people into doing things rarely works—certainly not in the long term. For example, doctors may try to scare a diabetic patient into eating more healthfully by describing the complications of advanced stages of diabetes. But telling someone they will end up with kidney disease, blindness, or the need of an amputation is likely to send that person into denial or into an emotional paralysis that hinders their ability to make positive, powerful choices. A manager who uses fear tactics to motivate his employees may get their compliance in the short term, but she will end up with a team that's suspicious, uncooperative, and quick to burn out. And an educator or parent who uses fear tactics can inhibit a child's confidence—the power that young person needs to go forth into the world and complete her own journey. Actually, research in both the fields of education and parenting shows that positive motivators and positive discipline get better results from children, and the same proves true for adults.

We need to let go of the idea that fear itself is a good way to inspire people. On the other hand, when we recognize fear for what it is, it serves as a wakeup call to the work we have to do within ourselves. When we know where our fears lie, we have access to important information that can help us begin to uncover the beliefs that seem to be holding us back. Fear is a road sign that points us in the right direction. When we see it, we need to turn toward it instead of speeding away. And we can do that with confidence, knowing that fear yields to faith when we use our insight and intuition to help us understand what is triggering the fear, do the emotional release work we need to do, and then set a new intention to focus on abundance and safety. We can free ourselves from the paralysis of fear through positive self-talk as well as by way of a number of spiritual tools that will help us transform the fear into faith in ourselves, faith in life, and faith in the divine.

To complete the process of transformation, we need the spiritual power of inspiration, our sixth power choice. The words "inspiration" and "spirit" come from the same root. Spirit is the breath of life; to be inspired is to draw in that powerful, life-giving breath and then use its power to do something creative and constructive. To fully access the breath of life, I believe we have to follow some sort of spiritual path. Now, I'm not proselytizing; how you define and act on your spirituality is a personal choice. You may go to a mosque, a temple, a synagogue, a zendo, or a church.

Inspiration

Or you may connect with spirit when you're working in your flower garden, hiking up a mountain, or sailing your boat on the ocean. Each of us is unique, and spirit speaks to us in different ways. Choose your own path—but do choose one. We all need something that inspires us, that uplifts us, that lifts our vision. Looking upward and reaching upward, literally and figuratively, helps us hold our intention and vision at the most elevated level.

Saints and sages throughout the ages have all shared wisdom that allows us to tap into this higher power because they understood how important it was to have access to that power. And while many people have come to understand that that power is somewhere outside us—in a far-off, unreachable heaven—many paths and teachers indicate that a higher power lives in the heart, that we're not separate from it at all. When we remember that, we stop feeling quite so small, or quite so alone, or quite so helpless—as if we don't have possibilities. When we know that we can look for inspiration, guidance, and encouragement—and know where to look—then we have found a way to step into our lives with true power.

THE SCIENCE OF SPIRITUALITY
We are beings of energy.
— William Collinge

I've always told my husband that the real reason that I married him was because he introduced me to a wonderful book: *Power vs. Force: The Hidden Determinants of Human Behavior*, written by Dr. David Hawkins. Dr. Hawkins used applied kinesiology—a process of testing validity where the subject is presented a yes or no question, and then the subject's extended arm is pressed down. The tested muscle remains taught if the response is true and becomes weak when the response is false. This process works regardless of whether the person being tested knows the true response or not. To calibrate the strength of various emotions and states of consciousness, Dr. Hawkins constructed a scale from 0-

1,000 that shows which emotions and states were more strengthening to a person's body and their life. Zero had the least power. One thousand held the most. With a score of 20, shame, is the lowest calibrated state. At the other end of the scale, enlightenment scores between 700 and 1,000. In the middle of the scale there's a line. Anything below the line causes us to lose power and strength. Anything above the line builds power and strength. The breakpoint is the shift between courage at 200 and neutrality at 250. The key to reaching the line and living above it is developing control of the mind and the emotions.

Remember the research we reviewed by Dr. Herbert Benson demonstrating the tremendous benefits of mind and emotional control using chanting as the tool? He found chanting words from a spiritual tradition, lowers blood pressure, improves the immune system, and increases the production of endorphins in the brain. Similarly young Gandhi's grandmother taught him to chant—*Hare Rama, Hare Rama*—which he credited for transforming him into the great national leader he became. That's a lot of oomph for your *om*—if you're chanting in the yogic tradition. Every spiritual tradition has some form of chanting as part of its practice. In some cases, like the Hindu or Buddhist traditions, it involves repeating a sound or a phrase over and over again. In other cases, such as in the Gregorian Christian Church, in original African religions, and in African-American Christian traditions, chanting involves a song that the congregation repeats together. I have also attended synagogues where the cantor led the congregation in songs and prayers in which the refrain is repeated. The prayerful chanting by the emir and congregants in mosques follows a similar pattern. Native American ceremonial songs also use the rhythm and vibration of chants.

The rhythm and repetition of chanting can be soothing and calming, but think about this as well: chanting creates sound that vibrates through the cells of your body. It literally moves you; it sets you in motion, so it makes sense that such a practice could make physical changes in your body.

Prayer, too, has been determined to result in specific physical outcomes. Dr. Larry Dossey, who was head of the Office of

Inspiration

Alternative Medicine at the National Institutes of Health, conducted studies and wrote several books on the relationship between healing and prayer, which he terms "nonlocal medicine"—a term based on Dr. Dossey's understanding that our mind extends beyond our physical body and transcends space and time. Dr. Randolph Byrd, a cardiologist at San Francisco General Hospital, also did some interesting work in this area. Dr. Byrd randomly assigned nearly four hundred patients to routine care or routine care plus prayer. The patients had no idea they were being prayed for; the people assigned to pray had no knowledge of the patients, and the hospital staff didn't know that a prayer study was underway. The results demonstrated that those who received prayer had fewer complications and better prognoses than those who didn't. Prayer, then, is an effective tool.

So why is spiritual power so important? Because it directly impacts the quality of your life and the lives around you. In 1995, the Oxman study showed that seriously ill patients who failed to draw comfort and strength from religious practice had as much as a 300 percent increased risk of death from the health issue they were facing. This implies that your connection with a spiritual practice can literally prolong your life—even in the face of catastrophic illness.

If we believe that there is a higher energy in the universe (particularly an intelligent and loving energy) that we have access to, we can imagine that, like all forms of energy—electricity, kinetic energy, fire, static, calories—this great universal energy can cause change in the things it comes into contact with. If we find ways to tap into that energy, it makes sense that it can make changes in our bodies and minds.

When people pray, they tend to practice speaking to a higher power—petitioning or asking for something, or expressing gratitude. But another form of communication with the inner self or that higher power is meditation. Meditation is a way to quiet your mind and spirit, emptying yourself of all those myriad immediate thoughts and allowing yourself a time of inner silence. Often, in these quiet moments, we receive insights and inspirations that may not have made it through our otherwise cluttered minds.

"Meditating has changed my entire life," said a sixty-two-year-old hypertension patient. "I feel relaxed and healthy all the time." He was part of a group of one hundred older African-Americans who practiced meditating twice a day, did muscle relaxation exercises, or changed their diet and exercise patterns. The people who changed their diets and did relaxation showed significant improvement, but the meditators showed a drop in blood pressure twice that of the other groups.

My spiritual teacher, Chow Chow Imamoto, wrote a book about self-healing in which she said that daily meditation brings peace, and peace, in turn, brings restored health. You can see the connection, right? Your body is going to do a lot better if you're not tensed up with your shoulders scrunched up to your ears and your face as tight as a prune.

Happily, the benefits of spiritual practice extend beyond health. My grandmother had a little framed needlepoint of praying hands on the wall in her New Orleans home that read, "The family that prays together stays together." It looks as if she was right. An extensive study at the University of Denver revealed that couples who share a spiritual life have more satisfying relationships, even after twenty years. Spiritual practice has inspired some of the most courageous acts of political transformation, whether it was the Quakers, who expressed peaceful resistance to war and violence; Ghandi, King, and the Dalai Lama, who preached nonviolent resistance; or a group of pacifists, who crossed the line to protest the School of the Americas, where U.S. military trained assassins. Believing that their faith demanded action, chanting "We shall overcome," they marched into guns, police dogs, hoses, and jail terms for their actions.

There's a lot that I could say to argue for the importance of spirituality, but to me one of the most important points is that spirituality always reminds us that we are one. That belief enables us to treat one another in the best possible way—with the most kindness, compassion, and generosity and with a willingness to give and expect the best from the other person. Daniel Maziaaz,

Inspiration

author of *The Angelic Way to Love*, says, "It is our oneness that we are all part of this body of the Divine, so that deep down inside we all love one another."

It is this love—this fire, this passion—that we want to tap into. What if you went home from work every night passionately on fire? Your relationship might get a lot better. If you showed up at work passionate about the job and on fire to get started, you might get that promotion and a raise. If you're running your own business and you're on fire, you're going to be magnetic—you're going to draw people to your business! Imagine what you'd be like if you were on fire and passionate about making the world a better place. You'd be unstoppable. We can do so much good when we are free of some of those stones in that bag on our back and when we understand that we're connected to the great, universal energy—and that the energy is love. Heart power, love, connects us—but only when our hearts are open. The thing that helps us to open our hearts is to be in tune with our intention, our inspiration, and our spirituality.

> ### POWER TOOL
> ### *DEVELOP A SPIRITUAL PRACTICE*
>
> *Here are some questions to help you get in tune with your spirituality.*
>
> - *What gives me the greatest sense of peace and energy?* Is it being outside? Is it hiking? Is it meditating? Is it going to church?
>
> - *How much time do you actually spend in spiritual pursuit?* Many of us know what gives us energy and makes us feel like the best we can be, but we don't make time in our lives to do that. We're too busy on Sunday morning to go to church; we have too many chores on Saturday to go to the beach or the

mountains; we have to get to work early so there's no time for morning mediation. There's got to be some balance. If we want to put our mental, physical, emotional, and spiritual lives in balance, we would conceivably spend 25 percent of our energy on developing our spirituality. But if we're only spending 1 percent of our time in spiritual pursuit, we're losing some power.

- *How can I enhance my spiritual growth?* Do I need to read? Take a class? Find a teacher?

- *Do I belong to a spiritual community?* Will such a community help me to strengthen my spiritual growth and offer me guidance? Whether we belong to a formal religious community or not, most of us need a spiritual community of some sort. None of us can do it alone all the time. Maybe you need to buddy up with someone or form a small prayer or meditation circle-some form of a spiritual support group that will be available to help you along, especially in those times when you're not feeling as strong as you ordinarily would be. We need to know that we are standing shoulder-to-shoulder with a community that can support us. But be careful about who you share your spirit with; I don't want anybody falling into cults here. You know you're in a cult when the your spiritual leaders tell you everything you should do, think, and wear; when all those rules don't allow you to move independently; and when their way and only their way is right. (I know: by that description, some established, traditional religions classify as cults. That may be the case.) Before you join any spiritual group, look within and examine

Inspiration

> why you are joining, what you expect from it. Ask a spiritual leader about any questions that arise for you. And then just trust what's in your heart. Your heart will tell you what's right. Trust your intuition.

༄

> ### POWER TOOL
> ### MEDITATION AND CHANTING
>
> *Many people think of meditation as sitting in some contorted position for hours at a time waiting for a bolt of lightning to strike. But meditation can take many forms and can be done just about anywhere; some people do it sitting, others walking. Some chant, some are silent. You can do it in groups or alone. Walking a labyrinth is a form of meditation. I read of one Buddhist chef who made mindful dishwashing her meditation. No matter how you do it, it's definitely an effective power tool.*
>
> *When I work with people who've never meditated before, I like to have them start with this meditation, which builds on the meditation we began with in chapter one. It's really brilliantly simple.*
>
> Light a candle.
>
> Sit in a comfortable place, breathe deeply, and relax..
>
> Focus on the flame.
>
> Imagine that the flame is inside you, and it is blazing brightly.

1
2
3
4

Power Choices

5. Then picture this flame surrounding you on all sides out to a distance of nine feet.

6. Simply relax in this field of light and energy imagining that you are falling back into a pool of light, letting the light support you just as the water in a pool would.

7. Let your mind emotions and body float effortlessly in this light. Continue for as long as you wish. That's it.

If you have a "monkey mind" or one of those King-Kong, off-the-hook minds that is running around all over the place, then you are going to need something else to capture your mind and keep it still long enough to have an effective meditation session. Chanting can help; it, too, is very simple.

1. Imagine something you want to change in your life right now. Hold that thought.

2. Next, create a mental picture of how things will look for you when that thing is changed, and then color your picture in shades of golden light.

3. Now raise your arms toward the sky. Why do you have your arms up? When you have your arms down at your sides, your center of gravity is in your abdomen, but when you lift your arms, your center of gravity shifts to your heart. In this position, we have more heart energy and are open to receiving what is being offered spiritually.

4. Now, while holding the thought at the back of your

mind, focus on your heart and repeat the chant we used in chapter five *"I am a success! I am a success! I AM A SUCCESS! I AM A SUCCESS!"* Chant it with conviction; really put some power behind it.

Repeat it until you begin to feel that you are embedding it into your heart.

Raising your arms and speaking the mantra aloud enables you to feel it physically and emotionally, which can help make it seem more tangible. Holding the thought in your mind as you repeat the chant helps you focus on your intention. The color of success and victory are gold; we value gold. That's why they give you a gold medal or a gold statue if you win an important award.

In fact, another mantra I suggest repeating is, "Everything I touch turns to gold." You don't have to be in meditation to do it. Just repeat it to yourself as you go about your daily tasks. Give yourself some little reminders. For example, tell yourself that every time you send an e-mail or go to the cash machine or hear a bell ring, you will repeat the mantra. After a while, the mantra will be a part of you, and when that happens, you'll start to see the truth of it manifest in many positive ways. The particular change you've focused on doesn't matter. You could picture any change, large or small; meditating, chanting, repeating mantras and affirmations will help bring it into fruition. Your mind is working for you, your feelings are aligned with what's on your mind, your body is engaged, and you are tapping into all the success that is available in the universe. That's a win-win situation.

BEVERLY AND KIRK

Not long ago I worked with a couple who was experiencing conflict because the husband, Kirk, had a hard time being loving and affectionate with his wife and their children. Beverly tearfully described how he deflected her attempts to kiss or hug him or to initiate sex. The only time they had a sexual encounter was if he initiated it.

When I asked him about when the pattern started, Kirk related the memory of being five years old and running to hug his mother only to have her push him away. He broke down in tears as he talked about it, "That's what she always did when I tried to hug her," he said. "So I gave up and stopped wanting to hug or kiss anyone, and I didn't let anyone touch me."

Beverly was tearful, too. She said, "I put up with this before working on myself, and now I need you to change too." She had been going to a 12-step program Marijuana Anonymous program, which had helped her realize that she didn't have to stay addicted to cope with her marriage. She had gotten in touch with her higher power and now she told her husband, "I have faith that your higher power will help you too." She asked if it was all right with me if they said a prayer; I was only too happy to lead them. By the end of the session, we could all feel the extraordinary new energy between the two of them as Kirk stood and made the decree, "I am ready to be a loving husband and father."

The following week they returned. During the session, Beverly put her head on Kirk's shoulder, and he put his arm around her. She said, "My prayers have been answered. Last week he would have pushed me away."

Beverly credits her prayers and the spiritual tools that she learned through her 12-step program for healing her marriage. She felt the group's support combined with the prayer and meditation tools she learned inspired her to continue to have faith in her husband and their capacity to grow together.

Inspiration

A SPIRITUAL LIFE ENHANCES PEACE
There is absolutely no doubt in my mind that [spiritual] exercises work.
— Dharma Singh Khalsa, MD

In 1980, Dr. Nereum conducted a study in which he gave a high-cholesterol diet to rabbits that had an inherited tendency to develop atherosclerosis. When he conducted the autopsies on the animals, half of the rabbits had severe atherosclerosis, and half did not. The research team was quite puzzled; they couldn't imagine what caused the discrepancy. Looking at every possible factor, they eventually realized that the animals were cared for by a very affectionate lab technician who was quite short-statured. The rabbits in the bottom cages—those she could easily reach—had received a lot of love and attention; the rabbits in the top cages had not. Did her attentiveness make a difference in the rabbits' health? Nereum developed another study to test the effect of being "hugged on" versus "business as usual." The rabbits that were hugged on had a 60 percent reduction in the amount of plaque in their arteries. The implication here is that love and affection—at the very least some kind of positive personal interaction—can have an impact on our well-being.

In humans, the ability to give and receive love begins in infancy. The purest love is the love of a child for their parent, but there are babies who are unable to cling or who are "difficult to soothe" and who seem to want to be left alone. The parents' feelings about one another, about conception, and about birth all play a part in the outcome for the baby. This process is what mystics would call the creation of karma. If your capacity to love is injured in infancy or somewhere along the way, your life journey involves healing those wounds in order to recover and to enhance your capacity to love.

This idea is expressed beautifully in the following quote by Robert Jaffe, MD, founder of the Jaffe Institute: "In a deep way, maintaining alignment means constantly returning to the Source of the love, peace and mercy. It is important for you to give these gifts to yourself and to others. But you must help yourself first. Send love and mercy for yourself. After you have helped yourself, then you can send mercy and love to another. As you learn to hold your alignment amidst all the challenges of this world, hopefully you will become the peace, the love and the mercy of God."

Dr. Jaffe's training of health professionals has at its core the need for healers to derive inspiration from spiritual practice, prayer, meditation, and opening their heart in order to truly meet the needs of their patients and clients.

MEG AND STUART

Meg and Stuart are a very spiritually evolved couple, both of whom are in 12-step recovery programs. Stuart's issues began in childhood when his parents divorced and his mother moved to California, leaving him in Ohio with his father. His father would scream at him, "How could you be so stupid!" and hit him for virtually any reason. Stuart became hypervigilant; like a soldier in a war zone, he was constantly scanning the perimeter for the next abusive assault. A bright and spirited child, he fought back. For his efforts to protect himself, at age sixteen, his father then remarried a woman who became the proverbial wicked stepmother. She encouraged his father to put Stuart out; Stuart's father complied.

Stuart found a gang of street kids who augmented his knowledge of drugs and alcohol, and he proceeded to anesthetize himself. He managed to find a steady job as a grocery worker and get through community college by the time he was twenty-five. Stuart found the 12-step programs, sobriety, and God. Since that time, he has developed a life committed to spiritual growth and community service, focusing on education. An exuberant and joyful person who lights up any room, he now tells anyone who will listen that the key to his success and happiness at home with Meg and at work with his students is God. His formula? Daily

Inspiration

meditation, twice weekly 12-step meetings with Meg, and the two of them holding hands each morning and evening for a brief prayer, which he and Meg find extremely uplifting, When they got stuck, another exercise that they could count on was the Remembrance Exercise, presented in chapter 3, which connects us with the divine in our heart.

Siddhartha

As with all things, moderation is the key. Even the Buddha had to learn that lesson. *Having left the princely life behind, Siddhartha renounced all worldly concerns and began a life of severe asceticism in hopes of gaining enlightenment. He ate nothing and eventually wasted away until he was no more than a skeleton with a few shreds of rags clinging to his emaciated body. But one day, in a flash of deeper understanding, it came to him that punishing his body wasn't bringing the spiritual upliftment that he had hoped for. Indeed, it was only killing him. He got up and bathed in the river, he accepted a bowl of rice from a sympathetic child, and he vowed to find enlightenment in a more humane way so that he might live to teach it to others.*

When he decided to eat and clothe and take care of himself, some of his followers castigated him as self-indulgent and weak. Impervious to their scorn, he sat under a banyan tree and vowed to remain there until enlightenment came. Through deep meditation he realized the eight-fold path and the four great truths leading to enlightenment. He achieved Nirvana and became an enlightened being. He could now enter the state of bliss and leave this world behind, but according to Buddhist teachings, Buddha elected to stay in this world to be of service to others.

The story of Gautama Buddha's life allows us to see the value of resigning from the need to look good for other people and having the courage to face scorn and ridicule in order to find a higher truth. This is also a beautiful example of choosing world service over personal achievement.

The Buddha's teachings have become one of the greatest sources of inspiration around the world, bringing Eastern values such as compassion, kindness, and nonviolence to Western seekers in a new way. Great Buddhist teachers such as Thich Nhat Hanh and the Dalai Lama join Thomas Merton and Bede Griffith in seeing the connection between Western and Eastern faiths. ☙

Spiritual Hunger

I've known what it is to be hungry, but I always went right to a restaurant.
— Ring Lardner

The hunger that drove Bede Griffith, spiritual teacher and author, to find an unusual spiritual path was not physical hunger, but spiritual hunger. I had the enormous good fortune to hear Father Bede Griffith speak shortly before he passed on a few years ago. He was eighty-five years old at the time, standing six-foot-five, hail and hearty, a dead ringer for Gandalf the wizard with his flowing white hair, white beard, and sapphire blue eyes. A strong and commanding presence, he lectured for two hours without a break.

He told the story about how he and his best friend, C.S. Lewis, left Oxford to become monks in a French monastery. Lewis didn't last long; he returned to Oxford to become a now-famous writer. Griffith stayed with the monastic order in France for twenty-five years, and from there the church subsequently sent him to India to found a monastery. As he began to study India's spiritual teachings, he said, "I have nothing to offer these people that is superior to their own spirituality, but I believe that by blending East and West we have something of great value." As a result of his life's journey, he stood before us in the traditional orange robes of a Hindu swami with a rope around his waist adorned with the wooden cross of his Christian order. Deeply moved by his talk, I went to him to ask a question that had long troubled me. "Father

Inspiration

Bede," I asked, "don't you think it is our materialism that holds us back in the West and hampers our spiritual progress?" He smiled and answered, "No, I think it helps because in the West you have so much and yet you still feel empty."

The emptiness is like a gnawing pain in the belly, which reminds us that we are hungry. But the pain gnaws at our hearts, which reminds us that we are spiritually hungry—and we need to keep seeking and searching until we find the spiritual connection we are looking for in life.

Sometimes spiritual hunger itself serves as a source of deep inspiration because it is so uncomfortable to live with that sense of dissatisfaction. But the hunger also serves another purpose, which is to notify us by its disappearance when we have reached the fountain of inspiration we seek and, having drunk our fill, we notice the absence of the hunger.

Death Teaches Kindness

Once there lived a rich, miserly man, his godless wife, and their one son. When the boy was sixteen, he died. After they buried him, the man and woman set up a shrine to honor him, and they followed the ancient Laotian tradition of bringing food and offerings to the grave each day for a full year. They adorned the shrine with the most beautiful items that money could buy; the food offerings were rich and plentiful—as befitted such a rich family.

One day, the maid was sent to deliver the offerings, but she encountered a sudden, fierce storm that made it impossible for her to continue to the altar. She huddled under a tree until the storm eased. On her way back home, she saw a Buddhist monk with an empty bowl in his hands. Without thinking, she donated all the food to him and continued on her way home. That night, the husband and wife heard their son speak to them, "I died a year ago, but I have not eaten any food until today." The next morning, the parents, quite excited, pulled the maid aside and demanded to know what had happened the day before. When they heard her story about the storm and the monk, they immediately headed to the temple to discuss the situation with the monks. The monks explained that possessions can never be taken into the afterlife. Only through service, donation, and respect could any gifts be passed on to the deceased. This stirred the hearts of the man and his wife. They were moved to build a huge, beautiful temple for the monks. They themselves went there often to pray and bring offerings. Their lives had been changed by the simple act of kindness that their maid had shown to a poor monk. ֍

LISTEN ALONG THE JOURNEY

To receive wisdom, quiet your mind and learn to listen. Peace, the door to your inner wisdom center will gradually grow and develop into your secret place of the most high. — Kimberly Marooney

Some years ago, the word went out to various spiritual centers in the San Francisco area that a swami from the Himalayas was on his first world tour after forty years in solitary meditation. I had to be there. I watched as the swami, who appeared to be a hale and hearty fifty-five-year-old, sprang swiftly up four flights of stairs since the elevator to the auditorium where he was to speak wasn't working. As we trudged up, far behind him, a number of us remarked that mountain living and meditation hadn't hurt his legs or his stamina.

Once we were all settled, he sat beaming and smiling in lotus position as he told us he was actually more than eighty years old (*Take me to that mountain*, I thought.). He explained that, respecting his father's wishes, he had first pursued a very successful career in engineering. But he had felt called to a spiritual way of life, which led him to leave his career and set up house in a small hut in the Himalayan Mountains. In his tiny hut, the swami meditated alone each day, consuming only one small bowl of rice supplied by villagers who lived at the base of the mountain. One day after decades in meditation, the message came that it was time to go out into the world and share what he had learned. The next day a man

Inspiration

from Canada knocked on the door of his hut and said, "I was directed to come and take you back to Canada with me."

"So here I am to tell you what I learned in these forty years sitting alone in deep meditation," the swami concluded. We eagerly anticipated the wise words he would say next, wondering how his profound wisdom would change our lives. And finally he spoke: "Love, love, love, love, love, love, love, love, love, love, love," he intoned over and over. "That's it. That's all I've learned." It was one of the most inspirational moments of my life.

On the mythic quest we call life, we pass from the choices marking our earliest turning point, investigation; to initiation as we receive the call to adventure; and insight as we move inward seeking to understand the baggage we carry with us. The midpoints, intuition and intention, lead us deeper still within our being, where the challenges of life must always take us. We journey, as did the sheroes and heroes of the wisdom teachings—Igraine and Pygmalion, Esther and Ruth, Merlin and Siddhartha—seeking answers to life's questions and cultivating our character, courage, strength, sensitivity, and loyalty to face the ordeals and tests we need to acquire self-mastery. As with Dorothy, who, at the final stage of her test confronts the wizard, it's time to turn toward home.

QUESTIONS
1. What gives me the greatest sense of peace and energy?
2. How much time do I spend in spiritual pursuit?
3. Do I belong to a spiritual community?
4. How can I enhance my spiritual growth?

POWER TOOLS

MEASURE YOUR ANIMA AND ANIMUS   1

Count how many times you exercise your "light side" traits each day.

2 **The Loving Mother Exercise**
To foster nurturing, do the Loving Mother Exercise.

3 **Develop a Spiritual Practice**
Finding a spiritual community can help you when you're not feeling strong.

4 **Practice Decrees**
Practice chanting inspirational and transformational decrees.

5 **Meditation and Chanting**
Practice chanting a mantra during your meditation practice.

Power Decree
I Am an Inspiration, Inspired by the Divine.

Let light and love and power restore the plan on Earth.
— The Great Invocation

Chapter Seven

Innovation
Returning With an Elixer for the World

It isn't what you have, but how much love you give that matters.
— Mother Theresa

LUCY AND WALTER speed toward the cemetery. Lucy can't believe that they have escaped the skateboarding goons once again, but she doesn't need a psychic to know that she hasn't seen the last of them.

"Start talking, Lucy," Walt demands. "What is going on here? Shouldn't we be headed for the police station, not the cemetery? Aren't those the guys who killed that old man on the street?"

"Walter, I'm not sure about anything right now except that I have to get to the gravesite," she says anxiously.

"What gravesite, Lucy? For god's sake, talk sense."

At that moment they pull up behind a funeral procession winding its way into the Holy Names churchyard. Lucy jumps out of the car and starts running. Walt ditches the car on the side of the road and rushes to catch up with her, hoping that whatever happens, he can help her.

They come to an empty grave bordered by a pile of dirt and several forlorn-looking folding chairs. "They're going to bury him here," she says.

"Bury who?" Walt demands.

"The Bag Man," she says.

Walt has no idea what she's talking about, but before he can ask, a formally garbed priest walks up with his Bible. "It'll be a few minutes before we start. Would you like to wait in the chapel?"

Lucy runs and throws her arms around the priest, crying. "I was right! It's you. I just figured it out. Oh, Daddy, Daddy! I can't believe it's you!" she sobs.

Walt is baffled. "Daddy? You told me your parents were dead."

"Shhhh," the priest tries to quiet Lucy. He guides her toward the chapel and nods for Walt to follow. They settle into a pew, Lucy and her father clinging to one another, and Walt standing a little off to the side, trying to give them some privacy but needing to hear something that will clear his confusion.

"Where is Mom?" she asks tearfully. He shakes his head; his voice is hardly a whisper. "She's gone. She died just last month," he sighs. "It's for the best. Anyway, you wouldn't have known her; she ventured out of hiding once hoping to see you and was scarred beyond recognition in an attack by Theodore's goons." Lucy clutches her father even more tightly, sobbing bitterly.

When Lucy calms a little, she starts talking. "I knew you couldn't be dead. I knew all along." Over the years—even when she sat beside the spot where her parents' remains presumably were buried—she knew somehow that those were not her parents' bones. "And I saw you in the chapel every time I came to this cemetery to visit your graves. There was something about you." She had always felt drawn to this silent watcher. "Why didn't you speak?" she asks.

"We would both have been killed instantly if I made any contact with you."

"But why now?" she says.

"You know the answer, Lucy."

"Because I escaped from the mental block I was using to protect myself—with a little help from the Bag Man. That was you, too. I finally put it all together—you weren't the Bag Man's physical body but his insides."

"This is not making sense!" Walt bursts out finally, unable to hold back his curiosity any longer. "Start at the beginning."

"It's really not as complicated as it sounds" Lucy replies. "My mom and dad were supposed to have died on a flight to Bermuda, like I've always said. But you," looking at her father, "went somewhere else."

"Yes, when the plane made a fuel stop, we slipped away and left two

blankets plumped up like we were sleeping there. We were afraid that we would be killed when we arrived on the island, but they went after the plane, instead. We were fleeing for our lives and hoping that by leaving you behind you would be safe."

"This guy Theodore is behind all this, isn't he?"

"Yes," her dad nods. "He isn't what he appears. He was once a member of my order of priests. We are forbidden to speak the name of the order to outsiders, but we serve the light, and he lost his way."

"You mean his shadow side took over, don't you?" Lucy asks as she shudders, remembering her close call with Teddy and his minions. "But what does the bag have to do with it?" she asks.

"The bag contains a rare collection of crystal tools, the most important discoveries we've made in our work with the light. They have extraordinary power," he goes on, quite excited at the thought of his work. "They were developed to increase a person's potential using light (think of it as universal energy) to manifest thoughts and visions instantaneously."

"I used to sit and look at the bag after you were gone, but I never opened it or played with it. Something told me not to—that it wasn't a toy. It's what you used to do your crystal experiments with," she says suddenly, remembering the geometrically perfect stones in the bag. "You used to glow with light sometimes when I peeked into your lab at night. When the Bag Man helped me create that light to defeat Theodore and the skateboarders, it all came back."

Finally, Walt's reserve breaks; he can't contain himself. "Okay, okay. I'm trying to be patient here, but I have no idea what you two are talking about. What's with the bag and the light? Please, please, put me in the loop here."

Lucy's father simply nods to Walt; then focusing his attention on Lucy, he gently urges her, "Lucy, I know that you hid the bag here; that's why I stayed close by to keep an eye on you and to stop anyone from disturbing it, but you are the only one who can retrieve it without severe injury or death because we tuned the crystals to your energy before we left. I sent you a mental image of an open hole at the back of the chapel where you could hide it. My teacher placed the stone over it; he's passed on."

"He was the old man," Lucy cries, "the one the skateboarders killed,

Power Choices

right?" As her dad nods, she continues, "He sacrificed himself so you could project into his physical body. When I was little, you told me a story about that technique before you left."

"It was the only way I could contact you without tipping off Theodore."

"It doesn't make a lot of sense to me, but let's get the bag out if it's here." Walt demands.

Lucy walks to the back of the chapel and starts counting the stone tiles in the floor. When she gets to seven, she beckons the two men over. "Come and move this stone," she says. It takes both Walt and her father to loosen the heavy stone, but they are finally able to lift it. There is the bag—an ordinary looking little girl's pink travel bag, moldy with age.

Lucy tries to hand the bag to her father who refuses it saying, "It's yours, but I couldn't give it to you until I knew you could handle it. All I could do was keep watch over it. You've awakened, and now you have enough power to use the tools and to protect yourself. You'll need it. Unfortunately, my enemies have never given up the hope that they could get hold of the stones. There's no telling how they might use the power those stones contain. We must make sure it's used for good. You must always be on guard. You'll have to work with the tools to discover their true power. It's different for each person, but I think you will have much greater results than your mother and I had."

Lucy's father pulls her close and embraces her, and before he can say a word, Lucy begins to cry again. His own voice seems to choke him, "I wish I could stay, Lucy, but my time is up. Walter, help her as much as you can, please. I can see how much you love her. And obviously she loves you too."

"Daddy. Daddy, please don't..." Lucy sobs as he kisses her cheek and hugs her. And then he disappears, completely, as Lucy and Walt stand there awestruck for a moment; then Lucy falls weeping into Walt's arms as he stares at the empty space in disbelief.

"I guess you can explain that too, one of these days," he whispers to Lucy, who is still clutching the pink bag tightly.

Lucy has come to the end of her unexpected and reluctant quest. The insight that she has gained have helped her to overcome emotional blocks and indecisiveness that had kept her stuck in her life. She has discovered power she didn't know that she had,

Innovation

found answers to nagging questions and reconnected with her family and her past. She now has a final decision to make, how will I put this power to use? As her father has admonished her, to guard it but use it for good.

WE NEED A HERO

Every child has their unique genius. If the teacher does not find it, the teacher has failed. — Motto over the entrance to the Sri Aourobindo School, Pondicherrry, India

Heroes in ancient myths were women and men who became strong, brave, and bold by taking on, however reluctantly, the challenges put before them, including monsters, giants, villains, Gorgons, and forests full of dragons. The physical challenges they faced symbolize the inner battles we must all fight. But in modern times, with dungeons and dragons relegated to video games, what are would-be heroes to do? There's still work for the heroic at heart—perhaps more work than ever.

The new millennium hero is a seeker—someone who is looking for the truth, for deeper understanding, for greater meaning in one's own life and in the lives of the people in one's community and culture. This hero steps out of the box—and pushes us out of the box as well, if we will go, by extending our ideas and taking us to the next level. Through their actions, this hero moves us all forward in a positive direction. Our "dragons" are the seemingly interminable conflicts in places like Sudan, Israel and Palestine, Haiti, and Iraq. Our "giants" are the clash between China and Tibet, North and South Korea, the United States and Cuba, even the Crips and the Bloods—some are the kinds of quarrels that have gone on for so long that few people really remember what all the fighting was about in the first place. Today's heroes are challenged to put a stop to these often deadly conflicts. Heroes are also needed to heal the kinds of personal, internal fears that turn to prejudices that then devolve into cultural "isms"—racism, sexism, homophobia, religious intolerance, and other forms of injustice. They have to use their heroic power to free themselves and to find solutions that will end homelessness and poverty; that will bring people to better physical and mental health; that will help people move away from rampant divorce, family violence, and addictions. A hero today is someone who is working to end unnecessary suffering. This work does not require swords and shields—at least not physical ones. These battles are fought in the hearts and minds of individual people.

By this definition, a seeker is automatically an innovator—someone who is a leading light, a trendsetter—because he or she is looking at things from a different perspective and asking the difficult questions in order to bring about change. Heroes have to take a new approach to things—because they see that the same old way of doing things will not help move people forward.

Some people might be under the impression that the heroism of physical giant-slaying would be more difficult than the kind of innovation we're talking about here. After all, innovation is a concept, an idea; it's not even a "thing." But look at how dangerous innovation can be: Martin Luther King, Medgar Evers, Malcolm X, and countless others were killed because of the innovative idea that people of all races should be treated equally. The Dalai Lama lives in exile because his idea that his people should be able to live and worship as they wish is a threat to the Chinese invaders of his land. Nelson Mandela was imprisoned for almost thirty years because he had the novel idea that black South Africans should not be treated as marginal citizens of their native country. Aung San Suu Kyi lives under house arrest and never saw her husband again—who died far from her in England—because she is committed to democracy in Burma, and social activist Rigoberta Minchu lives in exile under threat of death if she ever returns to her native Guatemala. Innovators put their lives on the line for their humanitarian beliefs. To risk your very life for the greater good—I don't know of any better definition of a hero.

The question we are seeking to answer in this book is, "How do we reach the point in our life where we can create *constructive* change in our world?" We must pass all of the signposts—and address all the challenges that we come to at each sign—so we can choose to be the most effective innovators possible. Whether you desire change within yourself, within your family, your community, your nation, or the world, innovation encompasses all of these.

CREATING BALANCE IN YOUR LIFE

We can be sure that the greatest hope for maintaining equilibrium in the face of any situation rests within ourselves.
— Francis J. Braceland

Like Lucy, we face many tests and many challenges as we travel along the road of life. We may not literally be pushed into a hole and have the kind of Alice-in-Wonderland experience she had, but we certainly have mental and emotional "holes" that we fall into, and our personal dramas are just as demanding. Among them is the challenge to achieve a balanced existence—physically, emotionally, mentally, and spiritually. That brings us again to the idea of balancing opposite energies—masculine and feminine (yin and yang), wisdom and truth, rest and activity, Eastern and Western perspectives, spirituality and science, and our inner and outer life. I have emphasized that in this book because finding balance is the key to our ultimate success: the ability to innovate. Let's explore the value of balance in choosing innovation.

The Master of the Estate

Once, not so long ago, not so far away, an owner of a small manor worked diligently to make a living from his holdings. Over time he built a vast estate, including a magnificent castle that necessitated hiring a large staff to operate and manage it. More than anything he desired to retire to his library in the tower to pursue his great love of esoteric study. While he'd been working so hard to build up his estate, his duties rarely permitted this indulgence. But now he could shut his door and delve into his reading, writing, and rumination to his heart's content after making just one more hire: an overseer to manage all of the other managers he'd employed. He found a suitable person in a man named Will. The master kept a watchful eye on Will for the first few weeks and found him so capable that he felt increasingly comfortable leaving the estate's management in Will's hands while he spent more time at his studies.

Will was a big, strong fellow with a shrewd mind, and he soon discovered that, with the master so absorbed, he was the sole power on the estate. He made himself quite at home. With his feet propped up and his arms behind his head, he issued orders to his liking. The other workers came to learn that Will had a foul temper. He raged at them if they made a mistake or otherwise displeased him, yelling and even throwing things. The servants feared him and avoided disturbing him at all costs.

One day Will was reclining on cushions, as was his usual habit, when there was a soft knock at the door. "Would someone get the damned door?" yelled Will. But the servants were all in the fields; so he arose, grumbling, and lumbered to the door. He was surprised to find a lovely young girl standing on the threshold, dressed in a simple but elegant gown and holding a scroll. "And who are you, my pretty?" he leered.

"My name is Love," she answered, "I have a message for the master."

"Well, I'm in charge here; I'll take it," Will replied.

"I'm so sorry," she said, "I can only give it to the master."

Will was enraged. "How dare you thwart my authority? Don't you know who I am? Get out of here!" And he slammed the door in Love's face. He sneered as he watched the lovely girl walk away, but the encounter put him in a particularly bad temper.

The next day, Will's mood hadn't lifted any. He lay fitfully on the cushions when again, a soft knock came again at the door. He smiled, "Ha, I'll bet its Love again, and she's come to her senses and is ready to give me the message." He rushed to the door. He'd been right. There stood Love once again, but the same scene ensued as she refused to surrender her message to anyone but the master.

Will's rage boiled over. "You idiot!" *he screamed.* "No one crosses me and gets away with it! Don't ever show your face around here again, or I'll make you sorry!" *Love turned and walked sadly away as Will continued his abuse and threats. Somehow she wasn't struck by the potted plants Will threw at her or even startled by the sound of them shattering behind her.*

But up in the tower, the master heard the crashing pots and Will's yelling; he ventured down to investigate. "Is everything all right here?" *he queried Will.*

Quickly closing the door and smiling as he always did with the master; Will reassured him, "Of course, Master, you know you have nothing to worry about when I am in charge. There was a beggar at the door, but everything is fine. You shouldn't interrupt your studies over any trivia that happens down here." *Will sent the master back to the tower.*

The master retreated, but he couldn't help feeling disturbed. "Maybe I really ought to spend more time downstairs," *he thought.* "Something's not quite right with Will; I almost felt that he was ordering me back to the tower. Maybe tomorrow I'll check on things."

Meanwhile, Will found a heavy club and hid it behind the sofa where he slept. All night, he paced the floor, muttering and cursing. "Just let Love show her face," *he raged. And all morning he was cursing, kicking anything that crossed his path—pets, furniture legs, servants who brought his food. By midday he was apoplectic. And then he heard the knock. Will grabbed the club and lunged for the door. There she was, as lovely, humble, and calm as ever.* "Give it to me!" *he screamed as soon as he saw her. When she shook her head no, Will didn't hesitate. With all the force of his size and his anger, he struck her.*

Again the master heard the noise and came running down. He recognized Love lying in the doorway, obviously dead. He cried out, "Love! Will, what have you done?" *Will spun around, still blind with anger and wielding the club. He lifted the club and struck the master a fatal blow.* ❧

In the preceding allegory, we see the danger of living a life that is out of balance. The estate owner spent so much time with his intellectual pursuits that he had neglected both his heart and his worldly affairs—and in the end, he lost both. He wanted so much to pursue the life of the mind that everything else was left by the wayside. Sadly, the result was the degradation of everything he'd worked for and built—and worse, the death of love. Because Will was out of control, representing a lack of self-mastery, the owner didn't get to see the fruits of his intellectual work either. Ironically, he might have wrought wonderful innovations had he maintained balance in his life and taken responsibility for his affairs.

Quite often I see people who have become so involved in their spiritual lives that they neglect everything else. You've probably seen them: They go to church every time the doors open, devote an inordinate portion of their budget to church activities, and spend much of their energy on religious pursuits. When there's a problem—their finances are in shambles, their relationships are crumbling, they're having a crisis of some sort—these are the people who say, "Why did God do this to me? Well, God will find a way." Now, understand that I don't have anything against people being devoted to their spiritual pursuits, but when a person turns things over to God without using the gifts and opportunities that their God has provided for them to help themselves; they are suffering unnecessarily as a result of imbalance, not to mention blaming God for their shortcomings. Over the years when I have helped people in this frame of mind, I have said, God is not going to make your breakfast for you. Even though it may seem that a life dedicated to spiritual pursuits alone is desirable, it can also lead to destructive imbalance if we ignore life's other demands. And there is nothing that says we can't be strong in our faith and spiritually devoted, and still be mindful of taking care of our mental, physical, and emotional needs.

I have often been called to do mediation and healing work for spiritual communities in which there have been conflicts or sexual improprieties that have torn the community apart. In particular, I frequently find myself helping these communities deal with the fallout when the spiritual leader has had an affair outside of marriage, had improper relationships with congregants, or is otherwise acting out sexually. Oftentimes, people say, "Well, he wasn't really a man (or woman) of God." In fact, the person may be spiritually advanced—may in fact have received a strong call to ministry or spiritual leadership—but has not done her or his emotional insight work or worked out his or her true intention. If a person hasn't developed all the other areas of life, then the fully developed area also suffers. In a case where a leader has exhibited such a weakness, the entire organization needs to heal—not just the person who did the acting out. This healing depends on the people in that community expressing their feelings and doing some deep emotional work to bring about the needed balance so that they have the wherewithal to cope with the crisis in their beloved community. Otherwise, their feelings, fears, and disappointments about the behavior of their "parent" can cause them to act out themselves in some way.

We live in the world, not in the heavens (not yet, at least), and there is much work to do here—work that requires us to pay attention to all aspects of our lives. It requires our minds and hearts and our physical and spiritual energies. One example of balancing the spiritual life with the practical can be seen in a habit of His Holiness the Dalai Lama. He has said that at the end of each day, he writes down every penny he spent that day. He says that this is an exercise in mindfulness. I think it represents a very interesting marriage between the spiritual world and the earthly world—and an innovative way of looking at the relationship between the two.

Similarly, one of my clients told me that everything in her life reached a new state of abundance when she realized that she was repeating her parents' workaholic patterns. Her innovation was to make some changes in her work life—working eight hours a day instead of sixteen; then she went to a three-day workweek. As a result of her changes she later told me, "Even though I was working less, I was working smarter, and the money/contracts/checks began to pour in. I have time for my husband, and we have renewed our passion." Her sense of joy and well-being exceeded anything she had imagined possible. She said, "I feel like I'm living my life for the first time, and everything just seems to flow." That's a sure sign that her energies are in balance.

When we travel life's journey following the guideposts and making positive power choices, we free up the energies that enable us to bring enhanced self-mastery to the business of daily life. Now we confront the ultimate question: what do we do with our hard-won wisdom, courage, and love?

KINDNESS AND COMPASSION

No act of kindness, no matter how small, is ever wasted.
— Aesop

The religion I practice is kindness.
— The Dalai Lama

The quality of kindness seems like such a simple thing. There's nothing complicated about it; it's easy to understand. Yet, we have only to look around us to see how much more of this "simple thing" we could use. Often, people are rude to one another—in our business transactions, on the phone, on the highways. We tend to be so focused on ourselves and so eager to make sure that we get our own needs met that we are willing to ignore the needs and feelings of others. We suffer from the emotional blunting that results from chronic stress, and we literally feel an intense inner pressure due to the constant experience that "there isn't enough time." For these reasons, the act of being kind becomes an innovation—a new, maverick way of being. And it's incredibly powerful and effective.

One of the biggest stumbling blocks to choosing kindness as a way of being is when we choose money and the acquisition of things over the development of our own inner substance and the appreciation of inner substance in other people. When we're so focused on "getting," it becomes difficult to be present with ourselves, to be in tune with our own feelings, never mind with other people. Our minds are constantly focused on where the next check is going to come from, how we're going to close the next big deal, what we're going to do to hit our jackpot—and then what we're going to do with it when we get it. There's no time to check on your elderly neighbor. You're moving too fast to ask how your office mate's root canal turned out. You don't have enough energy left at the end of the day to really listen to your child talk about her day at school.

The pull to do more, have more, be more is so strong in our culture that it takes a very brave person to opt out of the race. Those who do, face all kinds of stigmas. Karen, a very busy, high-level executive at a media organization got a taste of this at the going-away party for a colleague who'd decided to quit her job in order to stay at home with her young children. As she extended her well wishes to her departing coworker, Karen told her, "I envy you." Karen's job involves long hours and a good deal of travel; she often spends days at a time away from her own preschool-age son, and the separation is as difficult for her as it is for him. Later another office mate cornered Karen: "You didn't really mean what you said about envying her, did you?" Karen assured her that she did. The response was incredulous, almost hostile. "But you have a great career," the colleague said. "Why would you give that up?" She did not understand that, for Karen, work is important, but family is a priority. In fact, Karen finds that many of her colleagues are finding nannies and extended day-care settings so they'll be able to work more. Meanwhile, Karen is looking for ways to spend more time at home with her son. She knows that the pain she feels each time she leaves him is a signal for her to make some kind of change in her life. She's started counseling in an effort to free up her creativity so she can come up with an innovative plan that will enable her to make a living while she spends more time with her family.

But this isn't what most people do. Most of us do what Karen herself used to do: work long hours, make as much money as we can, and assuage our guilt by using the money to buy our children all sorts of toys and gadgets, expensive clothes, and lavish vacations. When we do this, we're unconsciously teaching our children that life involves only working, working, working, and spending, spending, spending—almost guaranteeing that they'll follow our pattern of workaholism. (There's another one of those intergenerational patterns.) We aren't teaching our children balance, and we aren't showing them how to take time to get in touch with themselves (another form of kindness), to enjoy the peace in nature, and to be kind to others.

It is in being awake to our own feelings and aware of our behaviors that our hearts become softened, and we develop compassion, mercy, and kindness. There isn't a single world religion that doesn't teach kindness. In fact, kindness and justice, mercy and compassion are all closely related and are exemplified in the lives of the heroes whose life stories we have examined.

MICHAEL AND ANGELA

My client Michael started psychotherapy with me after an "international incident" of sorts. He had gone to Hong Kong to represent his multinational company in an important bid conference, but he was feeling so out of it in the meeting that he embarrassed himself.

"I just couldn't focus my thoughts or think clearly," he said. "I knew I was making a fool of myself by the looks on people's faces. That trip was my chance to grab the brass ring; I would have no worries after that deal was in place. When I got on the plane to return home, I sank into my first class seat saying a prayer, 'God, just please help me.' When I landed, my wife picked me up and said, 'We have an appointment with a marriage therapist.' I figured she was bringing me here to tell me she wants a divorce."

"Maybe your prayers have been answered." I said. Then, on a hunch, I asked him how much he drank.

"Not that much," he told me. "I don't drink hard alcohol, just a few beers."

"How many?"

"Well, maybe eight to ten if we are out on the town."

Realizing his idea of "a few" had to be based on a childhood norm, I asked him how many beers his dad drank.

"Well, my dad had a problem. He brewed his own German- style beer and drank anywhere from twelve to sixteen bottles every night."

Michael's focus had been material gain, and the mad dash to grab the brass ring had created so much anxiety that he drank more and more beer to escape it. He didn't notice that the dependence on alcohol was creeping up on him. He had reached the point where he came home, drank until he fell asleep, and then repeated the behavior the next day. For all intents and purposes, Angela was a single mother to their two daughters. It was an act of heroic proportions that allowed Angela to pick up the phone and make their first appointment because, as you might have guessed, she was following her mother's pattern of "putting up" with her drug-addicted father.

Michael began going to Alcoholics Anonymous while his wife, Angela, went to Al-Anon. Each of them experienced profound change wrought by their work in their respective programs; their therapy brought them to a place of deep spiritual awakening. They were attracted to Buddhism and became leaders and teachers in their spiritual community. Michael left his job and now travels the world helping corporations to make good fiscal decisions that also honor human rights and the environment. Angela now creates magnificent paintings that reflect spiritual principles (compassion, kindness) and incorporate quotes from Buddhist teachings. Michael and Angela used innovation in their marriage as the jumping-off point for innovation in their spiritual and work lives, ultimately leading them to make beautiful contributions in the world.

INNOVATIVE LIFE PARTNERSHIPS

Marriage is the best spiritual path you will ever find.
— Stephen Levine

I cannot tell you how important the area of innovation is to me as it relates to life partnerships. The cost of shattered relationships extends to every aspect of our lives. We all know that most children of divorce suffer emotionally, in school performance and in their subsequent adult relationships. Breakups impact physical and emotional health (they get the second-highest score on the life stress units scale we discussed earlier), which of course throws careers off track and diminishes the positive impact that the couple or family could have in their community. Couples who split also lose out financially—especially the women with children—which has led to a movement to stop what is now being called the feminization of poverty. Even women who are doing well professionally and financially lose out because the laws that were designed to ameliorate the impact on divorced mothers are unequally applied to men who earn less but do not share equally the responsibility for children or the home.

The wonderful contributions that Angela and Michael made through their work would have been delayed or impossible if they had expended their energy on starting over after a marital split. In fact, the astonishing truth is that two out of three marriages that end in divorce could have been saved if the couple had sought qualified marital therapy. I would love to see an innovative movement to save relationships akin to the seat belt campaign that has saved so many lives. Okay, I confess I'm already working on it; care to join me? Relationships are one of the best paths of transformation available to us; I believe everyone could benefit from getting married and learning the skills to stay married if you really want to learn the virtues of patience, kindness, compassion, and how to love unconditionally.

Innovation

Quan Yin

In Eastern traditions, there is a beautiful and graceful goddess who embodies mercy and compassion. Various forms, names, and stories of this goddess of mercy have spread throughout many parts of Asia and even beyond the borders of the continent and the spiritual traditions encompassing Buddhism, Taoism, and Hinduism. Here, we will call her Quan Yin.

There are a number of stories about the generous life of Quan Yin. One of the more prominent tales describes her as a Buddhist who, through great love and sacrifice during her life, earned the right to enter Nirvana upon her death. Standing at the gates to paradise, she heard a cry of anguish from the earth below. Instead of accepting her place in Nirvana, she gave up the reward of eternal bliss, turning back to earth to find and soothe the source of that mournful cry. Another story holds that she fed starving people by giving them milk from her breasts, the drops of which manifested as grains of rice. In the end, she found her immortality in the hearts of the suffering because she was so willing to give. Her popularity has grown through the centuries, and now she is revered as the goddess who comforts the sick, troubled, lost, senile, and unfortunate.

FORGIVING YOURSELF

Forgiveness is the key to happiness.
— The Course in Miracles

What an example Quan Yin is of mercy and faith, giving up her heavenly reward to remain on earth and be of service here. Maybe we need a goddess in the West to remind us to - practice mercy because, unfortunately, most of us here focus on a god of judgment and punishment. This god can and does grant tender mercies, but we tend to focus more on his vengeance. I think of the "pro-life" activists who go to the extreme of bombing abortion clinics—taking lives in the name of saving lives—because they believe that God has judged those people to be sinners and that they must help God exact punishment. An innovative hero (with faith in a compassionate God) would look for ways to make abortion clinics irrelevant, obsolete. This hero would focus on educating men and women to be responsible in their choices and mindful of the way they use their bodies. His focus would be on helping people have the resources and skills to take care of the children they decided to have, and counseling people to forgive themselves and heal from the experience of unplanned pregnancy. A hero would help to find homes for the thousands of lonely children growing up in foster care and temporary shelters that turn them out, without help, when they reach eighteen. Yes, compassion, mercy, and forgiveness are very powerful.

This last idea—the idea of forgiving yourself—is an important one in any context. For most of us, the place we may truly need to practice mercy is with our self. Buddhist teachers Stephen and Ondrea Levine often work with people who are terminally ill or who are caring for people who are. Because these caretakers are prone to losing their boundaries and to ending up exhausted, the Levines remind them, "Have mercy on yourself; be merciful even if you are as yet unskillful."

The lack of skill the Levines speak of goes back to what I said earlier about people who are strong in one area but still have work to do in others. We may be strongly called to a certain purpose—in this case to help someone who is ill or dying—but we may have unfinished internal business that can get in the way of our providing the best possible assistance. That doesn't mean we shouldn't follow our call, but we also have to be aware that we may be confronted with our own very human lack of understanding or feelings that overwhelm us—our naked Achilles heel. It doesn't mean we're bad people, unfit to offer anything to the world; it simply means we have room to grow. I can remember warming the pew of the Southern Baptist church I grew up attending and

Innovation

hearing one of the ministers put it like this, "God isn't through with me yet. I have sinned and fallen short of the mark."

Even Mother Theresa seems to have made her share of mistakes, having received sharp criticism for her fiscal management, politics, and medical care—though it is a rare person who would question the purity of her motives. Does this mean that she should be condemned? Or is this a place to apply forgiveness and mercy? Your verdict may have less to do with the Catholic mother and more to do with how much healing of your own wounds you have accomplished. Those who have the capacity to forgive themselves find it easier to forgive others.

POWER TOOL
LOVE YOURSELF

This simple exercise will help you increase your self-love.

Stand in front of a mirror. Look directly into your eyes and say "I love you" to yourself, using your name. Say it twelve times, twelve different ways; change your voice and intonation each time.

You may be thinking, "No way. That's not something I would ever be comfortable doing." Good! *If you are comfortable with this exercise, and it doesn't feel at all strange then you don't need it. But do it anyway.*

Do this exercise every day, morning and night, after you brush your teeth. This is the place to use your courage to practice loving yourself. Do it consistently for just twenty-one days, and notice how you feel.

RIGOBERTA MINCHU

Born in Guatemala to a poor peasant family descended from the Mayans, Rigoberta Minchu began working on her family's farm when she was only eight years old. The grinding poverty and hard work were made much worse by the oppression that the ruling military regime forced on the Indian population. But Rigoberta didn't resign herself to this as her lot in life.

Through the Catholic Church, Rigoberta learned to read and write, and she became involved in social reform and women's rights work. She was following the example of her freedom—seeking family, many of whom were also involved in social reform. The military imprisoned and tortured her activist father; he was burned to death by the police while taking part in a peaceful protest. Rigoberta's brother was also tortured and killed. Her mother was tortured, raped and then killed while in police custody. There seemed to be no end to young Rigoberta's sorrow. Instead of crumbling, though, she worked harder for justice.

Rigoberta pressed on with her work and taught herself Spanish so she could tell the story of her people to the outside world, which she did in *I, Rigoberta*, the biography written on her life. She eventually had to flee Guatemala; fearing for her life, she continued organizing social reform from abroad. She made the most innovative choice possible, to return violence and hatred with peaceful resistance. This is what made Rigoberta a hero.

When the Nobel Peace Prize committee honored her, the president of the committee remarked, "There are those shining individual examples of people who manage to preserve their humanity in brutal and violent surroundings, of persons who for that very reason compel our own special admiration and respect. Such people give us hope that there are ways out of the vicious circle."

Innovation

OUTSIDE THE BOX

To love yourself is a truly revolutionary act.
— Dr. Cornell West

Heroes look outside the circle of their lives and think outside the box of accepted thinking and practices. Often they refuse even to see the box, soaring past its walls as if the barriers didn't exist. They can do it because somehow they believe that in the vast universe there must be a way to resolve any issue, correct any problem. Heroes make the transcendent choice to find a more humane approach—or as Virginia Satir would have said, a "more fully human approach"—to injustice and tragedy. The Dalai Lama in responding to China's devastating invasion of Tibet says, "Compassion for my enemy is the proper response, but nonviolent action must be taken to correct wrong acts."

In the terrible aftermath of Hurricane Katrina, many stories of heroism emerged. One that gripped me, as I watched a news report two days after the storm and the flood, was of the mother who, realizing that her husband could not hold onto her and their children said to him, "You have let go of me. Save the children." She pulled away from him and was swept into the floodwaters. This bereft father and husband openly wept as he told the story—as did the reporter who was interviewing him. As did I. The willingness to die for what we hold dear, whether our children or a just cause, motivated ordinary people like Nelson Mandela and Martin Luther King, Rigoberta Minchu and Las Madres de la Plaza de Mayo.

Aung San Suu Kyi of Myanmar remains under house arrest for countering the military regime that had violently crushed democracy in her land. She had opportunities to flee, but if she left, she knew she would never be able to reenter the country. For her, it was more important to stay in order to continue her father's work of liberating the country formerly known as Burma. Her sacrifice has been tremendous. She was separated from her husband and children. Her husband died of cancer in England without her ever having had the opportunity see him, to hold and comfort him during his illness. She doesn't know when she will see her children again. Her heroic struggle was recognized with the Nobel Peace prize.

Ireland's Betty Williams and Mairead Carrigan founded People for Peace in response to the hostilities between Northern and Southern Ireland. These two innovators decided to take a stand for peace after innocent children were killed in the conflict between the Protestant and Catholic factions in Northern Ireland. They risked their lives in standing for peace in the face of British and IRA forces. They were awarded the Nobel Peace prize for their efforts.

The first African woman to receive a Nobel Peace prize was Dr. Wangari Maathai, founder of the Greenbelt movement of Kenya. She is an environmental activist who not only organized African women to plant over twenty thousand trees but also works tirelessly to stop land-grabbing practices and to put natural resources to sustainable uses. She also strives to educate and empower women in the area of health and HIV prevention.

These heroes all rated their personal existence as less important than that purpose which they served—the good of others and service to the cause of a humane and peaceful life and a healthy environment for all.

THE COURAGE TO SERVE

Courage is the price that life exacts for granting peace.
— Amelia Earhart

Mitakaye Oyasin signifies a way of life for the Sioux people; in English it translates to mean "all my relations." This Lakota word is used to end and to begin all spiritual ceremonies. I first learned the word when I participated in an indigenous sweat lodge ritual. Upon entering and exiting a sweat lodge, you say *Mitakaye Oyasin* to direct the purification energy that is generated by the sweating, praying, and chanting to all those to whom we are connected.

In the traditions of indigenous people everywhere, "all my relations" means "all of life." When you hear Native people talk of

Innovation

Brother Wolf or Grandmother Moon, these aren't just quaint terms. The Native American worldview has always been that all beings on the planet are related—animals, plants, even the sun, moon, and weather. The earth herself is revered as our mother. Nothing exists that isn't closely connected with us. That means that when you interact with, say, a plant or an animal, you treat it with the respect and care with which you would want to be treated. Think about this in the context of Native peoples hunting, fishing, and gathering vegetables to eat. They did what they needed to do to feed, clothe, and house their families. But they respected the deer, the buffalo, the fish, and the sage. So when they took something, they only took what was needed; they gave thanks for it before and after they took it, and they used as much of it as possible, as wisely as possible.

Because they believe that everything is related, native peoples also believe that their "brothers" and "sisters" would be willing—if approached respectfully—to offer themselves in service to the tribe and its people, and that there would be no retribution for the warrior who killed a buffalo or for the woman who gathered herbs. Every being in the equation is offering a service to other "relations."

This idea of service is the culmination of every myth. The hero returns home after a long journey with the reward, the boon, the gift she has to offer as a result of the challenge she has faced and the triumph she has experienced. She has something of value to give to the people she cares about, including herself.

The strength we gain in the process of facing our trials is the strength we need to go forward and to be of service in the greatest way that we can. One yardstick that I use when I'm trying to decide whether or not to do a thing is: "How far will the light from this endeavor reach?" I read that line somewhere years ago—I wish I knew where—and it has served me well in making choices about projects that I will take on. For all of us, it is important to consider the best way to be of service for ourselves and for others. The following fable from Down Under beautifully portrays such extensive service; because of the selfless way in which it was offered, it brought about innovation that transformed all of life.

The Kiwi Birds

The Maori of New Zealand tell a delightful tale about how the kiwi birds lost their wings. *One day, Tanemahuta walked through the forest and noticed that his children, the trees, were becoming sick because the bugs were eating them. He talked with his brother Tanehokahoka, the father of the birds. "Something is eating my children," Tanemahuta explained, "I need your help. One of your children must come down from the forest roof and live on the floor so that my children and your home may be saved. Who among you will help?"*

No bird spoke.

Then Tanehokahoka asked each of his children the same question. Tui looked down at the cold dark earth and, shuddering in fear, said, "I'm afraid of the dark. I like it up here where it is bright." Pukeko responded, "It's too damp down there. I don't want to get my feet wet." Pipiwharauroa claimed, "I am too busy building my nest so I'm not available. Ask someone else."

With great sadness, the father of the birds realized that none of his children would make the sacrifice. But if none did, they all would become homeless. He looked at Kiwi. "E Kiwi, will you come down from the forest roof?" Kiwi looked at the sun filtering through the leaves, then looked at his family, and then looked at the cold damp ground. "I will."

Tanemahuta warned Kiwi that such a choice would change him. His legs would become strong so he could rip apart the logs, and his beautiful colored feathers would fade, and his wings would never again let him fly to the forest roof. Kiwi merely repeated, "I will." Tanehokahoka and Tanemahuta knew that this bird was giving them all hope.

Tanehokahoka then turned to the other birds and rebuked, "E Tui, because you were too frightened, you will now wear two white feathers at your throat forever marking you as a coward. Pukeko, because you would not get your feet wet, from now on you will live in the swamp. Pipiwharauroa, because you were too busy building your nest, you will never build another. You will lay your eggs in other birds' nests. But, my dear Kiwi, because of your great sacrifice, you will be the most well-known, honored, and loved bird of them all."

Kiwi is like one of our great heroes—someone who is best known because they dared to forgo their own gain to sacrifice for the greater good. What is also interesting in this story is that those who *refused* the call were changed in a way that tied them to their problem even more tightly. They bore inescapable reminders of their cowardice and fear. How like we humans who, upon refusing to grow and change, can count on facing the issue in a more intense and unavoidable way. When we fail to do something about our challenges today—whether it is refusing to make lifestyle changes that would protect our health, ignoring needed growth within our family, or ignoring situations in our community—we should expect to be faced with them tomorrow, only they will be harder. But when you embrace a challenge, you allow yourself to be changed for the benefit of all. ❧

POWER TOOL
LOVE ALL

This exercise ought to push a few buttons. As you walk or drive around for the next twenty-one days, think "I love you" about everyone and everything that you see. Yes, plants and animals too! I've had a lot of fun doing this, it changes my day completely when I do it. You'll see.

EMBRACING THE TRUTH

When we get stuck and seek to avoid a problem, our actions or lack thereof only make the problem more costly later. There is an inexorable movement in the universe that pulls us, pushes us, sometimes drop-kicks us, through shattering initiation to move forward on the journey of growth and evolution. The tragedy that evolved in New Orleans after Katrina makes this point. The Army Corps of Engineers had requested funds to repair the levee that held water back from this sub-sea level city. The cost to make the repairs was a fraction of the $100 billion estimated for cleaning and rebuilding after the city was destroyed. Now, not only will it cost billions more to rebuild, but a price has been paid in terms of the invaluable human lives that have been lost and the terrible suffering endured.

For many years, the hidden, insidious forces of racism and classicism have been at work, and we have turned away from the truth which Katrina revealed: here among us, our sisters and brothers in New Orleans have been suffering all along.

Buddhist teacher Frank Ostesseski (founder of the Alaya Institute) told me in a television interview for Link Television that he founded the Zen Hospice because serving those who were dying helped him to allow his heart to break, to let his fears and sadness be transformed into compassion. By embracing our feelings and our own suffering, we can better sense our own or someone else's, which opens us to deep spiritual transformation, which in turn transforms every area of our being.

Philosopher Jacob Needleman, interviewed on the Link Television channel (satellite dish only) on a program called *Lunch with Bokara*, said, "The only happy people I know are those who are of service." We can choose to be an innovator and to be of service by taking the lessons from our challenges and capturing the boon. Whether we consciously choose it or not, our journey continues to offer opportunities to grow through investigation, initiation, and all the other power choices. You can run, but you can't hide; this seems to be the law of life. Our life experiences are all weighed in the end by how much our hearts have grown in acquiring love, wisdom, and truth. This acquisition allows us to be the most creative and innovative in contributing our unique gifts to the world.

Ma'at

Weighing someone's heart was the ticket to paradise in Egyptian lore. *Ma'at, the Egyptian goddess of physical and moral laws, of order and truth, held the scales and made the decision. Since she instilled order over chaos, the Egyptians believed that if the pharaoh ever failed to live by and maintain* ma'at *(order and law), chaos would return to Egypt, and the world and all on it would be destroyed. Furthermore, Ma'at was the judge who would grant or deny eternal life to all who died. Legend says that when someone dies, Ma'at's ostrich feather—the accessory that heralds part of her fame and her role within Egyptian mythology—is placed on the scale with the deceased's heart. If the person's heart was as light as the feather, it was free of evil and sin and the person was granted eternal life.*

INNOVATIVE JUSTICE AND MERCY

As you journey through life, take a minute every now and then to give a thought for the other fellow. He could be plotting something.
— Dick Browne, Hagar the Horrible comic strip

We can certainly learn something from the story of Ma'at since our justice system is traditionally one in which we fail to consider the heart at all—our present judicial system needs heroic overcoming to make it fair and merciful. This is an area where creative innovation could work miracles. As it stands, people who are not criminals are often swept into the prison system undeservedly. Proving this point, since DNA became acceptable as evidence, hundreds of people have had their sentences overturned. Fortunate for them, but it proves how defective the justice system is. The facts show that guilty or innocent, you are more likely to have a favorable outcome if you are someone of financial means and of European ancestry. Together these factors result in a current U.S. prison population in the millions—the majority of the inmates being men of color.

Perhaps the greatest problem with our justice system is that it doesn't do anything to help remediate crime. People are released from prison having "paid their debt to society." In reality, most of them haven't done anything but sit in a cell, bored, endangered, their humanity slipping away day by day. By the time they emerge into the bright light of freedom, they are damaged and broken. Families are torn apart. Reputations are ruined. Even an innocent man released from prison bears the psychological scars from the experience and can never do enough to erase the stigma of having "done a bid." It's enough to make a person return to the criminal life—and many people do. Worse, their children are likely to do the same. The breakdown of family ties and support that occurs when a family member is sent away often results in a pattern of intergenerational imprisonment. It is a sad cycle: the family isn't strong enough to maintain constructive physical and emotional ties with the person who runs afoul of the law. And the judicial system's classist and racist application of the law takes away fathers, mothers, and other family caretakers from the communities and families that are already the most vulnerable. This further destabilizes the family, putting the next generation at risk for an encounter with the justice system.

Why would someone who has suffered the indignity of prison risk returning there? Why would sons or daughters, knowing the pain of living with a parent in prison, risk doing time? I believe the Biblical verse John 5:19 sums up the situation. "Verily, verily, I say unto you, the son can do nothing of himself, but what he seeth his father do; for whatever thing so-ever he doeth, these also doeth the son likewise." As we have seen in our chapter on insight, we are likely to repeat what we saw when we grew up. Because people who have been imprisoned are not rehabilitated and restored to their family and community, their children aren't given the support they need to cope with the absence of an imprisoned parent. It is time for a new kind of justice in the world—a kind of justice that includes both mercy and the ancient principles of restoration and maintenance of relationships within the community. Fortunately, such innovations are now underway.

In 1989, Brooklyn was the fifth most violent municipality per capita in the United States. The New York borough had nearly 750 murders between 1988 and 1989; a large proportion of the victims were children. Crime associated with drug use also skyrocketed. The community was desperate for a new solution—one that not only stopped offenders, but helped to prevent and reduce crime in the first place.

Desperation and compassion together can often lead to ingenuity. That's what happened in Brooklyn's Red Hook neighborhood. In June 2000, the Red Hook Community Justice Center, the nation's first multi-jurisdictional court, was born. A single judge at Red Hook hears neighborhood cases that would ordinarily go to three different courts—civil, family, and criminal. The court's founders realized that people's problems don't come neatly packaged under only one court's jurisdiction. Rather, the underlying and apparent problems faced by the people in Red Hook make up an intricately woven tapestry. At Red Hook, they chose to take on the whole, but they didn't stop there.

While guilty defendants are required to repay the community that they harmed through their crime, the court also addresses the underlying problems that led to their criminal behavior—perhaps addiction, homelessness, or lack of education. A typical sentence can include mandatory drug treatment, GED classes, job training, and community service, just to name a few.

When Judge Alex Calabrese, the presiding judge at the center, was asked how his previous role as a criminal court judge was different from his current role at Red Hook, he commented, "I feel that I can accomplish much more at the Justice Center. The options that I had at the Criminal Court were basically jail and no jail, with some women in drug treatment. At the Justice Center, I have a full range of services where I can release a defendant on the condition that he or she takes advantage of all these services. So you have a real chance at getting to the problem and preventing the defendant from coming back to the justice system."

So has this effort made a difference? Absolutely. The results of community surveys indicate that the quality of life for Red Hook residents improve each year, perceptions of the criminal justice system are also improving, and there is an increased amount of support for the Red Hook Community Justice Center. In fact, over 80 percent of the people surveyed indicated that they would use the services—job training, victim services, drug treatment, law-related education, and mediation—housed at the Justice Center.

This community approach to justice is at the core of many African religions, which emphasize the importance of restoring balance through adjudication and protecting relationships and the community—all by restoring everything to its rightful place. For example, in his book *African Religion*, Laurenti Magesa tells the story of a woman who stole chickens from another woman in the village. The thief was found out and brought before the village. She was ordered to sit down with the person she robbed and figure out how to make restitution. You see, when she committed a crime, she was not sent away from the community, rather through the restitution, she was bound more closely to the other members of the village. They in turn, learned to forgive and forget.

Bishop Desmond Tutu used this community-based style of justice in the Truth and Reconciliation hearings in South Africa after apartheid ended. Bringing his deep Christian faith in the power of forgiveness together with the African view of justice, he guided the new nation of South Africa through a period many had predicted would lead to a massive blood bath. Instead, all sides faced the painful, in some cases horrifying, abuses that took place under the old racist regime. There is still much work to be done to steer the country into safe waters as the people continue to recover from their troubled past, but restorative rather than retributive justice has set the country on the right path.

The area of spirituality is another area where the healing balm of heroic innovation is needed. The power choices of investigation, initiation, insight, and intuition make it easy to see that much mischief has been practiced in the name of God. Clearly, most wars are fought in the name of religion. Once a leading guru of southern India, Sathya Sai Baba, was asked why this is so, and he replied, "This is not God's will. If you want to know God's will, you must not listen to the voice of politicians but to the voice of your own conscience—which is God's voice speaking in your heart."

The power of innovation could increase our alignment with our religious beliefs. All religious traditions teach love, but do we really practice love? In the name of religion, many unwittingly practice classism, sexism, racism, homophobia, and oppression; we inflict suffering on our brothers and sisters without holding ourselves accountable for the harm we may have triggered. You may remember the case of Matthew Shepherd, the young man beaten to death by other young men of his town because he was gay. The many ministers who speak out against gay marriage would never directly advocate murder; yet they are unwittingly sowing the seeds of such crimes by preaching oppression in the form of homophobia. On more than one occasion I have sat with an aching heart as a minister preached a sermon in which they proclaim God made Adam to be with Eve not Steve. I believe in the intent of this quote from the *The Gates of Prayer* by the Central Rabbinical Committee of America: "You may not stand by as your neighbor bleeds." Thus, I find myself unable to avoid reminding these ministers that there were once laws that made it illegal for enslaved African-Americans to marry because slaves were considered subhuman—not men and women with the right to marry. Interracial couples were also legally forbidden to marry. As the Canadian Prime Minister pointed out in his address following the legalization of gay marriage in Canada, "We can't cherry-pick rights." Either every human being has rights, or one day, we could all be vulnerable to someone deciding we are on the wrong side of an arbitrary fence. When you look at history, you discover that at some point we've all had our turn as the oppressed.

I have often wondered, as I read the stories of Jesus of Nazareth who ministered to the poor, adulterers, lepers, and prisoners, where he would be ministering if he was alive today. It seems clear to me that he devoted himself to practicing love, mercy, and non-judgment; he would not be condemning anyone. What an innovation it would be if we all subscribed to love as a practice.

The status of women is another area in need of innovation in our society and indeed globally because abuses against women occur everywhere. For example, women's rights issues range from violent crimes to political, social, and religious oppression. Women are still often denied meaningful roles in religious organizations today. The ancient reverence for the feminine aspect of the divine has all but disappeared, leaving in its wake the imbalance of masculine power. The result is a lack of feminine nurturing, receptivity, and creative influence—qualities that support compassion and fairness. This calls to my mind the scene of Padme's funeral procession in *Star Wars: Return of the Sith*. We watch as the dead body of the feminine, bedecked with flowers, is borne away while the masculine shadow side of Anakin dons a black mask and cape to become Darth Vader, a dark lord.

Recent changes in the status of women in the Middle East, such as the election of the first woman official in Afghanistan, the first woman pilot in Saudi Arabia, and discussions regarding women's rights in Iraq herald a positive change to allow women more choices. In Brazil the election of Benedita de Silva from Rio de Janeiro, the first woman of African decent elected to serve as senator, focused the attention of Brazilians on the needs of the poor, Afro-Brazilians and the barbaric murders of homosexuals and street children. So much more needs to be done here at home and worldwide to return the balance of masculine and feminine power. We can each play a part by encouraging the nurturing creative qualities within our own being and in our own life.

The disparity in spiritual circles doesn't stop with women. Those of different classes don't worship together for the most part, nor do those of different races. As Martin Luther King, Jr. observed, Sunday morning is the most segregated time of the week in the United States.

Innovation

Dr. Howard Thurman, a hero of mine, took on the issue of making religion more inclusive after an interracial and interfaith group of spiritual students who wished to broaden their understanding of all faiths invited this innovator to come and speak with them. Dr. Thurman had already served as the chaplain at Morehouse and Boston colleges, and he was recognized as Dr. Martin Luther King's spiritual mentor. Along with Dr. Harold Fisk, Dr. Thurmond and that group of students decided to integrate Sunday mornings not just racially but religiously as well—honoring all traditions as sacred. They founded the Church for the Fellowship of all Peoples, the first interfaith and interracial church in the country. That was sixty years ago, and Fellowship Church continues its mission in San Francisco to promote integration of every sort and to work actively for social justice.

The church is thriving under the leadership of the Reverend Dr. Dorsey Blake, a champion of human rights, equality, and the social-justice work that typifies Fellowship Church. Among the unsung heroes I know, Dr Dorsey Blake tops my list. Born in Kansas City, Missouri, he is the fourth of nine children born to a dedicated homemaker and a minister father who was the first African-American to attend Rockhurst College in Kansas City, Missouri. The future theologian received his first initiation into the need for social justice at age eighteen when his brother was killed in a racial incident. Dr. Blake once described the incident in one of his deeply insightful sermons; he related his emotional experience, the shock, the pain, the inability to believe that he would never see his brother again, and how he forever after had a sensitivity to those who were oppressed. While a student at Brown University, he met Dr. Martin Luther King Jr., and a fire ignited. From that pivotal time of his work in the civil rights movement, he has held to his mission, keeping always before him his goal of bringing justice and freedom to all people, including the freedom to worship as the constitution promises and humane values dictate, but also the freedom to live without the tyranny of the "isms".

This is the kind of innovation we need more of.

Creating Happiness

Whenever she had to warn us about life, my mother told stories that ran on like this one, a story to grow up on.
— Maxine Hong-Kingston

My colleagues in my holistic practice have broadened my understanding of the interlocking pieces of our nature as human beings. Why do I have a holistic practice? Diane Ricksecker, MPH, an energetic healer and transformation coach, says it well, "Each healing tradition, whether it addresses the mind, emotions, body, or spirit (or any combination thereof), enables us to envision more of the pieces of the jigsaw puzzle that makes up our lives. The more pieces we see, the easier it is for us to pull them all together, align them properly, and lead healthier, happier lives."

When I asked the chiropractors on our team, Dr Galina Nayfeld and Dr. Eilina Feygina, if they could tell whether a person was suffering emotional distress based on the physical symptoms they presented, they both responded, "Absolutely." In fact, they told me emphatically that if a person's systems are in balance, that person is happy.

Speaking of happiness, I can remember feeling quite miserable in my early life and having a host of physical complaints from cystitis to chronic insomnia to nebulous aches and pains a young person would not be expected to have. Clearly my emotional state and my physical distress were linked. My own life story sometimes surprises me as I reflect on it. I see that I have largely overcome the obstacles of childhood turmoil and, through persistence, determination, and the help of many wonderful teachers, achieved many of my personal goals, including a wonderful family life and spiritual development. One of the proudest moments of my life was when my older daughter organized a "no hatred here" day of silence at her high school after the Matthew Shepherd murder. Giving me more opportunities for motherly pride, my youngest daughter also consistently championed the underdog and was the confidant and justice keeper for her friends as she grew up. When

Innovation

I look at my children, I think with satisfaction that the long years of work I did on myself paid off. If you are a parent, breaking dysfunctional family patterns so that your children don't have to repeat them is the most rewarding innovation.

I once thought, "I'll never spend twenty-five years at this spiritual development stuff," but I did, and it's become a way of life; for me it's the only game in town. If you think, "It'll take too long," I say to you, hopefully, that you're going to live those years anyway; you might as well go for what you want. So many extraordinary and innovative things have been accomplished by those who stepped up when no other choice would do. Those innovators have created miracles that cause me to marvel. I thought I would never see apartheid end or the Berlin Wall come down or the end of the war in Angola or Nicaragua or Ireland. Yet they have all arrived.

Retreats, therapy, trips to India, Al-Anon, the Hoffman Institute, Reichian therapy, and a number of gifted mentors and teachers have all been part of my personal healing work. I still have work to do, such as not reacting from my childhood patterns when my husband does or says something I don't appreciate. I have to pay more attention to balancing my life so that it includes down time to relax and play and to transition to more creative projects that I want to take on. I still need to work on myself—inner work is never finished—but, oh, I feel so much freer than in years past. Because for twenty-five years, I have worked with these power choices in my private practice with hundreds of clients and with thousands of seminar and workshop participants around the world , I can confidently recommend that you use them as your signposts. I only wish that I had known about them earlier. If I had recognized some of my challenging experiences were guideposts—signs that I needed further investigation or that I was undergoing an initiation—I might have chosen to work with them, not run from them. That would have made my path much easier.

One of my favorites, the following parable has helped me to transcend many challenges in my life.

Four virtues threw a formal ball. Love, Patience, Hope, and Charity were all there making grand entrances on the red carpet in their designer gowns and ensuring that all the other virtues were having a great time. Hope noticed that a thin and pale-looking virtue in a sadly outdated gown had arrived. No one seemed to know who this poor little virtue was. Finally Charity went over to her and said, "Excuse me dear, do I know you? You look familiar, but I can't place you."

"Oh yes, we've met," said the virtue, "but it's been quite a while. I don't get asked out much. My name is Gratitude."

I recommend the radical innovation of practicing gratitude. If you do that, then you are truly a hero because gratitude shifts us from negative to positive thoughts and feelings in an almost magical way.

Gratitude is a power in and of itself. Senator Barack Obam'a electrified the Democratic Convention in 2004 when he expressed his gratitude in a powerful way: "I owe a debt to all of those who came before me." His speech made him an overnight hero to many.

You are a hero just by making the power choices to keep growing and to increase your awareness and by striving to reach higher. Your light gets brighter with each effort that you make. You are not alone; there are many of us climbing, step by step, the winding narrow path that leads us to the mountaintop of the best within us—the reunion with the divine in our hearts.

In Hindu teachings, Indra, king of the gods, vanquished a giant dragon that threatened to destroy the world with his thunderbolts. *When the monster shattered, all the waters of heaven burst free, replenishing the moisture the monster had drained away from the earth. The hero was celebrated far and wide by the grateful inhabitants of both earth and heaven; indeed, Indra himself was quite elated with his success.*

He decided to build a lavish palace for himself and soon became obsessed with the effort. His demands on the royal craftsman, Vishvakarman (himself a god), became so excessive that the craftsman, fed up with Indra's insistence on a bigger and more lavish palace each succeeding day, turned to Brahma for help. Brahma assured Vishvakarman he would take care of it and sent the craftsman back to work.

Innovation

The next morning, a young boy about age ten arrived at the door of Indra's palace. He spoke with the wisdom of a guru as he challenged Indra by stating that no previous Indra had ever succeeded in completing such a magnificent palace. The child went on to recount for the disbelieving Indra all of the Indras he had known until Indra felt quite uneasy. The child then began to laugh.

"What is so funny?" Indra asked him.

"Oh, the ants," he replied, "each was once an Indra, just as you are."

An army of ants marching across the floor stunned Indra. Coming to his senses and realizing—in the scheme of things and the grand sweep of time—that he was insignificant. Indra amended his plans for his palace and devoted himself to spiritual service. He is a reminder to us all that in the end we are all part of the web of life, therefore all inextricably linked to one another. As the mystics say: *we are all individual drops in the ocean of life.*

LOVE, SIMPLY

Love all. Serve all.
— Sathya Sai Baba

Following the signposts along our journey, we have passed each of the seven key markers posing the choices that advance our progress. By making the conscious choice to investigate, we become truth seekers. Accepting the call to initiate, we embark on the adventure that opens the door to growth. The choice to gain insight gives us the self-knowledge critical to making needed changes in who we are and how we are in the world. Proceeding to go deeper still and choosing to tap intuition, we enter the inmost cave, the seat of inner guidance. At this point we are ready to do battle with the inner forces arrayed against us—the negative thought patterns and habits of our own minds—and now is the moment to choose a new intention. Coming into the home stretch, inspiration lights our path with renewed energy and light. In making this choice, we ourselves also become an inspiration.

Having learned the lessons on our journey, we can make the most of them by sharing them with others, by choosing to create innovation in our personal behavior, in our family, our work, our community, and the world. At whatever level of service to which we feel called, innovation is an uplifting choice.

The wonderful thing about learning to work with the power choices is that each choice can be applied to every facet of our lives. At some point, we're all going to run into some challenge or trouble with some aspect of our lives. It may be with our careers, our financial situations, our health, or our relationships with lovers, children, friends, colleagues, or family members—but somewhere along the line, we'll face a test with some important part of our lives. The good news is that we have the power choices that can guide and support us through that challenge.

For example, when our career is stalled, we may need to investigate why we're not being promoted or given plum assignments, then initiate the changes that we need to make to present our talents and gifts in a better light. Mothers are noted for tapping into their intuition when it comes to dealing with their children, but perhaps Mom needs to take the next step and examine what her intentions are with regard to her children's lives. Certainly, if something is not quite ideal in one aspect of our lives, it's worth looking at through the prism of the power choices.

We've all known people who have life paths that seem paved with gold. You've heard it said—you may have said it yourself—"That person seems to live a charmed life. Nothing bad ever happens to him." But that's probably not true; what you're seeing is an illusion. Everyone has challenges. Everyone. But there are people who know how to transcend those challenges with greater ease. They've figured out how to work through them quickly, quietly, and efficiently, so that by the next time you see them, the problem seems to have disappeared. But that is the power of power choices—they're really terrific tools that enable us to move along our life path with fewer stumbles and tumbles. They help us traverse the miles more quickly. We don't have to take the long way around; we can go right through the ordeal and come out the other

Innovation

side having learned our lessons.

All the power choices free us to be our highest and best selves and to fulfill the ultimate purpose of our life. Dr. Deepak Chopra once said in an interview with Oprah Winfrey when she asked him what the purpose of life is, "Life has only one purpose, to learn to love unconditionally." When we travel on our life journey, following the signposts that our lives provide for us—and making positive power choices along the way—we clear the path to make the ultimate power choice, which is love. Ultimately, if we work on making the power choices a part of our lives, we will come to be concerned with little other than how can we give and receive more love—at work, at home, in our families, within ourselves. It's a powerful thing—no, actually, it's the powerful thing—that we all desire and strive for, whether we realize it or not. And it's what we need. The Beatles sang, *"All you need is love. Love. Love is all you need."*

And they were right. If you have it—can tap into it and use it and give it to others—everything in your life will turn out bright.

Choose to live full out with all you've got, by practicing unconditional love for yourself, for every human being, for mother earth, and for the divine. I humbly pray that my journey will be of benefit to you and call you home to the divine within your self.

With every experience, you alone are painting your own canvas, thought by thought, choice by choice. — Oprah Winfrey

QUESTIONS

1. What innovation would I need to balance all four levels of my consciousness—physical, emotional, mental, and spiritual?

2. What innovation would I need to balance my masculine and feminine polarities (for example, practice listening to develop more feminine receptive power)?

3. What innovation would deepen my spiritual awareness?

4. What innovation can I be a part of so I may be of service to others or a just cause (such as the environment or animal rights)?

POWER TOOLS

1. LOVE YOURSELF
Do this simple exercise consistently for just twenty one days, and notice how you feel.

2. LOVE ALL
Practice this exercise regularly, and it will change the way you see everyone and everything.

3. STRENGTH IN NUMBERS
This power tool will give you even more impact in the world. Join a group (start your own if you want) to address an issue that you want to solve. There is strength in numbers.

POWER DECREE
I AM INNOVATION IN ACTION! I AM A SUCCESS!

I know you're out there. I can feel you now. I know that you're afraid... afraid of us. You're afraid of change. I don't know the future. I didn't come here to tell you how this is going to end. I came here to tell how it's going to begin. I'm going to hang up this phone, and then show these people what you don't want them to see. I'm going to show them a world without you. A world without rules or controls, borders or boundaries. A world where anything is possible. Where we go from there is a choice I leave to you.
— Neo, *The Matrix*

Selected Bibliography

Adiswarananda, Swami. *Tagore: The Mystic Poets*. Skylight Paths Publishing, 2004.

Allende, Isabel. *The Stories of Eva Luna*. Bantam Books, 1991.

Aron, Elaine N. *The Highly Sensitive Person: How to Thrive When the World Overwhelms You*. First Broadway Books, 1998.

Benjamin, Medea, and Maisa Mendonca. *Benedita daSilva: An Afro-Brazilian Woman's Story of Politics and Love*. Food First Books, 1997.

Bercholz, Samuel, and Sherab Chödzin Kohn. *An Introduction to the Buddha and His Teachings*. Barnes and Noble Books, 1993.

Brady, Ignatius. *The Writings of Saint Francis of Assisi*. Arti Grafiche Antica Porziuncola, 2004.

Brown, Dan. *The DaVinci Code*. Doubleday, 2003.

Cameron, Julia. *Walking in This World: Practical Strategies for Creativity*. Rider, 2002.

Campbell, Joseph, and Bill Moyers. *The Power of Myth*. Broadway Books, 1988.

Chang, Stephen T. *The Complete System of Self-Healing: Internal Exercises*. Tao Publishing, 1986.

Coelho, Paulo. *The Valkyries: An Encounter with Angels*. Harper Perennial, 1995.

Collinge, William. *Subtle Energy: Awakening to the Unseen Forces in Our Lives.* Warner Books, 1998.

Collins, Larry, and Dominique Lapierre. *Freedom at Midnight.* Avon Books, 1976.

Diallo, Yaya, and Mitchell Hall. *The Healing Drum: African Wisdom Teachings.* Destiny Books, 1989.

Easwaran, Eknath. *Mantram Handbook.* Nilgiri Press, 1988.

Faber, Adele, and Elaine Mazlish. *Siblings without Rivalry: How to Help Your Children Live Together So You Can Live Too.* Avon Books, 1988.

Fadiman, James, and Robert Frager. *Essential Sufism.* Castle Books, 1997.

Follmi, Danielle, and Olivier Follmi. *Wisdom: 365 Thoughts from Indian Masters.* Harry N. Abrams, Inc., 2004

Ford-Grabowsky, Mary. *Sacred Voices: Essential Women's Wisdom through the Ages.* Harper Collins Publishers, Inc., 2002.

Fox, Emmet. *Sermon on the Mount: The Key to Success in Life.* Harper San Francisco, 1989.

Frazer, James. *The Golden Bough: The Roots of Religion and Folklore.* Avenel Books, 1981.

Gaer, Joseph. *What the Great Religions Believe.* Signet, 1963.

Gass, Robert, and Kathleen Brehony. *Discovering Spirit in Sound Chanting.* Broadway Books, 1999.

Goodrich, Norma Lorre. *Priestesses.* First Harper Perennial, 1990.

Greene, Liz, and Juliet Sharman-Burke. *The Mythic Journey: The Meaning of Myth as a Guide for Life.* Fireside, 2000.

Gurian, Michael. *The Soul of the Child: Nurturing the Divine Identity of Our Children*. Atria Books, 2002.

Hall, Manly P. *First Principles of Philosophy*. Friends United Press, 1989.

Hawkins, David R. *Power vs. Force: The Hidden Determinants of Human Behavior*. Hay House, Inc., 2002.

Hay, Louise L. *Heal Your Body*. Hay House, Inc., 1982.

Hill, Napoleon. *Think & Grow Rich*. Fawcett Crest, 1960.

Hill, Napoleon, and W. Clement Stone. *Success through a Positive Mental Attitude*. Pocket Books New York, 1977.

Imamoto, Chowchow. *I Am You Are: A Simple Guide*. Designs of Light, 2000.

Jewell, Terri L. *The Black Woman's Gumbo Ya-Ya: Quotations by Black Women*. The Crossing Press, 1993.

Khalsa, Dharma Singh. *Brain Longevity: Regenerate Your Concentration, Energy, and Learning Ability for a Lifetime of Peak Mental Performance*. Warner Books, 1997.

King, Godfre Ray. *Unveiled Mysteries* (Original). Saint Germain Press, Inc., 1995.

Knight, Christopher, and Robert Lomas. *The Hiram Key: Pharaohs, Freemasons and the Discovery of the Secret Scrolls of Jesus*. Arrow Books, 1997.

Ladinsky, Daniel. *Love Poems from God: Twelve Sacred Voices from the East and West*. Penguin Compass, 2002.

Lerner, Harriet. *The Dance of Anger: A Woman's Guide to Changing the Patterns of Intimate Relationships*. Harper Collins, 1997.

Levine, Stephen, and Ondrea Levine. *Embracing the Beloved:*

Relationship as a Path of Awakening. Anchor, 1995.

Lhalungpa, Lobsang P. *The Life of Milarepa*. Shambhala, 1984.

Lorenzini, Chiara. *The Life of St. Clare*. Arti Grafiche Antica Porziuncola, 2001.

Maalouf, Amin. *The Crusades through Arab Eyes*. Schocken Books, 1984.

Magesa, Laurenti. *African Religion: The Moral Traditions of Abundant Life*. Orbis Books, 1997.

Marooney, Kimberly. *Angel Blessings: Cards of Sacred Guidance and Inspiration*. Merrill-West Publishing, 1995.

Matt, Daniel C. *The Essential Kabbalah: the Heart of Jewish Mysticism*. Castle Books, 1995.

Maziaaz, Daniel. *The Angelic Way to Love*. 1994.

Moffatt, Bettyclare. *Soulwork: Clearing the Mind, Opening the Heart, Replenishing the Spirit*. Wildcat Canyon Press, 1994.

Muktananda, Swami. *Play of Consciousness: A Spiritual Autobiography*. Syda Foundation, 1994.

Muller, Wayne. *Legacy of the Heart: The Spiritual Advantages of a Painful Childhood*. Fireside, 1992.

Murphy, Joseph M. *Working the Spirit*. Beacon Press, 1994.

Myers, David G. *Intuition: Its Powers and Perils*. Yale University Press, 2002.

Narayan, Kirin. *Storytellers, Saints, and Scoundrels: Folk Narrative in Hindu Religious Teaching*. University of Pennsylvania Press, 1989.

Obama, Barack. *Dreams from My Father: A Story of Race and Inheritance*. Three Rivers Press, 2004.

Paul, Jordan. *Becoming Your Own Hero*. Hara Publishing, 2003.

Pearl. *Step by Step We Climb to Freedom and Victory*. Naturegraph Publishers, Inc., 1983.

Prophet, Elizabeth Clare. *The Art of Practical Spirituality*. Summit University Press, 2000.

Real, Terrence. *How Can I Get Through To You? Reconnecting Men and Women*. Scribner, 2002.

Russell, William F. *Classic Myths to Read Aloud*. Crown Trade Paperbacks, 1989.

Schwab, Gustav. *Gods and Heroes: Myths and Epics of Ancient Greece*. Pantheon Books, 1974.

Shlain, Leonard. *Sex, Time and Power: How Women's Sexuality Shaped Human Evolution*. Penguin Books, 2003.

Smith, Huston. *The Illustrated World's Religions: A Guide to Our Wisdom Traditions*. Harper San Francisco, 1994.

Stone, Merlin. *Ancient Mirrors of Womanhood: A Treasury of Goddess and Heroin Lore from Around the World*. Beacon Press, 1984.

Thompson, Robert Farris. *Flash of the Spirit: African and Afro-American Art & Philosophy*. First Vintage Books, 1984.

Thurman, Howard. *The Luminous Darkness*. Friends United Press, 1989.

Waite, Linda J., and Maggie Gallagher. *The Case for Marriage: Why Married People Are Happier, Healthier, and Better Off Financially*. Broadway Books, 2000.

Wilfried. *The Mother: A Short Biography*. Sri Aurobindo Society, 1986.

Wilhelm, Helmut. *Heaven, Earth, and Man in the Book of Changes*. University of Washington Press, 1977.

Wilhelm, Richard, and Cary F. Baynes. *The I Ching or Book of Changes*. Princeton University Press, 1976.

Wilkinson, Tanya. *Persephone Returns: Victims, Heroes and the Journey from the Underworld*. Pagemill Press, 1996.

Wilson, Barbara Ker. *Scottish Folk-tales and Legends*. Oxford University Press, 1993.

Wolman, Richard N. *Thinking with Your Soul: Spiritual Intelligence and Why It Matters*. Harmony Books, 2001.

Yamamoto, Eric K. *Interracial Justice: Conflict & Reconciliation in Post-Civil Rights America*. New York University Press, 1999.

Ywahoo, Dhyani. *Voices of Our Ancestors*. Shambhala Publications, Inc., 1987.

Moving from Distress to Success

Whether you are:
• Experiencing significant stress, depression, marital, family or career issues and want relief or
• Seeking support to take your life to the next level of success, wholeness, love, joy and peace

Then professional psychotherapy or well-trained success coaching will provide the useful, supportive tools you are looking for to improve your life. In fact, taking these steps can be magnificent Power Choices to unlock a happier, healthier you.

Power Choices Certified Coaches & Power Choices Success Groups

Power Choices Certified Coaches, trained to facilitate Power Choices Success Groups or One-on-One Coaching, are becoming increasingly available throughout the country. For further information on how to locate a Power Choices Coach near you or on how to become a Power Choices Coach, contact us by calling us at 415.775.4866 or write us at *love@docwade.com*.

Finding a Local Therapist

To locate a qualified therapist in your area, please contact:
• American Psychological Association: 1-800-964-2000 or www.apa.org
• National Association of Social Workers: www.socialworkers.org
• American Association for Marriage and Family Therapy: www.aamft.org

Power Choices Seminars

Do you want to take your life to the next level? Imagine more success at work, at home, in relationships, with money, and best of all more joy and more peace in your life. If you answer yes, then you definitely want to experience the power of positive transformation first hand by attending Power Choices Seminars. These seminars offer dynamic, hands-on and above all practical tools to make every day your best day ever.

• **To Host a Power Choices Seminar**, call Heartline Productions at 415.775.4866.

• **To Attend a Power Choices Seminar**, visit www.power-choices.net or www.docwade.com for the most recent calendar or call the Heartline Productions office at 415.775.4866.

Heartline Productions

Heartline Productions, Inc. was founded by Dr. Brenda Wade to create seminars, television programs, films and written materials that enhance healing, success and transformation.

POWER CHOICES DECREES & AFFIRMATIONS CD

This CD features each of the Power Decrees from the Power Choices *book set to lively music. Using the principle that repetition programs the mind, chant along with the decrees to establish a positive and powerful mind set.*

Audio CD: $16.00 plus shipping

LOVE LESSONS: A GUIDE TO TRANSFORMING RELATIONSHIPS

"We were divorced five years when we read Love Lessons. Now we are happily remarried."
—AS and WS
Baltimore, MD

Dr. Wade's first book, coauthored with Brenda Richardson, Love Lessons (Amistad Press, 1993), leads couples in trouble through a step by step healing program based on the 12 steps of Alcoholics Anonymous. You'll learn how to break old patterns and establish healthy new ones.

Paperback: $12.95 plus shipping

WHAT MAMA COULDN'T TELL US ABOUT LOVE:
HEALING THE EMOTIONAL WOUNDS OF RACISM AND CELEBRATING OUR LIGHT

"A powerful, moving and life-enhancing book that will help readers reconnect with the past and move forward into the future. It will change lives and hearts."
—Harriet Lerner, PhD
Author of *Dance of Anger*

What Mama Couldn't Tell Us About Love (Harper Collins, 1999), also coauthored by Brenda Richardson, focuses on breaking the emotional chains of racism through holistic transformation and celebrating new victorious life patterns.

Paperback: $13.00 plus shipping

To Order and see the entire product line, visit the website:
www.docwade.com
To Order by Phone: Call 415-775-4866

BRENDA WADE, PHD

Best known for her love-centered approach to transformation, Dr. Brenda Wade is a San Francisco-based psychologist, TV host, author, and dynamic international speaker. Dr. Wade with Tamara Jeffries authored the newly released *Power Choices: 7 Signposts on Your Journey to Wholeness, Joy, Love and Peace* which clearly outlines seven choices we can all make to meet life's challenges and create a breakthrough out of what seems to be a break down. The *Power Choices PBS Pledge Special*, released nationwide, highlights four Power Choices and features tools from the book.

Dr. Wade is known to national audiences as the host of the nationally syndicated television show *Can This Marriage Be Saved* and co-host of *Real Personal* at CNBC. She has appeared in prime-time specials with Peter Jennings and as the regular psychologist for *Good Morning America*. Dr. Wade has also appeared on many shows such as *Oprah*. She is a featured writer for Essence magazine and contributed to the popular Ladies Home Journal column "Can This Marriage Be Saved?" She is a sought-after international speaker and hosts the San Francisco Bay Area community affairs program *Black Renaissance*.

Dr. Wade has previously co-authored with Brenda Lane Richardson two books: *What Mama Couldn't Tell Us About Love* (Harper Collins) which focuses on healing the wounds and celebrating the strengths of African American Women, and *Love Lessons* (Amistad Press) which leads couples of all backgrounds through a step by step healing program based on the 12 steps of Alcoholics Anonymous.

Visit Dr. Wade's website at www.docwade.com or www.powerchoices.net for more information.